Quiet Mind,
Fearless Heart

Also by Brian Luke Seaward, Ph.D.

Hot Stones and Funny Bones: Teens Helping Teens Coping with Stress and Anger

Health of the Human Spirit; Spiritual Dimension for Personal Health

The Art of Calm: Relaxation through the Five Senses

Stressed Is Desserts Spelled Backward: Rising above Life's Challenges with Humor, Hope, and Courage

Stand Like Mountain, Flow Like Water: Reflections on Stress and Human Spirituality

Health and Wellness Journal Workbook (second edition)

Managing Stress: A Creative Journal (third edition)

Managing Stress: Principles and Strategies for Health and Well-being (fourth edition)

Quiet Mind, Fearless Heart

The Taoist Path
through
Stress and Spirituality

BRIAN LUKE SEAWARD, Ph.D.

WILEY

John Wiley & Sons, Inc.

Published by John Wiley & Sons, Inc., Hoboken, New Jersey
Published simultaneously in Canada

The author gratefully acknowledges the following for permission to quote from: page 34, *If Life Is a Game, These Are the Rules: Ten Rules for Being Human* by Dr. Chérie Carter-Scott, Broadway Books, © 1998; page 91, translation from *Tao Te Ching* courtesy of Josh Zhou; page 117, "Stand Like Mountain, Flow Like Water" by Brian Luke Seaward, © Health Communications Inc. Reprinted with permission; page 165, "Beauty Poem" from *In One Era and Out the Other* by Samuel Levenson. Reprinted by permission of SLL/Sterling Lord Literistic, Inc. Copyright 1996 by Samuel Levenson; page 226, "The Winds of Grace" by Brian Luke Seaward, © Inspiration Unlimited. Reprinted with permission. All rights reserved.

For general information about our other products and services, please contact our Customer Care Department within the United States at (800) 762-2974, outside the United States at (317) 572-3993 or fax (317) 572-4002.

Wiley also publishes its books in a variety of electronic formats. Some content that appears in print may not be available in electronic books. For more information about Wiley products, visit our web site at www.wiley.com.

Library of Congress Cataloging-in-Publication Data:
Seaward, Brian Luke.
   Quiet mind, fearless heart : the Taoist path through stress and spirituality / Brian Luke Seaward.
      p. cm.
   Includes bibliographical references and index.
   ISBN 0-471-67999-2 (pbk.)
   1. Spiritual life. 2. Stress (Psychology)—Religious aspects. 3. Taoism. I. Title.
   BL624.S4226 2004
   299.5'144—dc22

                                                              2004014378

Printed in the United States of America
10 9 8 7 6 5 4 3 2

For Donna and Scott Mefford

CONTENTS

ACKNOWLEDGMENTS

First and foremost, I would like to thank Susan Lee Cohen of the Riverside Literary Agency, who, upon seeing my FedEx package one summer day, opened it, read the contents, and immediately signed me on. Susan, you are truly a gift, and I thank the universe for having our paths cross. I look forward to many more literary ventures with you. Special thanks go to Tom Miller, my editor at John Wiley & Sons, who has been a blessing to work with—Tom, thanks for holding the vision and sharing your wisdom, which enabled this book to reach its greatest potential. I am forever indebted to my friend and colleague Deepak Chopra, who is the divine manifestation of infinite possibilities. A big bear hug to Larry Dossey, M.D., Nien Cheng, and Candace Pert, Ph.D., for their wonderful endorsements of this book as well. Special thanks to Sean Hepburn Ferrer, you're the best! Long live the spirit of your mom, Audrey Hepburn. Words of gratitude go to my personal assistant, Marlene Yates, who read the manuscript more times than she ever thought possible but also told me that the content was so rich, she got more out of it with each reading. A fortune cookie's gratitude to my friend Josh Zhou for his translation of the *Tao Te Ching* passage. My deepest gratitude to the special people who shared their stories with me, which added vitality and color to this book. Special thanks goes to Mark S. Johnson. You are one good *hombre* for touching up my photos. *Pura Vida*! Heartfelt thanks to Peter Vegso and Gary Seidler at Health Communications Inc., who gave the book *Stand Like Mountain* a home years ago. Gratitude to Javier Saws at Eversound Music too. Thanks to the spirit of Lao Tzu, Joseph Campbell, and all the wisdom keepers whose insights are woven into this book. As always, special thanks to my friends, family, and fans, too numerous to mention, who have been so generous with their support over the years. Thanks for making this a better world in which to live.

Introduction

The Best of Times,
the Worst of Times

Your joy is your sorrow unmasked . . . the deeper that sorrow carves into your being, the more joy you can contain . . . Verily you are suspended like scales between your sorrow and your joy.

—KAHLIL GIBRAN, *THE PROPHET*

It's likely that Charles Dickens was not well versed in the Taoist philosophy when he began his classic novel *A Tale of Two Cities* with the now infamous paraphrased line "It was the best of times, it was the worst of times." The truth is, you don't have to study Taoism to appreciate the concept of balance. Balance is an inherent aspect of life. It's ubiquitous throughout all cultures and has been expressed in the wisdom of every language since the dawn of humanity. Words such as *inner peace*, *equilibrium*, *stability*, *homeostasis*, *coherence*, and *steadiness* all speak to the philosophy of Taoism. Lao Tzu just happened to be the first to describe this philosophy—quite eloquently, I might add—more than two thousand years ago in his book *Tao Te Ching*. Dickens's phrase, however, strikes a harmonic chord in the heart of almost everyone, because deep down inside, we know that both good and bad moments can coexist, for better or worse, on any given day and sometimes in the same situation.

With the rapid changes taking place in our society today, you might find it hard to acknowledge, let alone appreciate, the positive aspects of life, particularly if you watch the nightly news. Current research suggests that over one-third of the American public takes antidepressants. Sixty-three percent of the American population is overweight. The average American carries approximately

$8,000 of credit card debt, and, sadly, episodes of violence at grade schools and colleges across the nation have not decreased since the 1999 massacre at Columbine High School. Yet stress is not just an American curse; it's a global phenomenon. From Sao Paul, Brazil, to Johannesburg, South Africa, and beyond, people's lives are out of balance and are becoming even more so. If Lao Tzu were alive today, my hunch is that he would be a bit disappointed.

"May you live in interesting times," is often cited as a Chinese curse, and we would all agree that these are indeed interesting times. Yet, even so, I often think, "God, it's a great time to be alive." I know I am not alone in this sentiment. Many people say that we are living in a remarkable time right now, and they see this "curse" as a blessing. Truly, our attitude is the paintbrush with which we color the world. At no time in human history has so much knowledge (particularly, through the Internet) become so accessible to so many people. As the saying goes, "With knowledge comes freedom!" Based on the e-mails I receive from around the world, the information superhighway is buzzing with activity, as curiosity seekers and gung-ho Internet surfers seek answers and spiritual insights to help them make sense of this crazy world, and do it gracefully.

Conversely, in the last couple of years and even this morning, I have heard comments, speeches, and editorials about the dire shape of the world today. It is no exaggeration to say that we are poised in a very precarious position. Our growth has exceeded our capacity to sustain ourselves, our freedom has outstripped our responsibility, and we are now causing irrefutable damage to the biosphere we call home, with problems that range from global warming to genetically modified super foods. This brings to mind Woody Allen's tongue-in-cheek comment: "More than any other time in history, mankind faces a crossroad. One path leads to despair and utter hopelessness. The other to total extinction. Let us pray that we have the wisdom to choose correctly."

From ancient Egypt comes an axiom, "As above, so below." It suggests that the microcosm and the macrocosm are tightly intertwined. Not only is balance an issue for each individual, it's necessary for the entire world. Both wonderful and horrific times await humanity. To be quite blunt, the world is out of balance. Putting it back into balance may seem like a daunting task, yet it's not impossible. Self-improvement, like charity, begins at home. From China, an ancient proverb cautions that to bring peace to the world, one must first bring peace to one's heart. *Quiet Mind, Fearless Heart* is more than a cute mantra to promote inner peace; it's a philosophy by which we can live our lives in balance, uniting the divine spirit with the human spirit to overcome personal adversity, thus bringing peace to the heart and the soul.

For nearly three decades, I have gathered nuggets of wisdom about stress and human spirituality. Over the years, I have shared these insights in settings that range from college classrooms and corporate boardrooms to a host of national and international conferences and workshops. My journey has been nothing less than ecstatic. I have learned that the relationship between stress and human spirituality is so strong, it would be a travesty and a great disservice not to address it. I learned early on that stress-management courses and seminars are natural vehicles in which to demonstrate this association and to augment personal growth by integrating various aspects of human spirituality into everyday life. Today, with our feng shui'ed houses and the ever-increasing popularity of yoga and tai chi classes, we may take this for granted; however, things were quite different back in the seventies.

For instance, in 1970, it was rare to hear the word *spirituality* in everyday conversations. To the contrary, people were actually debating whether God was dead! To show you how far things have come, now you can hear the word *spirituality* in conversations taking place anywhere from the frozen food section of your local grocer to late-night talk-radio phone calls. Moreover, decades ago, you would have been hard-pressed to find human spirituality addressed anywhere, other than in religious texts and a few self-help psychology books. If, thirty-odd years ago, someone had told you that there would be a popular book on the market titled *Spirituality for Dummies*, you would most likely have either raised an eyebrow or keeled over with laughter. So common is the word *soul* in book titles nowadays that a classic joke in the field of health psychology asks, "Who knew the soul was so fragmented?" While some things are slow to change, it's encouraging to see that the topic of human spirituality is now seriously being addressed in both medical schools and corporate boardrooms (Enron, Worldcom, and Tyco, notwithstanding!). There are even conferences and associations on the topic of spirituality in business (for example, check out www.spiritualityinbusiness.com).

An expression states that every generation has to reinvent itself. If you don't believe this, look around at today's hairstyles, slang, clothing, fashion, and music. (Remember your parents' or grandparents' initial reaction to the Beatles? It's probably not too dissimilar from your reaction to Eminem or any band that plays "techno.") Does the same hold true for spirituality? Does this aspect of human nature need to be reinvented for the twenty-first century? In some regards, yes, because spirituality is experiential. The topic of spirituality has a uniqueness all its own. Although the tenets of spiritual wisdom can never be reinvented, surely they can and must be reinterpreted, as guidance for the troubled times of each generation. Every new experience demands that we readjust the lens through which we see the world and try to make sense of things. It therefore stands to reason that we need to continually return to sources of wisdom for guidance. Without a doubt, these insights will serve as a compass on the path of our human journey.

The *Tao Te Ching* is but one source of ageless wisdom. Unlike writers of other books who use the word *Tao* in the title and scatter quotes from Lao Tzu's writings throughout the text, I have chosen to follow the spirit of Tao by using a more subtle approach, by elaborating on the essence of balance, simplicity, and harmony that is found not only in the *Tao Te Ching* but also in many writings, East and West, with the same universal message.

Because I've given many seminars and presentations on the topic of stress and spirituality, people often ask me about my religious upbringing. They inquire, "Are you Buddhist?" "Were you raised Catholic?" "Are you a Christian?" One woman insisted that I was Jewish, and once a man said, "You don't look Hindi, but you surely are well versed in the Hindu Vedic scriptures." I merely smiled. Rest assured, the ageless wisdom found in these pages knows no one particular religion. In its own subtle way, human spirituality permeates all belief systems, to their very core. Although I could share my background with you, in the past I found that by my doing so, people began to perceive this wisdom through my eyes, rather than through their own. To be honest, my religious upbringing is not important. In the prophetic words of one of my favorite luminaries, the theologian Matthew Fox, "We are living in a post-denominational age now." So, my background for now shall remain a mystery.

When my first book, *Stand Like Mountain, Flow Like Water*, came out in 1997, it rode the second, or perhaps the third, wave of books on the topic of spirituality. This wave included everything from angels, aliens, and bountiful helpings of chicken soup to new clues in the search for the Holy Grail. What made my book distinctive, however, was its focus on the unique relationship between stress and spirituality. After I wrote *Stand Like Mountain*, I did not intend to revisit this issue (I naively thought I had written all that I could say). Yet a confluence of factors (e.g., letters from readers, workshop participants' comments, the Columbine High School massacre, and, of course, September 11, 2001) enticed me to once again drink from the waters of "ageless wisdom" and put pen to paper, or, more specifically, fingers to keyboard and further explore the insights from various wisdom keepers regarding what the philosopher Aldous Huxley called "the perennial philosophy." Among the many events that inspired me to write this book, I would like to share two with you.

Not until the end of the spring semester in 2000 did I learn that several survivors of the Columbine High School shooting were in my stress-management course at the University of Northern Colorado. Wanting to keep a low profile, they never mentioned their experience in class. These seven students had dodged bullets in the cafeteria and the library of Columbine High School that notorious April morning. Several months later, they enrolled in my class, hoping to reclaim a sense of inner peace that had been lost that day. On the last day of class, each of these students specifically thanked me, and one expressed her thoughts this way: "I have been in therapy and counseling since last April, simply grieving. Thank you for putting all the pieces together, including that which was missing for me: the health of the human spirit. Up until this class, I was living in a fog. It's lifted now, and I feel that I can actually go on with my life, walking in balance. Please keep sharing your message of hope."

Perhaps equally poignant was a man who walked into a bookstore in North Carolina, during a signing for my second book, *Stressed Is Desserts Spelled Backward*. He waited patiently in line, and when he approached my table, he politely asked whether I would autograph his copy of *Stand Like Mountain*. The book in his hand was so worn, it was barely recognizable. As he placed it on the table for me to sign, I could see that this man had traveled many miles on the human journey. Smiling, he opened the book to the page he wanted autographed and said, "I've read this book through several times. It's been a big help to me." He paused for a moment before continuing, "I was an alcoholic when I picked it up two years ago; I have been sober ever since. I came here to personally thank you." He expressed the same wish that others had: "Please keep spreading your message of hope and inspiration." From these and other encounters, I realized that if you can positively affect one person's life, you have made the world a better place. So, once again, I drink from the waters of ageless wisdom, and the result is *Quiet Mind, Fearless Heart*.

In the spirit of one of my heroes, Joseph Campbell (*The Power of Myth*), a man who certainly understood the relationship between stress and spirituality, this book is divided into sections that resemble the classic template of what Campbell called "the Hero's Journey." *Part I: Into the Unknown* frames our departure from the familiar into a brave new stressful world and the problems often associated with that departure. *Part II: Crossing the Threshold* highlights the ageless wisdom of the dance between stress and spirituality and features several stories of everyday heroes who perform the dance masterfully. *Part III: Life in the Balance* contains abundant how-to advice to help you build a solid foundation or an action plan, using effective coping skills to victoriously meet the challenge of life's stress and thus celebrate your own heroic qualities. *Part IV: Back Home Again* brings you home to a hero's welcome, with a few inspirational stories that promise that you, too, can complete the journey and return home as "the master of two worlds." To support the theme of balance, sprinkled throughout the book are exercises, action plans, photographs, meditations, and poems to engage the right brain, help the left brain to process and reintegrate the information, and remind us of what we already know. It is my hope that *Quiet Mind, Fearless Heart* can reawaken your slumbering spirit, help you build a foundation of balance in your life, and enable you to regain a sense of personal homeostasis, so that the *winds of change* become the *winds of grace* that will allow your spirit to soar!

PART I

Into the Unknown

"A journey of a thousand miles begins with the first step," wrote the Chinese philosopher Lao Tzu, as sage advice to fellow travelers on the Taoist path. The renowned mythologist Joseph Campbell often referred to the first stage of "the Hero's Journey" as "the call to adventure," a step that all of us must take, many times in the course of our lives. The cautious first step into the unknown, however, is typically accompanied by fear—so much so, that it can immobilize us, make us want to refuse the call, rather than answer it. This part highlights our departure from the known into the unknown, from the familiar to the unbalanced brave new world we now find ourselves in, and the common dangers of getting stuck or lost on the way.

The Winds of Change Are Brewing

*W*hen we forget our stories,

then we forget our dreams.

When we forget our dreams,

we lose our spirit.

—MAORI SAYING

R emember when the world seemed like a simpler place to live? Not long ago, stores were closed on Sundays. Only girls wore earrings. There were just three television networks (four, if you could get PBS). Cell phones were considered science fiction. Only NASA engineers and MIT professors used computers. Some cows were a bit unhappy, but none were mad, and there were seven words you could never say on television. That was then. Things are quite different now!

The stormy winds of change are blowing fast and furious today, and, by all accounts, they show no signs of stopping. Change has always been part of the human landscape, but the rate of change occurring today, from near-instantaneous telecommunications to terrorism, genetic engineering, and globalization, is unparalleled in human history. Future shock has arrived, throwing everything out of balance. Experts suggest that we will see as much dramatic change in the next three to five years as our grandparents saw in a lifetime. Are you ready for this?

If your answer is no, you're not alone. Add to this list more social changes, such as nanotechnology, rapidly infectious diseases, and cloning, as well as any personal dramas that you might go through, whether a death in the family, the end of a marriage, or being downsized out of a job, and your pace of life has just accelerated tenfold. Social changes only increase your levels of personal stress. The winds of change are blowing at gale force, so it's best to batten down the hatches by using your inner strength.

Believe it or not, if you stay anchored to your inner resources (e.g., faith, optimism, courage), it is possible to stay calm in the eye of the storm. Yet most people, distracted by the newest technology craze or a plethora of shallow media events, find it hard to recognize their strengths, let alone make use of them. Whether welcome or unwelcome, change is often associated with stress, because with change comes uncertainty, and uncertainty breeds fear. Fear clouds the mind and robs the heart of its highest potential. Let there be no doubt that we are living in a time of great fear.

Nestled up against the foothills of the Rockies, Boulder, Colorado, may not be your typical town, but like everywhere else in America, the winds of change blow here regularly. Renowned for its mountain splendor and subtle mystique, "the Republic of Boulder" is sometimes described as ten square miles surrounded by reality. At the cash register of my favorite local bakery, there is a sign taped to a huge teacup. Unlike most signs that read "Need a penny, take a penny," this one says "If you fear change, leave it here." Every time I go in, I notice that the bowl is overflowing with pennies, nickels, dimes, and quarters. I'm not sure whether people contribute their pocket change out of jest, guilt, or authentic fear, but without a doubt, not only is change brewing, like the pocket change in this teacup, it is overflowing. Change is inevitable, and with change comes fear, particularly fear of the unknown. Granted, while a little bit of change (e.g., new restaurants, new music, etc.) can interrupt life's monotony, by and large, people don't like change because it is perceived as stressful. As the expression goes, "The only person who likes change is a wet baby."

The weather from hell. Traffic from hell. The stock market from hell. Have you noticed how popular hell has become lately? Hell is the metaphorical symbol of stress, and whether it's frozen over or breaking loose, there seems to be no shortage of turbulent winds these days, all of which precipitate feelings of personal stress. Everywhere you go, people are tense, frustrated, and pushed beyond the limits of their patience. Take a look around. Listen closely. People talk as if they have Tourette's syndrome, or they complain like Andy Rooney on *60 Minutes*. He gets paid to whine, though; the rest of us do it for free.

A Lesson from Churchill

Perhaps the first time the world's inhabitants were acutely aware of global stress was during the height of World War II. But even before the atomic bomb was dropped on Japan, ushering in the age of nuclear destruction, Britain was continuously being bombed by the Germans in the famous "Blitz." Winston Churchill, the prime minister of England and a man known to never mince words, shared this thought with his countrymen: "If you're going through hell . . . keep going." Though slightly humorous, his message holds profound wisdom. In times of great strife, we often want to throw in the towel and give up. Many people, when confronted with stress, whether of the mountain or the molehill variety, admit defeat without even trying. Churchill's message was clear. Hell isn't meant to be a permanent refuge or a final destination, so keep moving.

The Hero's Code

At a recent dinner party I attended, the conversation was abuzz with personal strife and national calamities: the death of a mutual friend, a newly discovered cancerous tumor, and a hellacious divorce, as well as the stock market crisis, high school shootings, and weather storms of biblical proportions. Eight of us sat around the table, sharing moments of our lives, perceptions of the global village, and our visions of the next decade. With each new topic of the conversation, we tried to make sense of the rapidly changing world we live in, as well as determine our best course of action while individually navigating the shoals of impending disaster. It didn't take long for us to realize that stress was a recurring theme in every aspect of our lives. In the midst of our apparent abundance and prosperity was the inherent knowledge that things were terribly amiss.

Mark put down his wine glass and asked, "Is it me or has anyone else noticed that the planet earth has become a runaway train?" His question went unanswered for a few moments. Then the dining room became vibrant with conversation on how to take command in a situation where control is a tempestuous illusion. With a wary eye on the future, we came to a simple consensus that the only way to deal with the turbulent times ahead was to have a clear mind and a brave heart with no trace of fear, for it made no sense to either fight with anger or surrender in disgust. We had too much living to do. Before we drove back to our respective homes, we made a pledge to return to the same dinner table in a few months, like knights returning to King Arthur's round table, to share with the group how we had slayed a personal dragon or two, found the mythical Holy Grail, and, in doing so, made the world a better place to live.

Brave New World Revisited

A hush fell over the crowd as the speaker walked up to the microphone. It was the spring of 2004, and the topic was "Global Change," a glimpse into the next decade through the eyes of one of the country's foremost futurists, Dr. Paul Kordis. His presentation was an eloquent synthesis of keen insights poised at the vanguard of what the next decade holds in store for earth's inhabitants. Dr. Kordis spoke of the advances in microchip technology, political upheavals, nanotechnology, the application of the Human Genome Project, newly revealed secrets from the Hubble space telescope, the bioengineering of food, and more. At the conclusion of his talk, he specifically addressed the fear that will accompany these changes, as paradigms crumble and belief systems collapse. "We have entered a time in the history of humanity when our capacity to use this technology has exceeded the consciousness to question whether it should indeed, be used. I am afraid to say there is no stopping it." Kordis paused to view the attentive audience. "Welcome to a brave new world," he said without a hint of cynicism.

In 1939 the book *Brave New World* rolled off the presses. It described a future utopian society—ironically, one not without problems. Its author, Aldous Huxley, like other science fiction writers of his time, used literature to make a philosophical point about many things, including spiritual hunger and the pursuit of happiness. Huxley died in 1964, but if he were alive today, he would most likely not be surprised to see the advances in computer technology, cloning, and mind-altering pharmaceuticals that he envisioned so many decades ago. He might, however, be disheartened to know that with these changes, humanity's potential is far less than realized. Apparently, his warning went unheeded.

Like so many other science fiction books, Huxley's work wasn't so much a vision, as it was a spiritual wake-up call. Ever the philosopher, Huxley intuitively knew the dangers of a world that neither acknowledged nor fully embraced the spiritual dimension of life. In a later book of nonfiction titled *The Perennial Philosophy*, Huxley explored the deeper issues of human spirituality by synthesizing ageless wisdom derived from several of the world's cultures, traditions, and religions. Reality, he explained, is a shrouded mystery, hidden from people who are neither pure of heart nor light in spirit—in essence, those who are victims to personal events, by not learning from them or moving on with life.

People who travel the human journey with a pure heart and a light spirit, no matter what comes their way, will master the human condition. Huxley believed that while life is never easy, when one is armed with a pure heart and a hungry spirit that's willing to learn, the trials of the human journey are always rewarding. His call to action is as important today as it was when he first wrote *Brave New World* about half a century ago—given the state of current global changes and personal strife, coupled with futuristic technology, perhaps even more so.

A growing majority of people believes that brave or foolish, we truly have entered a "New World." In many ways, though, the more things change, the more they remain the same. Yet regardless of the personal issues and the global events that lie ahead, we still have valuable inner resources to cope with change. Patience, compassion, honesty, faith, humor, forgiveness, and a score of other human attributes have helped us deal effectively with personal crises and cope with stress throughout the course of human history. I call these inner resources "muscles of the soul." When we use them in trying times, they manifest as grace. To quote a familiar expression often attributed to Ernest Hemingway, "Style is grace under pressure." Undoubtedly, adapting to personal and global change in today's world without animosity, resentment, or fear takes grace.

The Way of the Tao

If one word describes Nien Cheng, it is grace. I was first introduced to Nien in 1987 through her book *Life and Death in Shanghai*, a remarkable, heroic story of the human spirit's triumph over indescribable adversity. With the rise of communism under the rule of Mao Tse-tung, all Chinese intellectuals who spoke English were accused of being spies. Nien had been educated in London and had lived in Australia as the wife of China's ambassador; she then took an assignment for Shell Oil in Shanghai after the death of her husband. Her past became highly suspect to the Communist Red Guard. In 1965, at the age of fifty-six, she was falsely accused of being a spy and imprisoned in solitary confine-ment for over six years. She endured horrendous living conditions and physical torture. She was never allowed to see her family, including her only daughter, Mei Ping. A U.S. détente between Nixon and Mao opened a window of opportunity in 1972, and several prisoners, including Nien, were released. Upon learning the unspeakable fate of her daughter, she made the decision to leave China forever, first immigrating to Canada, then relocating to the United States. If you were to meet her today at age ninety, you would see the scars on her wrists from shackles she was forced to wear. But more important, you would be struck by her sincere smile and bright eyes, conveying grace and dignity and giving no hint of the utter hell she endured.

While serving on the faculty of the American University in Washington, D.C., I invited Nien to be a guest speaker for my stress-management class in the spring of 1992. She graciously accepted. A wonderful friendship developed afterward, which over the years has been cultivated with letters, phone calls, and e-mails. When I return periodically to the nation's capital, we visit over lunch or dinner. Conversations with Nien are never boring, as she is well versed in many topics that range from politics, health care, and gardening, to current issues and world events.

Sitting in her living room sipping tea one afternoon, I asked whether she had seen the movie *Crouching Tiger, Hidden Dragon*. Her face lit up with a big smile. "Oh, yes," she said, "I liked it so much, I saw it twice. You know, long ago, this was how they made movies in China: flying on rooftops and such. As a young girl, I loved to see them. Then Mao Tse-tung took over, and they stopped making these films. The communists," she said with a faint laugh, "they have no sense of humor." Humor, I learned, was one of Nien's many inner resources.

I mentioned that I, too, had seen it twice and was quite taken with the philosophical theme, as well as with the movie's plot. Pouring more tea, Nien looked up to make eye contact and asked whether I was familiar with the concept of Taoism. Like many people in the mid-seventies, I first became aware of the Taoist philosophy by reading Fritjof Capra's book *The Tao of Physics* while attending college and again, years later, while reading *The Tao of Pooh*. Taoism is rather hard to explain, so rather than risk embarrassing myself, I politely shook my head, hoping that Nien would share her insights. She did.

"We have a philosophy in China called Taoism." She paused to collect her thoughts, before attempting to explain the unexplainable. "Taoism is not a religion, it's merely a practical way of life: living simply, living a life of balance and harmony." She looked out the window. "So many things are out of balance today." She took a sip of tea, then shared her experience of being interned in Shanghai's Number 1 Detention House. It became obvious to me that not only her faith in God but her subtle discipline of patience, integrity, and persistence, as expressed through the Taoist philosophy, had enabled her to survive such a terrible ordeal.

A Sage Named Lao Tzu

Many people are aware of the Taoist yin/yang symbol, a ubiquitous icon spotted everywhere in America, from bumper stickers to tattoos, yet few know the origin or the concepts of this ancient Chinese philosophy. As the author of the acclaimed book *Tao Te Ching*, Lao Tzu is credited with recording the tenets of Taoism well over two thousand years ago. Although little is known about him, some people believe Lao Tzu to be a contemporary of the renowned philosopher Confucius (551–479 B.C.). It is understood that Lao Tzu wrote this manual of virtues, often called the wisest book ever written, for the rulers of the Zhou dynasty. Over time, as Taoist concepts were integrated into Buddhism, the Zen style of Buddhism became popular in the Orient. Through the centuries, the *Tao Te Ching* made its way into the hands of the general public and is now accessible the world over. Although Taoism originated in China long ago, its popularity stems from the fact that the concepts of balance, simplicity, patience, and harmony are universal to the human condition.

The *Tao Te Ching* was a manual for living a life of balance, in harmony with the divine force of the universe. When translated into English, the Tao is perhaps best described as "the Way" or "the Path." Many people think that George Lucas based his concept of "the Force" on the Tao, as the two seem nearly identical. Through countless observations of the natural world and human nature, Lao Tzu imparted his wisdom in richly worded poetic verse of eighty-one passages. His intention was to transform consciousness to its highest potential. It would be incorrect, however, to think of the Tao as a list of simple rules or dogma. The complexity of Taoism comes through its application to daily life, including the most simple acts of breathing and walking. A fundamental tenet of Taoism states that taking time to cultivate the inner landscape of the soul promotes an external harmony under any set of circumstances. If you read a translation of the *Tao Te Ching*, and there are many, you cannot help but notice a sense of the divine that connects all things as one. For this reason, a strong, but subtle mysticism also infuses the Tao.

In the book, *365 Tao*, the author, Deng Ming-Dao, writes, "Those who follow Tao would first think to know themselves well. They believe that the outside world is only known in relation to an inner point of view. Self-cultivation is the basis for knowing Tao. Although Tao may be glimpsed in the outer world, individuals must sharpen their sensibilities in order to observe the workings of the great."

A Chinese proverb states, "When there is peace in the heart, there will be peace in the world." The American version suggests the following wisdom: let there be peace on earth and let it begin with me. When there is peace in the heart of each soul, there will be peace in the world. In the words of another great sage, Mahatma Gandhi: "To change the world, we must first be the change we wish to see."

It's fair to say that under the influence of chronic stress, balance is called into question. Taoism isn't a panacea for stress. It merely offers suggestions for bringing aspects of life back into balance by going with the flow, rather than fighting the winds of change. Following the way of the Tao provides a sense of empowerment that allows us to overcome the most hellacious obstacles without animosity or anger—in essence, to walk the human path gracefully.

Recently, a 113-year-old Floridian was asked about the secret to his longevity. His answer embodied the wisdom of the Tao: "When it rains, I let it."

A Crazy Little Thing Called Stress

The moment I walked off the plane, I was greeted by a man holding a sign with my name on it, who then escorted me to a limousine. I had just flown out to Hollywood to tape a talk show on stress. Los Angeles, the epitome of stress, was nothing less than frenetic, from the airport to the freeways to the heart of the city. When I walked into the studio, I thought, "You'd need an ax to cut through the tension in this place." People were running around like crazy: beauticians from the makeup department pranced all over, producers roamed the halls in search of the show's hosts, nervous guests paced the floors in their dressing rooms, and security guards with earphones and mikes raced around like the president's Secret Service, trying to keep everything in order. I sat patiently in the "green room," waiting to go on, and within minutes was escorted to the stage and quickly seated. After a brief introduction, the first question I was asked was "Dr. Seaward, what is stress?" At the time, it was hard to give a comprehensive answer in a sound bite, but I have more time now, so here is a more thorough answer.

Although there are many different definitions of stress, the one that I like best states that "stress is any change you encounter in your life." Today the words *change* and *stress* are often used synonymously, particularly in light of global terrorism and the national terrorism alert code. As a rule, people feel threatened by change. We don't like change because it tends to disrupt our comfort zones, which can include anything from our daily routines to our thoughts, opinions, and attitudes about all aspects of life. Like the tectonic plates that shift and crumble during a violent earthquake, change can dramatically shift the foundation of our lives and quite literally move the earth on which we walk.

There are many definitions of stress. Each definition depends on which expert (e.g., psychologist, sociologist, physiologist, or theologian) you talk to. The word *stress* comes from the field of physics. In the simplest terms, "stress is the force or pressure applied to an object, enough to bend or break it." If you have ever been emotionally distraught or overwhelmed beyond belief, you surely know what this feels like. Professionals in the field of medicine tend to see stress as "wear and tear" on the body, and sure enough, there is a strong association between stress and disease. Therapists and counselors in the field of psychology define stress as the "inability to cope with problems," as well as "the loss of emotional control." People with a more spiritual approach say that "stress is the absence of inner peace." Quite honestly, all of these insights together, when examined through the mind-body-spirit equation, only begin to approach the essence of what stress really is. Ironically, stress is almost as complex to define as it is to resolve. An ancient Chinese proverb offers this insight: tension is who you think you should be. Relaxation is who you are.

Where There's Unresolved Stress, There's Ego

Barely a household word a few decades ago, stress is now as American as apple pie and as common as the use of cell phones. In fact, stress is ubiquitous across the planet. Even the World Health Organization calls stress "a global epidemic." It doesn't matter where you live, how much money you make, what you do for a living, or how dysfunctional your parents were when you were growing up—everyone has stress. Stress, quite aptly, is called the "equal opportunity destroyer." Like change, stress has always been part of the human landscape, but in our rapidly changing world, problems, both big and small, now form momentous headwinds. Sadly, the average person seems to have neither a clear reference point to achieve balance, nor a lucid perspective from which to avoid this deluge and take full command of his or her life.

The stress people feel today comes not only from a multitude of outside sources, such as the lack of job security or the looming threat of terrorism, but also from the internal voice of the ego, which constantly interprets both personal and global events. The ego itself can cause a tremendous amount of stress. If you were to hold a bunch of stress experts captive in a room and not release them until they came to a consensus, they most likely would say that stress, real or imagined, is a "perceived" threat to our physical, mental, emotional, or spiritual existence. Note that the word *perceived* is in quotes, because two people can experience the same situation, yet one may find it nonthreatening, while the other is freaking out. Ultimately, stress is based on your interpretation of each event, as well as your reaction or response to it. The ego reacts, the soul responds. Both reactions and responses are conscious choices; however, responses require a clear conscience, brought forth by a calm mind. This is what Aldous Huxley hinted at when he referred to a "pure heart." And people who say, "I don't have stress, I give stress," are only fooling themselves—they are time bombs waiting to go off.

With a little prodding and encouragement, these same stress experts will admit that some stress is actually healthy, but beyond that point—which, of course, varies from person to person—stress can be quite harmful. In simple terms, chronic unresolved stress is deadly. Eventually, it kills. On the other hand, healthful stress is inspiring, motivating, and, yes, even euphoric. Downhill skiing comes to mind, as does falling in love. Unfortunately, most people who ricochet through today's stressed-filled world are well beyond the point of motivation and excitement. They are heading toward burnout, which can manifest as either fear or anger.

Stressed Mind, Angered Heart

Not long ago, I went to a movie theater to escape the real world of cares and worries by entering into a world of fantasy. Despite the fact that the movie was a comedy, anger was brewing in the aisles. About halfway into the flick, a cell phone went off, and the man beside me proceeded to whisper loudly into his hand for the next few minutes. People around me seemed irritated, but no one said anything. When the credits began rolling on screen, the man sitting next to me stood to leave. In a moment of polite assertiveness, I said, "Excuse me, but the next time you come to the movies, would you consider turning off your cell phone?" He glared at me as if I had tossed a verbal hand grenade and said, "Get a life!"

Astonished but composed, I looked him in the eye. "What did you say?"

He yelled a profanity and quickly walked away.

To live a life without stress is just not possible or even desirable. To live a life full of stress, however, is neither normal nor healthy. Balance is essential. It may sound rather clichéd, but coping well with stress comes down to one thing: your attitude. I have met scores of people who, on the surface, have enviable lives. They have more possessions than they can use and more money than they can spend, yet they are anything but happy and stress free. Conversely, I know many others whose lifestyles appear less than desirable, as measured by the "American dream," yet they have the world in their pockets. It's not that they don't have stress. They do. They just don't hold onto it. By cultivating a winning attitude, they have learned to adapt. They acknowledge stress, work to resolve it, and then move on. In tomorrow's world, survival of the fittest will mean the person who adapts well to stress by going with the flow. This is conscious evolution. To be ready for tomorrow, however, we have to start today.

Many sociologists suggest that living in America, the land of milk and honey, the land where dreams come true, has its downside. It has made us soft, perhaps even spoiled. Living a comfortable life tends to weaken our resolve when challenges, both big and small, come our way. Let there be no doubt: human life is full of ups and downs. Lao Tzu foretold this long ago. His advice was to see the bigger picture and the cycles that make up our lives. More often than not, though, unresolved stress creates a sense of myopia, and we miss the glorious big picture.

The quality of life in America is at an all-time high, while people around the globe struggle to make ends meet and earn only dollars per month. Surely, they are laughing at our contemporary stress "problems" (particularly, at the use of Botox to reduce the effects of aging). However, some Americans have lived long enough to know otherwise. While walking my dog in the local park, I happened to meet Al, an eighty-five-year-old man who takes his dog, Shadow, out to get his morning exercise. He confided that in the days of the Depression there was a lot of stress but not like there is today. "We take so much for granted today. It seems to me that no matter how good life is, people always complain. I am old enough to remember the Great Depression. People today don't know how good they really have it."

Fight, Flight, or Delight?

In a Los Angeles museum stands the skeleton of a six-foot-long saber-tooth tiger with an equally long tail. If you use your imagination a little, it could be scanning the crowd of tourists for its next meal. Chances are, at the intersection of Hollywood and Vine, many millennia ago, this same cat might have snacked on a human being for lunch. A distant relative of the saber-tooth tiger is the mountain lion, and today they roam freely, from the foothills of the Sierras to the Front Range of the Colorado Rockies. Every couple of years, newspapers report that someone was chased by a big cat with a long tail. This really is quite rare. For the most part, the felines are more afraid of us than we are of them, yet a chance meeting can occur and with it, stress.

For every human who became lunch meat for tigers, lions, and bears eons ago, many more escaped. What allowed them to survive these animals' predatory instincts is called the "fight-or-flight response," a survival dynamic that dates further back than anyone knows. The fight-or-flight response gives you a practical choice when you're cornered by something bigger or more dangerous than yourself. You could either stick up your fists and draw blood or, more likely, head for the hills until the danger was gone. Because of our human physiology, we have the ability to do both— at the same time.

Like a fire alarm that rings in the middle of the night, the fight-or-flight response begins with a mental perception that something is amiss. Within milliseconds, the heart starts pumping blood to the extremities. Blood pressure skyrockets to aid the blood's movement to the large muscle groups. The skin becomes sweaty to cool the core body temperature, and a rush of hormones, from epinephrine to cortisol, is secreted to pump sugar and free fatty acids into the blood for energy. All of this (and a lot more) occurs immediately in your body, enabling you to avoid immanent death. This is the sole reason for the fight-or-flight response—physical survival.

With the exception of a chance unscheduled meeting with a mountain lion or quickly passing through a burning building, it's safe to say that (terrorism notwithstanding) most of us rarely find ourselves in the grip of physical danger. But the fight-or-flight response is ready and waiting, in case we ever need it. So, imagine how inappropriate it is for us to trigger this survival alarm when stuck in rush-hour traffic, debugging a computer virus, or coping with a tax audit. With rare exceptions, the fight-or-flight response is an antiquated survival method in today's high-tech world of computer crashes and poor cell phone reception. What was once a valuable asset at the dawn of humanity has now become our greatest liability, threatening our health and well-being. The association between stress and disease is astonishing.

Wired for Stress, Programmed for God

In 1990 the medical establishment dedicated the entire decade to the study of the human brain. With the use of MRI technology and other high-tech methods, long-hidden secrets of brain physiology were brought to light, including what happens during the stress response. In his book *The End of Stress As We Know It*, the researcher Bruce McEwen highlights some of these new insights, such as the fact that a preponderance of stress hormones is believed to inhibit new brain cell growth. Moreover, we now know the exact regions of the brain that are responsible for emotional thought processing, the specific effect of stress hormones, and the intricate relationship between the brain and the endocrine system. Perhaps it's no surprise to learn that we are indeed hardwired for stress.

Referring to the stress response as "allostasis," McEwen says, "The physiological systems that support allostasis follow a basic pattern that's been used quite successfully, for about 400 million years. Surely, these provisions did not evolve for the purpose of causing illness." McEwen admits that for stress, as we know it, to end, there has to be a change in consciousness, or what he calls "positive health." Positive health begins with a conscious response to stress and manifests as many healthful behaviors, such as engaging in cardiovascular exercise, eating a healthful diet, and getting adequate sleep; in essence, living a balanced life.

We may be wired for stress, but, according to Andrew Newberg, M.D., we are also wired for spirituality. In his book *Why God Won't Go Away*, Newberg describes information from brain-imaging data collected from both Tibetan Buddhists and Franciscan nuns, practicing meditation and contemplative prayer, respectively. A SPECT (single photon emission computed tomography) machine shows the way that blood flow to the prefrontal cortex, which correlates with neuronal activity, indicates how people register a transcendent or mystical experience. Newberg found that when the brain is denied typical sensory information, the censor of conscious thought is unplugged, and thus space and time are perceived differently. Meditators often describe this enhanced conscious state as having touched infinity or "being one with everything." The clinical search for the cerebral "G" spot in the brain has led to a new discipline called "neuro-theology," the study of the neurobiology of spirituality. Meditation of any type that promotes the relaxation response seems to enhance these euphoric experiences. Emerging leaders in this field of research have reached a consensus that everyone has the brain circuitry to elicit a mystical experience. Once again, the balance of yin and yang can be achieved through simple brain chemistry.

Mountains and Molehills

There is a world of difference between the stress of locking your keys in your car and that of coping with terminal cancer, but the way some people describe their problems, you would never know it. The mind, in cahoots with the ego, has a great way of exaggerating things to produce the worst possible effect and the greatest amount of sympathy. Molehills quickly become mountains. Just as many people climb Mt. Everest these days, there is no shortage of people ranting about all kinds of catastrophic problems, most of which are molehills. As the expression goes, don't sweat the small stuff; you'll just get wet.

In simple terms, there are two kinds of distress: acute and chronic. Acute stress is very intense but very short term. At the most, these events may last about twenty minutes. Anyone who has ever been pulled over for speeding is familiar with this kind of stress. The list of acute stressors is nearly endless. Ironically, once the problem is over, our memory of it quickly fades and life goes on (until the next encounter). For this reason, acute stress, as intense as it might be, is not a major concern, in terms of its health risk. The problem today lies with chronic stress.

It would be nice if chronic stress lasted only minutes, but, typically, it results from issues and problems that persist for weeks, months, or years. Sometimes they may last even decades. Examples include, but are not limited to, bad marriages, terminal illness, a hostile work environment, addictions, elder care, financial problems, and rebellious teenage kids. At first glance these and similar problems seem insurmountable. Avoiding them, however, is not an option. A Zen proverb reminds us that often "the best way out is through." Stress must be confronted diplomatically, so that we can gracefully move on with our lives.

Despite the abundance of people claiming victimization, enough brave souls have learned to dismantle, circumnavigate, or climb over these obstacles and move on with their lives to show the rest of us that it can be done gracefully. We all have the same potential. If you were to ask people who overcame their stressors about their secret of success, you might hear this sage advice: if your mind got you into this mess, use your mind to get you out of it. These people refuse to see themselves as victims of their situation, and while they would not necessarily call themselves heroes, others surely do.

A Time for Heroes

I lifted the mike to speak and asked the audience members to call to mind a hero in their favorite book or movie. Seated in front of me, a large group of eighth-graders who were enrolled in a health class eagerly raising their hands, offering all kinds of answers.

"Harry Potter," yelled one.

"Frodo Baggins," shouted another from the back of the room.

"Ariel, the Little Mermaid," said a young girl in the front row.

"Neo in *The Matrix*," said a fourth.

"Stanley Yelnats," said a fifth, and as he mentioned this name, I saw the students began to smile, comparing Stanley to Neo. The movie *Holes* had just opened, and from the sounds of it, every kid in the auditorium had seen it.

Ever since the 1999 shootings at Columbine High School, I have been invited to speak to middle and high school students about coping with stress. One school, in particular, has brought me in several times a year to work with teens, in a class called Health Quest. In addition to teaching the kids about anger management, humor therapy, and meditation, I spend a full class period sharing Joseph Campbell's wisdom of the Hero's Journey: how to be a victor, not a victim, to life's problems.

After explaining the difference between a celebrity and a hero, I mentioned a few recognizable names.

"Lance Armstrong?" I asked.

"Hero," they yelled in unison.

"Rosa Parks?" I asked.

"Hero," they again yelled in unison.

"Brad Pitt?" I said.

"Celebrity," they shouted back.

"He's my hero," a girl in the front row said loud enough for the entire group to hear. Everyone giggled.

The Hero's Journey Revisited

Joseph Campbell's name became a household word in the late 1980s, when he appeared in a five-part series with the PBS host Bill Moyers. The show was called *The Power of Myth*, and it explored the format for every great story ever told, a format as old as story-telling itself, and that which is used, with some variations, in novels, television shows, and movies today.

Campbell dedicated the better part of his life to studying the myths and the stories of nearly every culture, past and present, on the planet. Despite the differences in language, culture, climate, and history, he was amazed at the similarity in the structure of these stories. Campbell left no stone unturned when looking behind the message of each story. He found not only astonishing parallels (e.g., virgin births, resurrections, journeys, healings, etc.) but remarkable patterns, in terms of character development. Regardless of its origin, each story spoke to the nature and the triumph of the human spirit. Extrapolating to the human condition, Campbell often referred to each person's life, regardless of gender, as "the Hero's Journey." Perhaps it's no surprise that stress and tension can be found in every story. Apparently, it thickens the plot.

While historians and storytellers haven't kept a running tab on acute stressors over the ages, they have done an excellent job with chronic stress and people who deal well with it. In fact, not only is the stress response embedded deep into our DNA, but the means to solve and resolve problems are encoded as well. It's just that we forget (perhaps it's stored in the inactive strands of the double helix.) Regardless, the retelling of the Hero's Journey serves as a constant reminder to awaken our slumbering spirits and figuratively make our way back home. Now, more than ever, we need heroes.

Having studied the myths and the legends of all ages, from Ulysses in ancient Greece to Dorothy in Kansas, Campbell noticed this interesting trend: in each myth there is a hero, and although the face of the hero may change from story to story, the plot remains nearly identical. In his book *The Hero with a Thousand Faces*, Campbell highlights the progression of the hero's journey, which, as it turns out, mirrors our own lives' sojourns. The three stages of each journey include the departure, the initiation, and the return. As we take a closer look at each stage, please pause for a moment to ask yourself where you are on your hero's journey.

- *The Departure*: The first step in any adventure is to leave your place of origin, which, metaphorically speaking, means change. The departure is a "call to adventure," where you leave your place of comfort and venture into the unknown. Whether it's departing on a ship, as Ulysses did, or on a spacecraft like Luke Skywalker did (George Lucas was a student of Campbell's), every hero must leave home to find himself or herself. In Campbell's words, "The call to adventure signifies that destiny has summoned the hero and transferred his spiritual center of gravity from within the pale of this society to a zone unknown." The departure stage is also called severance or separation, because in some stories, the reluctant hero may be unwillingly forced into a situation. Campbell cites Adam and Eve's exit from Eden as the epitome of a reluctant departure. There are many, many more. If we step outside of the classic myth tale into ordinary life, departure may begin with the first year in college away from home, the death of a parent, the loss of a job, or the end of a marriage. Some people begin their departure simply by driving to work each day. Departures can occur in a great many ways, and fear is never far behind. With the first step out the door, across the threshold, the journey has begun.

- *The Initiation(s)*: Traveling down the road far away from home, crossing many thresholds, the hero is always put to the test. Campbell calls this stage "the road of trials." For some people, the trial may be a dragon (a metaphor for fear); for others, it may be a symbolic river to cross (the River Styx). And for yet others, it may be an evil witch, a wicked stepmother, a daring rescue, or the betrayal of a close friend. In the legend of King Arthur, initially, it was the apprenticeship with Merlin and then the infidelity of his closest friend, Lancelot. Dorothy had the Wicked Witch of the West to contend with, and Frodo Baggins had the ring. In truth, all initiations are personifications that mirror the hero's ego, which he or she must ultimately overcome.

  In your life, initiation can manifest in a thousand ways, including a debilitating injury, the boss from hell, or an abusive alcoholic parent. Some people refer to this life chapter as a rite of passage. Others call it "baptism by fire." In every mythological story, the hero must demonstrate strength, courage, patience, and willpower, to overcome adversity and do it gracefully. Nobody likes a cocky hero. If we fail with the first test, another will appear, until we are strong enough to conquer it and move on. Rest assured, there are many, many tests. Campbell also noted that on every journey there is spiritual assistance, for although each journey is a solitary venture, we are never alone. Frodo had Gandolf, Dorothy had the Good Witch of the North, and we have an undeniable connection to the divine source of the universe, one that is always present.

• *The Return Home*: At some point in the journey, usually upon the success of the initiation process, the hero must return home (even if home is nothing more than a sense of inner peace or homeostasis). Frodo Baggins made it back home. So did Dorothy and the fish Nemo. Even Jesus made it home. Upon crossing the threshold of return, the hero shares the wealth of wisdom and riches acquired on the road. Symbolically, the return home may be accompanied by a trophy of sorts: magical runes, the Golden Fleece, or the medusa's head, all of which convey a pure heart. Campbell points out that there may be a reluctance to want to go home, either because of feelings of shame or, more likely, lust for additional conquests. But return we must, to complete the story. The stage of returning home is also called incorporation, where the returning hero is accepted by his family and peers as an equal, and everyone benefits from sharing his wisdom. Thus the hero becomes a master of two worlds: the one he conquered and the one he has returned to. The return phase offers a promise that all ends well. In the course of one's life, there are many journeys and many trips back home.

Campbell was of the opinion that the power of storytelling, whether around a campfire under the stars or in an epic story on the silver screen, is to remind us that we are participating in our own hero's journey. In all of these stories, the hero successfully overcomes adversity. With arms stretched overhead in the now-familiar Rocky pose, we become the victors, not the victims, of our circumstance. What do Lucy Ricardo, Pinocchio, Maria Von Trapp, Lance Armstrong, and you have in common? According to the template of the hero's journey, a lot. And Campbell had a bit of advice to his fellow travelers. In what has become his most famous quote, Campbell encouraged everyone to "follow your bliss" (a similar expression is "follow the Tao"), suggesting that if your heart and mind are aligned, the journey is truly headed in the right direction.

More Than Fictional Heroes

As I wove Joseph Campbell's insights into the presentation to these teens, students eagerly called out examples of each stage of the Hero's Journey: from Dorothy in *The Wizard of Oz* to Luke Skywalker in *Star Wars*. They quickly grasped the concepts of each stage. To emphasize my point, I added a new name to the list: a real-life hero. As fate would have it, while driving to school that day, I heard on the news of a young man named Aron Ralston, who had gone hiking in Utah several days earlier, only to get his right hand and forearm pinned under a huge boulder—a tumultuous initiation, of sorts. For days, unable to move, he contemplated his ordeal. When it came down to it, he had only one choice. In order to save his own life, he did the unthinkable and amputated his arm with a pocketknife. The road of trials continued as he rappelled sixty feet down the rock face with one arm, to successfully make his way home. That was the day he became a hero. In an interview with the *Rocky Mountain News*, Aron said that his will to live was stronger than his will to die. Willpower, an undeniable inner resource, is a muscle of the soul.

EXERCISE
Your Hero's Journey

Briefly reflect on your own personal journey and where you are at this time in your life. With life being complex as it is, it may seem like you are on many journeys, all at the same time, but integrate these together and take a moment to describe the details of the stage where you now see yourself.

Stage one: The Departure

_____

_____

Stage two: The Road of Trials

_____

_____

Stage three: The Return Home

_____

_____

The Power of Myth

Before his death in 1988, Campbell grew increasingly concerned that many people were losing contact with these sacred stories and the wisdom they contained. There was a time when myths were passed down from parent to child and generation to generation, not merely for entertainment purposes but as ageless wisdom to guide the child on his or her life journey, serving as a wake-up call to the human spirit. Stories from the Bible, the *Bhagavad Gita*, and other sacred scriptures, as well as scores of legends, fables, fairy tales, and folklore, all serve the same purpose: to remind us that we have what it takes to gracefully overcome adversity and make it back home in one piece.

According to Campbell, the tradition of gleaning wisdom from these stories is slowly vanishing in the American culture. With the exception of classics like the *Lord of the Rings* trilogy, it certainly has become diluted in Hollywood's shock-and-awe approach to entertainment. In his discussion of *The Power of Myth*, Campbell related our state of increasing spiritual hunger to our lack of connection to mythological stories. As he explained, when a society forgoes the power of myth and instead replaces it with information, technology, or perhaps nothing, that society becomes less civilized and more destructive. In a few, simple words: perpetually stressed.

Knowing the power of myth, Campbell had an optimistic outlook on the journey of humanity, because he knew the end of the story. "We are at this moment participating in one of the very greatest leaps of the human spirit—to a knowledge not only of outside nature, but also our own deep inward mystery—the greatest leap ever," he said.

Whether we know it or not, we have all embarked on the Hero's Journey: a spiritual quest in human form in an attempt to reach our highest potential. Like stories, fables, myths, and fairy tales told over the centuries, the message of this book serves to gently nudge you from your slumber, helping you get back on the road and eventually home again—in one peace.

The Rules for Being a Hero

As I finished my presentation and made my way out of the auditorium, an eighth-grader approached me.

"My parents are going through a messy divorce, so I can relate to all of this pretty well. I thought you might like this," he said, handing me a piece of paper. "It's called the Rules for Being Human, but after listening to you today, it could just as easily be called the Rules for Being a Hero. Thanks for coming today. You put everything in perspective." I opened the folded paper and read the following:

TEN RULES FOR BEING HUMAN

1. You will receive a body. You may like it or hate it, but it will be yours for the entire period this time around.

2. You will learn lessons. You are enrolled in a full-time informal school called life. Each day of this school, you will have the opportunity to learn lessons. You may like the lessons or think them irrelevant and stupid.

3. There are no mistakes, only lessons. Growth is a process of trial and error and experimentation. The failed experiments are as much a part of the process as are the experiments that ultimately work.

4. A lesson is repeated until it's learned. A lesson will present itself to you in various forms until you have learned. When you have mastered the lesson, then you can go on to the next lesson.

5. Learning lessons does not end. There is no part of life that does not contain lessons. If you are alive, there are lessons to be learned.

6. "There" is no better place than "Here." When your "There" has become "Here," you will simply obtain another "There" that will again look better than "Here."

7. Others are simply a mirror of yourself. You cannot love or hate something about another person unless it reflects something you love or hate about yourself.

8. What you make of your life is up to you. You have all the tools and the resources you need. What you do with them is up to you. The choice is yours.

9. Your answers lie inside of you. The answers to all of life's questions lie inside of you. All you need do is look, listen, and trust.

10. You will forget all of this.

—Chérie Carter-Scott

A Time to Remember

At the same moment that I smelled an aroma of burning sage and cedar, a loud clap of thunder filled my ears. I was about to introduce Michael, a revered Lakota elder, to the conference participants who had assembled to study the art and science of complementary medicine. Michael looked at me and smiled. We both knew the power of offering cedar to cleanse and balance, and we also knew the healing power of thunder. In the time-honored tradition of seeking the sacred wisdom to be shared, on behalf of the entire group I presented to Michael a pouch of tobacco, which he graciously accepted. As I extended my hand in gratitude, I thought of Joseph Campbell, who had embarked on his journey to explore mythology through a similar encounter with a native elder when he was a teenager.

Michael began his eloquent talk with a mythical story of creation, about the spider spirit who weaved a world of creation around the planet earth. Then he spoke of the four directions, the four colors, the four totem animals, and the symbolic meaning that wove all of these aspects together. Once again, the power of myth was resurrected.

"We tell these stories so that we don't forget who we are or why we are here, so we don't forget our sacredness. All life is sacred," he said. "Unfortunately, there are many who have forgotten, even those from my own tribe. I come to honor the sacred hoop and share this wisdom because now is a time for all planetary citizens to remember who we are and why we are here." His comments were punctuated by loud claps of thunder. "The spirits are speaking," he said. "Their voice is a clarion call to remember."

Of course, sometimes we do forget or, worse, fail to listen to the words that keep us on course. This is known as "falling asleep on the spiritual path." Drifting off course may initially seem a bit liberating, but as the winds of change pick up, the emotional barometric pressure begins to increase to a point where feeling lost overcomes feelings of self-reliance, and hope begins to turn to despair. As the clouds move in, a bleak moment attempts to lure us into the dark night of the soul. This, too, is part of the Hero's Journey.

2

Under Pressure

*Giving up is the final solution
to a temporary problem.*

—GERTA WEISSMAN KLEIN

Checking my voice mail after a trip to Asheville, North Carolina, I retrieved a message from a college buddy. "Hey, friend," it began. "I have some bad news. I hate to leave this on your voice mail, but seeing as how you will be gone for a few days, I feel compelled to tell you this. Roger [a mutual friend] has died of an apparent suicide. Call me as soon as you can." Within a few days, the details crystallized to a more clear picture of Roger's demise. Deluged with personal debt and unable to secure a stable professional foothold, Roger decided that the best solution was to take his own life. Upon arriving back home, I discovered an e-mail from my deceased friend, sent days before he checked out. As it turned out, neither I nor anyone else was able to open the attached file, so I never knew what words he tried to share with me before he took his own life. I can only imagine the pain he must have been going through to commit this act of self-destruction.

It's sad to say, but Roger did not hold a monopoly on this kind of pain. Current statistics suggest that as much as one-third of the American population is on antidepressants. Alcoholism, drug addiction, self-mutilation, and suicide are just some of the more popular ways that people cope with their stress today. Through these tactics, people merely avoid the problems at hand, rather than work to resolve them. For stress to be dealt with effectively, no matter how much pressure is bearing down on us, avoidance is rarely a viable option. In the short term, avoidance might seem like the right thing to do, but in the long term, it causes us to get emotionally stuck. Seeing no immediate way out, we may want to throw in the towel and call it quits, leaving the Hero's Journey unfulfilled. Gerta Weissman Klein thinks otherwise. Gerta is a Nazi concentration camp survivor who shared her story as part of the living testimonies in the Holocaust museum in Washington, D.C. After describing her terrible ordeal and her escape, she ended her story of triumph with these heroic words of advice, "Giving up is the final solution to a temporary problem."

Nothing New Under the Sun?

If you listen closely to people's conversations, you might notice how they tend to be stuck: not processing every aspect of a given situation to make sense of it, but rehashing thoughts and feelings, which, in turn, only validates their stress. This becomes a real-life version of the movie *Groundhog Day*, which starred Bill Murray— where every day is a repeat of the last one. As often happens in this case, people are either glued to a past event because of some level of resentment or are frozen in the future because of their fear of something that might happen. Like a recurring dream, these frustrations and fears tend to dominate not only our conversations, but, as Daniel Goleman suggested in his acclaimed book *Emotional Intelligence*, they literally hijack and stifle our positive thoughts as well. The Tao cannot move freely through a fear-based heart.

In what is often called the Universal Law of Attraction, a critical mass of negativity forms, and like a magnet, our mental focus begins to attract more things to complain about. As a result, we get caught in a whirlpool of negativity, from which it is very difficult to escape. While it's true that analyzing our thoughts about past or even future events can be useful, repeating the same old mental tapes is a complete waste of time and energy. Common sense dictates that we need to learn all there is from the situation and then move on. Common sense, however, is not that common, particularly when pessimism takes hold. If we stay stuck in this mind frame of negativity, the consequences are rather staggering, specifically with regard to how thoughts and feelings ultimately affect our physical health. Sometimes all that is needed is a new perspective. In the words of Marcel Proust, "The real act of discovery is not in finding new lands, but in seeing with new eyes." Attitude, once again, is the paintbrush with which we color our world.

Years ago, I was given a book written by Leo Buscaglia called *Living, Loving and Learning*. As many authors do, Buscaglia recounted several childhood memories. One of his most vivid memories, and hence one of mine from the book, was his description of family dinner conversations. Every night, his father asked the kids what new experience they had to share, what one new thing they'd learned that day, what they had seen through new eyes. Buscaglia admits that coming up short, he often excused himself to fetch the encyclopedia and pull out some item of interest. He then returned to the table and shared his mental fortune. Over time, what he really learned from his father's perpetual question was to sharpen his sense of perspective, curiosity, and risk taking. Moreover, he learned to seek life's passion in the present moment.

Being moved by that story, I often ask friends, colleagues, and students the same question. Mostly, I am met with blank stares. Sometimes I get football scores, stock market tallies, and weather updates. Rarely do I get anything that remotely resembles curiosity or adventure. When I pose the same question to kids, however, I gratefully take a seat for at least ten minutes while I get an earful. Children have a knack for living in the present moment. They can find a whole planet in a blade of grass and an entire universe in a forest. As a rule, adults have a hard time living in the present moment. Saddled with responsibilities, they tend to be preoccupied with the past (guilt) or the future (worry). Having a quiet mind and a fearless heart means rising above the confines of past frustrations and future worries to live in the present moment. Is this really possible? Sure! As the author Tom Robbins once said, "It's never too late to have a happy childhood!" There really are new things under the sun; we've just got to take risks and go out and explore them. Here is the Taoist translation: being stuck is a choice of perception.

Uncomfortably Numb

Long ago, I heard a story about how Indians train elephants in Asia. When the elephant is very young, the owner ties a very thick rope around its leg and attaches the rope to a strong, tall pole. As strong as the elephant is, the rope is always stronger. After countless attempts, it resigns itself to the confines of the rope. As the elephant matures, a thinner rope is employed. At the elephant's full maturity, the smallest rope is used. At this point, the elephant is surely strong enough to break the flimsy rope. But because of its conditioning, the elephant assumes that the rope is always stronger than it is and never tries to escape. Sadly, this conditioning process is not unique to elephants. There is an important lesson here: we are often prisoners of our own mental conditioning.

As infants, we are given protective boundaries by our parents, and for good reason. Then, as children, we employ countless means to exercise our freedoms, but our efforts are often caught in the net of limitations we impose on ourselves. Furthermore, as adults we perpetuate our childhood insecurities (e.g., I cannot draw), thus limiting our true potential. Just like the adult elephant, we resign ourselves to the length and the strength of the rope. Ironically, with maturity the limitations are miniscule, but, like the elephant, we are fooled into thinking otherwise. The good news is that a conditioned mind can be reprogrammed.

With regard to being caught in the undertow of life's problems, some questions come to mind. The first is, "Why are you stuck?" or "What is holding you down?" The second is, "How do you get unstuck?" Since the rest of this book is dedicated to getting unstuck, let's examine why some people choose to stay stuck. A colleague of mine with a practice in internal medicine shared this soliloquy, which sheds significant light on the issue:

"You know, there are people who come see me who don't want to be healed. They actually enjoy their illness. Oh, they would never admit that. In fact, these people would most likely deny it. But if you were to unlock the door to their unconscious minds, you would find out that their illness gives them some level of recognition, a strange kind of notoriety. Perhaps its even control over a spouse or a child. This baffles the hell out of me and my colleagues, because our job is to cure them, yet *they* interfere with the healing process. Some patients may say that they want to be healed and go through all the motions and the efforts to reach the elusive golden ring of health, but somewhere along the way, they sabotage themselves. The desire not to be healed is far greater than the wish to be cured, and this secret desire wins out every time. In essence, their identity is wrapped up in the disease. Boy, is the ego a powerful sucker!"

His comment reminded me of my favorite lightbulb joke: How many psychologists does it take to change a lightbulb? Answer: one, but the lightbulb really has to want to change! Whether it's an illness, a dying relationship, or a bad day at the office, the same explanation applies. Unless the mind is totally committed to change, the wheels of limitations just keep spinning in place.

Breaking the Spell of Limitations

I once attended a presentation by a renowned healer who offered advice on how to get on with our lives, should we find ourselves "stuck." When it came time for questions, a woman in the audience stood up and shared a touching story of great personal loss and anguish. The audience was quite moved, but the speaker wasn't. She merely said in a loud voice, "Get over it!" The audience was stunned. Some people laughed nervously, while others whispered their displeasure. Without missing a beat, the speaker continued with her presentation.

What initially may have seemed like harsh words was, in effect, more of an incantation: a means to break the spell of misery and grief. Reflecting on the episode, I realized that in the tradition of myths, fables, and fairy tales, the hero often has a spell cast on him (typically, by some witch). It usually takes a magical feat by the hero to break the spell. Remember, it's not the hero's role to stay stuck in a situation for long because there is a task to accomplish, followed by a homecoming. Fairy tales aside, given the power of the mind, the idea of spells is rather intriguing. Once again, as the saying goes, if your mind got you into this mess, use your mind to get you out of it. The message is that if we can place a spell over ourselves, then, likewise, we have the power to break it. If we cannot break it ourselves, then we can call for divine assistance, as the founder of Alcoholics Anonymous, Bill W., discovered, by calling on his Higher Power.

Mind Over Matter Every Time

Consider this. The average person has over forty thousand thoughts roaming through his or her mind on any given day, perhaps even more. As impressive as that might sound, there's a catch. About 80 percent of these thoughts are repeats from the previous day, week, month, or even year. Here is another catch. Most of these repeated thoughts are perceptions, attitudes, beliefs, and opinions about our personal day-to-day situations or interactions with other people, and the majority of these thoughts are stress-related—unresolved issues of either anger or fear. Like a summer full of reruns on television, our mind is practically frozen on the remote control button of the Recurring Thoughts & Feelings channel. This is anything but A&E!

Here is a new thought, so please read this carefully. Scientists who study human thinking processes—particularly, intentions such as prayer and various forms of healing—are coming to the conclusion that our thoughts and feelings are actually a form of vibrant energy. Stated simply, consciousness is a vital and powerful form of energy. The mind isn't merely a consequence of neuro-peptides being released from brain cells, as some people have hypothesized. Rather, the mind is a limitless bank of conscious energy, which uses the brain as its primary organ of choice. With most thoughts being repeats from a previous page in the book of our lives, it appears that for the most part, the average person's energy is poorly spent on taking one step forward and two steps back, thus causing the individual to lose ground on the Hero's Journey. Given the possibility that our thoughts and feelings are indeed a form of energy, the question begs to be asked, "How and where do you choose to spend your energy?" If we spent a little more time observing our thoughts, we'd realize pretty quickly that we throw away a lot of good energy. Perhaps this behavior pattern is best described as "mind *under* matter."

Bernie Siegel, M.D., who is best known for his book *Love, Medicine and Miracles,* has studied the attitudes, the perceptions, and the feelings of cancer patients for years. He noticed a trend with terminal cancer patients who seem to turn things around and live for years, even when the best medical experts advised them that they had only weeks or months left. So, what's their secret? It appears that the patients who reversed their bouts with terminal cancer had a shift in attitude. Instead of feeling helpless, they grabbed the bull by the horns, tamed the beast, and took it for a joyride. Once again, it's a simple case of the ageless wisdom: mind over matter. In what has now become one of Siegel's more popular quotes, he states, "Thoughts are energy, they can kill or heal." While the disease of cancer is more complex than we currently understand, Siegel's wisdom certainly goes beyond the four walls of the local hospital into all aspects of our lives. Harnessing the power of our thoughts and feelings is germane to our careers, our families, our friends, and everything we do. In the broadest sense, thoughts and feelings are energy; they can move us forward on the journey or make us stall indefinitely. The good news is that we are free to choose our own thoughts.

I once had a student who turned in a journal summary project with the title "Best Friend." In the paper, she said that by observing her thoughts over the entire semester, she noticed a behavior pattern that stopped her in her tracks. She saw herself sabotage her own best efforts regarding her relationships, her career, and her family with a cynical attitude, sarcastic comments, and negative, self-defeating thoughts. She had learned that she was her own worst enemy. After this epiphany, she gradually turned her thoughts and attitudes around, by using optimism and acceptance. In doing so, she became her own "best friend" and has remained so ever since. She closed her journal summary with some sage advice: "I learned that if you find that your life's not flowing, then stop stepping on the hose."

Ego This!

When Freud coined the term *ego*, he placed a big X on the map of the mind, giving credence to a topic of discussion that dated back to antiquity: the issues of identity, control, and manipulation. If you need a quick refresher course on Freud's concepts, he suggested that the ego's main purpose is to avoid pain and promote pleasure. The ego, in the role of mind's censor, has quite a few control cards (he used the term *defense mechanisms*) to draw upon in its bag of tricks—everything from rationalization and projection to sublimation and sarcasm. So, in every situation where we find ourselves stuck, let there be no doubt that the ego is behind the scenes, doing what it does best: casting spells to manipulate our thoughts and perceptions to keep things under control and inhibit personal growth. Unless the ego relinquishes control, the spell won't be broken and "getting over it" won't happen easily.

I have a close friend who works every day to keep moving and not get stuck in an emotional tar pit. By any measure, he's quite a success, but his secret for inner peace comes from a Tibetan proverb that states, "Once you have conquered the enemy within, no external force can harm you." Jon has added a mantra that helps him with this goal: "Keep in mind, I'm from New Jersey, so I might have to translate, but every day I tell myself not to be an asshole." Taoist translation: Jon is working on taming his ego, and he's doing a great job with it. Every day, Jon conquers the enemy within.

A Lesson from Jane Goodall

One of the best definitions of emotional health I've ever come across goes like this: emotional well-being is the ability to feel and express the entire range of human emotions (from anger to love) and to control them, not be controlled by them. Anger is an emotion; so is fear. Despite all that you've heard or read, these are not bad emotions. First and foremost, they are survival emotions. Anger elicits an urge to fight; fear manifests as flight. Together, they constitute a part of the spectrum of consciousness that is employed to avoid physical danger. In terms of physical survival, anger and fear and all the many feelings they generate are meant to last only seconds, perhaps minutes—long enough to get out of harm's way and then move on with our lives. In terms of physical survival, neither anger nor fear is a negative emotion. In fact, they are considered healthy emotions. However, they can certainly become negative if they persist longer than the time that's necessary for us to return to safety or if they are employed for nonphysical threats.

In her inspiring book *Reason for Hope*, the primatologist Jane Goodall describes her many adventures in the jungles of Tanzania, studying chimpanzees. Goodall explained that nearly a whole year had passed before she ever saw the chimpanzees display signs of anger. At first, she thought that perhaps this was one species that truly had no aggression. Upon closer observation, though, she discovered that chimps do indeed have tempers. But unlike their human counterparts, the expressions of anger are barely noticeable. The reason she easily overlooked this behavior was because the episodes of anger were extremely short—one, maybe two seconds—and whatever the problem, it was over. Moreover, Goodall observed that immediately after the brief altercation, the chimps went back to hugging and grooming. Regardless of where you stand on the evolution/creation argument, of this you can be sure: when it comes to resolving anger issues, it appears that chimps are more evolved than we are. Humans are known to harbor feelings of anger for weeks, months, years, and even decades. The question begs to be asked, "Which is the more evolved species?"

Safety in the twenty-first century is far different than it was thousands of years ago. Terrorists notwithstanding, today's safety issues are strongly tied to financial stability, intimate relationships, career objectives, and work-life balance, with traces of anger, fear, or both running rampant through each issue. Thoughts and feelings that, millennia ago, focused on present-moment issues are now heavily filtered through the lens of the ego, serving past memories and future worries as well, thus contributing to prolonged periods of stress. Unresolved issues of anger and fear help no one. Moreover, research is conclusive that unresolved anger and fear suppress the integrity and the function of the immune system. As we now irrefutably know, the body becomes the battlefield for the war games of the mind.

Although several types of roadblocks occur on the path of life, as a rule, they typically fall into one of two categories: issues of anger (fight) and issues of fear (flight). Both of these emotions, when left unresolved, are deeply rooted in the seat of the ego. Recall the dynamics of the stress (fight-or-flight) response. The stress response is a preparation for motion: to either defend your territory or run like hell. Some people suggest that the flight response also includes the act of hiding. Hiding for any prolonged period of time is another way of getting stuck.

EXERCISE
Identifying Your Stressors

Here is a quick exercise to check your personal challenges and take inventory of your life journey right now. This is similar to taking inventory of your stock portfolio and, these days, perhaps just as unsettling. Grab a pen and a piece of paper, and make a list of your top five stressors. As you review your current state of affairs, ask yourself what issues, problems, or concerns you are facing. If you have less than five, consider yourself lucky; if more than five, just list the first five that come to mind. Write these down, and describe them in a few words. When you finish this list, identify the primary stress emotion (anger or fear) associated with the stressors, and estimate how long each problem has loomed on your personal horizon.

	STRESSOR	DESCRIPTION	ANGER/ FEAR	DURATION
1.	_____	_____	_____	_____
2.	_____	_____	_____	_____
3.	_____	_____	_____	_____
4.	_____	_____	_____	_____
5.	_____	_____	_____	_____

The Gilded Cage Is Rusting

Sam won't admit that he's hiding. Instead, he might say that he is just biding his time. But fear is what's behind the biding. Sam has worked for his company for fifteen years. In five more years, he'll be able to retire. The problem is, he's bored out of his mind at work, and five years seems like an eternity. The position he's created for himself has become a gilded cage. He has scouted out different job possibilities, but if he were to take any of them, he'd also take a cut in pay—basically, half of what he's making now— plus a huge reduction in vacation time and other benefits. As the main breadwinner in his family, he would have to sell his house if he took a cut in pay. And there would be other lifestyle inconveniences. So, he says that he feels like he's between a rock and a hard place: if he stays, he's miserable; if he goes, he's miserable. So, he figures that he'll stay and stick it out five more years. *Stick* is the present tense of *stuck*.

J O U R N A L I N G   E X E R C I S E
Unwritten Letters

The following journaling exercise is a vehicle to help you get unstuck and back on the road again. Note: this journal theme, above all others, has been cited as people's favorite theme to help them get unstuck and start to heal their unresolved feelings.

Many times, we want to say something to someone we love, like, or just know well. For one reason or another, whether it be anger, procrastination, or not finding the right words at the right time, we part ways. As a result, those special feelings never seem to be resolved. One of my college students had a former boyfriend who took his own life. He specifically mentioned this student in the note he left behind and his words haunted her for what seemed like an eternity. After counseling, she decided to write him a letter expressing her anger, sorrow, loneliness, and love. Her letter initiated the resolution process and her path toward inner peace.

Resolution through letter writing has been the theme of a great many books, plays, and movies. In a made-for-television movie, *Message to My Daughter*, a young mother with a newborn baby discovers that she has terminal cancer. As part of her resolution process, she records personal messages to her daughter on several cassette tapes. Many father–son relationships also fall into this category, where men feel that their sons might never get to know them in their own lifetimes. It is a common theme found in movies, plays, and books because, as the expression goes, "Art imitates life."

Perhaps because of recent advances in technology, from the cellular phone to the microchip, Americans are writing fewer personal letters. Sociologists worry that future generations will look back at this time period, the high-tech age, and never really know what individuals were actually feeling and thinking, because there will be so few written records. Moreover, psychologists agree that many patients today are troubled and unable to artic- ulate their thoughts and feelings, which results in unresolved stress.

This journal entry revolves around the theme of resolution. When you take pen in hand, it allows your mind to carefully process not only the words but also the feelings aroused by unresolved issues associated with the person to whom the letter is written. Following are some suggestions that might inspire you to draft a letter to someone whom you have been meaning to write to. Now is your chance.

- Compose a letter to someone you were close to who has passed away or perhaps someone with whom you have lost contact for a long period of time. Tell that person what you have been up to, perhaps any major changes in your life, or changes that you foresee in the months ahead. If there are unresolved feelings toward this person, try to express your thoughts and feelings in appropriately crafted words so that you can resolve them and come to a lasting sense of peace.

- Write a letter to yourself. Project yourself to a point in time a decade from now. What advice would you give yourself, with the wisdom you have gained from these years?

- If you have a son or a daughter, what would you like to share with your child now, in the event that for some reason, you do not have the opportunity to do so later? What would you like your child to really know about you? For example, perhaps you would share things about yourself that you wish you knew about your parents or grandparents, which are now missing pieces of your life.

- Write a letter to anyone you wish for whatever reason.

EXERCISE
The Seven Veils Meditation

The following meditation has become a favorite among workshop participants, for helping them to move through barriers that seem to keep them immobilized. If you feel stuck in a particular situation or with a specific person, read through this meditation and, afterward, see whether things begin to loosen up enough to allow you to get moving with your life again. As with any exercise, more than one exposure may be necessary for you to experience the full effect. It may also help to have a friend read it to you.

Introduction

The greatest obstruction on the human highway is our own fear and anger. Fear and anger manifest in human thought and behavior in a great many ways. It has been said that both fear and anger are projections of the ego. In its finest measure, the ego is the bodyguard for the soul; at its worst, it is the greatest impediment toward spiritual growth. Fear and anger are nothing more than illusions. They are exaggerations that the ego uses to move into a position of control. In the Eastern culture, it is said that once these veils of illusion are removed, we are in the presence of the divine.

The following meditation is a soul-searching exercise to lift these veils of illusion and return to the source of unconditional love. Assuming that there are seven veils, use this meditation exercise to change any of your lingering perceptions of disconnection to one of complete harmonious union with the divine, however you conceive this to be. (Please note that you may need to do this meditation several times to feel its full effects, as some veils may be too heavy to lift with the first attempt. Also, if you'd like to use a different metaphor, such as a door or a window, feel free to do so.)

Sit quietly in a comfortable position, with your spine in complete alignment. Close your eyes, and focus your complete attention on your breathing. Take several slow, deep breaths, and come to a place of calm stillness. As you sit, become aware that in front of you are several veils, layers of consciousness that you wish to slowly pull back, for what lies beyond these veils is a view of unparalleled beauty and profound wisdom. This beauty, this wisdom beckons you, but first the veils, one at a time, must be drawn.

The First Veil: Fear

The first veil to dissolve is the veil of fear—fear of the unknown, fear of failure, fear of rejection, and, perhaps most common, fear of death. Fear manifests in a great many ways. Take a moment to search your mind to identify which elements of fear obscure your vision. Ask yourself, "Which aspects of my life fall prey to fear?" Identify one specific fear that surfaces to your conscious mind. Slowly, bring yourself face-to-face with it. In this place of comfort, ask yourself, "Why am I afraid?" Take a deep breath and relax. As you do this, let this thought and the feeling of fear escape as you exhale. In place of the fear, feel a sense of courage. Then see the veil of fear as translucent until it completely disappears, either dissolving into thin air, parting in two, lowering to the ground, or evaporating like fog. To encourage this process, once more take a deep breath and repeat the phrase "I am at peace with my fear, I now release my fear and bring love to my heart once more."

The Second Veil: The Wall of Anger

Anger manifests in a great many ways, from impatience to rage and hostility. Guilt, envy, jealousy, and indignation are also aspects of anger. Search your mind to identify which aspect of anger presently obscures your vision. Which aspects of your life fall prey to anger? Identify one current episode of anger. Slowly, bring yourself face-to-face with it. In this place of comfort, ask yourself, "Why am I angry? What expectation wasn't met?" Take a deep breath and relax. As you do this, let this thought and the feeling of anger escape as you exhale. In place of the anger, feel a sense of forgiveness residing there now. Then see the veil of anger as translucent until it completely disappears, either dissolving into thin air, parting in two, lowering to the ground, or evaporating like fog. To encourage this process, take a deep breath and repeat the phrase "I am at peace with my anger, I now release my anger and bring love into my heart once more."

The Third Veil: The Roadblock of Greed

Greed initially arises out of need, but the ego, expressing insecurity, senses that there never really is enough. As such, the feeling of greed feeds upon itself to keep searching and acquiring more—more possessions, more accolades, more anything, to provide a sense of security. In truth, we are the source of our security. No amount of possessions, money, or compliments will ever fill the void of insecurity. Search your mind to identify which aspect of greed presently obscures your vision. Which aspects of your life fall prey to greed? Identify one current episode of greed in your life, no matter how big or small. Bring yourself face-to-face with it. In this place of comfort, ask yourself what it is in you that feels the need to acquire security through external sources. Take a deep breath and relax, letting this thought and feeling escape as you exhale. Instead of greed, feel a sense of security and stability. Then see the veil of greed as translucent until it completely disappears, either dissolving into thin air, parting in two, lowering to the ground, or evaporating like fog. To encourage this process, take a deep breath and repeat the phrase "I am at peace with my sense of greed. As the source of my security, I now release any feelings of greed and bring love into my heart once more."

The Fourth Veil: The Obstruction of Laziness

Laziness is a stoppage in the flow of the lifeforce of spiritual energy. While it may be nice to stop on the spiritual path and take in the view (this is actually encouraged), a pause that refreshes is not meant to be a twenty-year nap. Inertia builds upon itself, making it harder to start moving again, should the rest be too long. Laziness appears most commonly in the face of addictions, for what begins as an attraction soon becomes a distraction. Some people say that by our very nature, human beings are addictive; however, this needn't be the case. We must walk the spiritual journey in the balance of freedom and discipline. So often, we forget the latter. Search your mind to identify any aspects of laziness, from low motivation to the shadow of an addiction. Which aspect of laziness presently obscures your vision? Which aspects of your life fall prey to inertia? Identify one current episode of laziness or lack of discipline in your life. Bring yourself face-to-face with it. In this place of comfort, ask yourself what it is in you that has allowed this inertia to persist. Take a deep breath and relax, letting this thought and feeling escape as you exhale. In the place of laziness, feel a sense of passion and inspiration. Then see the veil of laziness as translucent until it completely disappears, either dissolving into thin air, parting in two, lowering to the ground, or evaporating like fog. To encourage this process, take a deep breath and repeat the phrase "I am at peace with my sense of laziness, yet I vow to keep the life force of energy moving. I now release any feelings of laziness and bring love into my heart once more."

The Fifth Veil: The Curtain of Desire

Desire is a tether that encumbers dreams and wishes, never letting them get off the ground. Desire is the hand that holds the arrow of intention, yet refuses to let go as the string of the bow is pulled, for fear of losing control. Desire begins as a feather but quickly becomes a rock, pulling even the strongest inspiration down. The opposite of desire is detachment, letting go. The Buddha said that of the four noble truths, desire was the cause of greatest suffering. Take a moment to search your mind to inquire where desire resides. Is there a spark of desire with attachment that presently obscures your vision? Which aspects of your life, your relationships, your values, or your purpose in life reside in the shadow of desire? Identify one personal goal that is tethered to the chain of desire. Bring yourself face-to-face with it. In this place of comfort, ask yourself what it is in you that allows this desire to keep your dream in bondage. Take a deep breath and relax, letting this thought and feeling escape as you exhale. In the place of desire, feel a sense of faith that all will turn out as it should in the divine game plan. Then see the veil of desire as translucent until it completely disappears, either dissolving into thin air, parting in two, lowering to the ground, or evaporating like fog. To encourage this process, take a deep breath and repeat the phrase "I am at peace with my desire, and in recognition, I release my desires with my wishes and dreams and bring love into my heart once more."

The Sixth Veil: The Mask of Pride

Mistake not happiness for pride, nor jubilation in the glory of one of life's many fine moments. Pride is the insatiable ego dominating the limelight of the soul's present moment. Pride is approval seeking, an addiction all to itself. Pride is self-love turned sour. Pride is a consuming need for adoration; if some is good, more is always better. Pride is not self-esteem or worthiness. Pride is conceit, on its way toward arrogance. Take a moment to search your mind to identify any aspects of pride that obscure your vision. Which aspects of your life fall prey to pride? Identify one current episode of pride in your life. Bring yourself face-to-face with it. In this place of comfort, ask yourself what it is in you that has allowed modesty and humbleness to take a back seat to praise. Take a deep breath and relax, letting this thought and feeling escape as you exhale. In the place of pride, feel a sense of godliness that seeks no praise. Then see the veil of pride as translucent until it completely disappears, either dissolving into thin air, parting in two, lowering to the ground, or evaporating like fog. To encourage this process, take a deep breath and repeat the phrase "I am at peace with my sense of pride, yet I vow to turn the passion of pride into humbleness, to serve rather than be served. I now release any feelings of pride and bring love into my heart once more."

The Seventh Veil: Conditional Love

Conditional love, the thinnest of the seven veils, is often mistaken for unconditional love, which is why it is the last of the seven veils to dissolve. Let there be no mistake, the ego desires love. But in an effort for reciprocation, the ego places restrictions and limitations on love. Ifs and whens are the loopholes for love's retraction. The ego places restrictions on the expectations of love as a protection, in the event the goods aren't delivered. So we hold love in reserve, just in case. And like cut flowers, love soon wilts because the source of sustenance is missing. So common are acts of conditional love that they often go unnoticed. Some people say that humans are incapable of the feat of unconditional love. Yet any mother can tell you how possible unconditional love is. Love isn't ours to give, so much as it is ours to share. We are conduits for divine love, when our hearts are open at this time. Search your heart to identify any conditions you place on the love you share with others, such as on your love for family, friends, pets, and even strangers. What conditions of love presently obscure your vision of the vista that lies beyond this last veil? Which aspects of your life fall prey to conditional love? Identify one current episode of conditional love. Bring yourself face-to-face with it. In this place of comfort, ask yourself what it is in you that has allowed these conditions to persist. Take a deep breath and relax, letting this thought and feeling escape as you exhale. In the place of control, feel a sense of compassion. Then see the veil of conditional love as translucent until it completely disappears, either dissolving into thin air, parting in two, lowering to the ground, or evaporating like fog. To encourage this process, take a deep breath and repeat the phrase "I am at peace with my sense of conditional love, yet I now vow to share my love unconditionally, freely. I now release any feelings of control and bring unconditional love into my heart once more."

Now open your eyes and observe what you see with each person you meet today.

The Pause That Refreshes: Breaking Free and Moving On

Sean is a mechanical engineer for a high-tech medical firm in San Francisco. For the last year, he has been unhappy with his job—specifically with the lack of company loyalty, integrity, and employee appreciation. He had been toying with the idea of quitting for the last six months. That's what it looked like from a distance. An inside look revealed that he was mapping out a strategy to start his own consulting company, with everything from business cards and letterhead stationary to a dedicated fax line, contract forms, and a Web page. In addition, during that six-month period, he bankrolled a sizable amount of each paycheck to ensure a smooth financial transition. Like a sailor reading the winds, Sean cut loose from the mother ship and hoisted his sails for new horizons. When everything was in place, he declared independence and resigned from the company. His boss was surprised, as were many of his fellow colleagues, but inside, Sean was beaming.

Meredith is another person who's beaming. About a year ago, she lost her husband to cancer. He had just retired, and they'd planned to spend the next several years traveling around the world. All of those plans and others evaporated with the news of his pancreatic cancer. The shock of losing her husband was devastating. I remember her telling me that "Nothing anyone can do can prepare you for the loneliness of losing a spouse."

I first met Meredith at a social function in town about three months after the funeral. As might be expected, it was no exaggeration to say that she was visibly struck with grief. After the event, Meredith approached me near the coatrack and asked for some advice. I told her that grieving was not only normal but healthy. Yet for every memory that came to mind, I suggested that she make a plan to do something new and different until a new routine had been established.

As normal and healthy as grieving is, prolonged grieving can be unhealthy and is perhaps the epitome of being stuck. At some level, Meredith discovered this. I happened to pull up to a gas station recently, and across the island, Meredith was filling her tank. I walked over to her and immediately noticed a sparkle in her eyes that I had never seen before. We exchanged hugs and smiles, and she told me what she had been doing the last several months.

"I was in Ireland last April. Boy, was it incredible!" she said.

Before I could ask any questions, I got a jubilant five-minute travelogue of the Emerald Isle.

"What's next?" I inquired.

"Oh," she said, "I'm glad you asked. I am flying to New York City in September. I have always wanted to go and see some museums and take in a few Broadway shows." She got into her car and rolled down the window. "I'll send you a postcard," she said, driving away. Sure enough, two months later, I received a postcard of the Statue of Liberty, a symbol of her newfound freedom.

There is a huge difference between being stuck and doing nothing about it versus pausing to survey the situation before you make your next move. Taking time to collect your thoughts, weigh your options, and devise a strategy is not the same thing as being stuck, although anyone will tell you that taking time out to catch your breath can seem momentarily overwhelming. The pause that refreshes is actually several breaths, each one symbolically representing a series of options and backup plans that will ensure your momentum up the next hill before you can begin coasting once again.

What's So Bad about Feeling Good?

In the early 1970s, when Hollywood first began to make movies for television, I discovered a show called *What's So Bad about Feeling Good?*, and it has since become one of my favorites. It starred Robert Morse and Mary Tyler Moore as two hippies living in New York City. The story begins with a sailor in South America who smuggles a toucan aboard his ship, headed for the States. Unbeknownst to the sailor, the toucan is carrying a highly contagious virus. Unlike the West Nile virus, this unique microbe makes people euphorically happy. By the time the ship gets to New York City, the entire crew is floating on cloud nine.

As the ship docks, the bird gets loose and eventually lands on the windowsill of Morse and Moore's pad. Infected immediately, the two leave behind their hedonistic lifestyle and begin what can best be described as a fairy tale. Soon, the whole city is infected. Crime disappears; drug, alcohol, and tobacco use becomes nonexistent; and New York City, as well as other cities, starts to look like nirvana—that is, until the government steps in. Apparently, when the alcohol and tobacco use evaporated, so did the tax base, which worried the elected officials. So, an immunization was created and secretly put into the gasoline, which, via multitudes of combustible car engines, mixed with the city's air pollution, and within days, everything was back to normal. Well, almost normal. As it turns out, some people, like Mary Tyler Moore's character, never caught the virus in the first place. It seems that she was already happy, but, being caught up in all the problems of city life, she forgot it. The toucan simply reminded her of what she already knew. It awakened her soul.

The reason I liked the movie so much is because of its subtle message. Optimism is a trait that we all have; it just tends to become dormant if we get stuck in the negativity of each day's issues. Ironically, it seems that there is a virus going around the country today, but unlike the toucan's virus, this one is a highly communicable, fear-based virus. It spreads through rudeness, sarcasm, impatience, negative conversations, catastrophic news headlines, and any other means it can use to proliferate. But like the character whom Mary Tyler Moore played, we don't have to be passive victims to this virus. We can make a conscious choice to become unstuck and start moving. What's so bad about feeling good? What's so bad about feeling balanced? Absolutely nothing!

Out of a Rut, into a Groove

What's the difference between a rut and a groove? An engineer might say the depth of the hole you find yourself in, but in the context of the Hero's Journey, the real answer is your attitude. As the saying goes, "Attitude is everything!"

You feel a sense of liberation when you're free from the rut of despair and perhaps feel even more freedom when you're in the flow of life. Attitude is the first step to get you out of the rut and into the groove. What is the winning attitude to make this happen? Any thought, feeling, or perception that unlocks you from the bondage of fear or anger (and all of the many ways that either of these emotions can manifest). A winning attitude is not a feeling of competition. It is a sense of self-reliance and empowerment.

A Final Story about Moving On

One day while listening to National Public Radio, I heard an interview with the screenwriter and director Allison Anders. Her movie *Things Behind the Sun* was about to air on a cable network, and she spoke about various aspects of the movie's theme and production. In the course of the interview, Allison was asked about an episode early in her life, in which she had been raped, and how it had affected the rest of her life. She commented that it certainly was one of several key life moments, but when the radio host persisted, Allison said this: "This event was about one hour of my life. It's not my whole life." Like Gerta Weissman Klein, Allison has learned how to cross the threshold of roadblocks and continue gracefully on her hero's journey.

• • •

The Taoist path through stress and spirituality has many thresholds for us to cross. More than a series of tests to build character, they are attempts to polish the rough edges of our soul. In essence, each threshold, disguised as a stressor, is a lesson in consciousness that will help the human spirit to evolve. The recognition of this symbiotic relationship between stress and spirituality is the Taoist hallmark of the Hero's Journey.

PART II

Crossing the Threshold

Stress and spirituality are inseparable partners on the Hero's Journey, for wherever there is stress, there is always divine guidance—when we take the time to listen. As a Chinese proverb reminds us, "When the pupil is ready, the teacher will come." The hero with a thousand faces, as Campbell called our spiritual essence, is also equipped with a thousand inner resources to help us cross the threshold of the unknown and deal with whatever challenges lie ahead. Crossing the threshold successfully is the transition from despair to hope, from fear to courage, and from doubt to faith. This part highlights the ageless wisdom that describes the dance between stress and human spirituality and contains stories of several everyday heroes who have learned to use these inner resources (muscles of the soul) to meet each and every challenge successfully. By example, they lead us further on our own journey with a quiet mind and a fearless heart.

3

Stand Like Mountain,
Move Like Water

God, grant me the serenity to accept

the things I cannot change,

the courage to change the things I can, and

the wisdom to know the difference.

—Reinhold Niebuhr

So common is the concept of balance that we tend to take it for granted. Yet so powerful are the intricacies of balance that when we are reminded, it often takes our breath away. Such is the power of opposites, which, when united, form a whole. This is the subtle yet powerful message of the Tao, the union of opposites leading to wholeness through balance and harmony—lessons that are quite easily observed in nature. The seeds of Taoist philosophy were first planted in the Chinese culture, but like all truths found in the depths of ageless wisdom, its message is both timeless and universal. Even the book of Psalms in the Bible is loaded with pearls of Taoist wisdom.

Carl Jung once said that the philosophies of the East and the West were so vastly different that he assumed the two would never meet eye to eye, nor would the culture of one adopt the signatures of the other. So I wonder what he would think today, if he saw countless Americans having their houses feng shui'ed or saw how commonly the yin/yang symbol appears on clothing and tattooed bodies. I myself was surprised when a military student walked into class one night wearing combat fatigues. On the top of his left shoulder was the now-familiar half-black, half-white Taoist circle. When I asked him whether he knew what the symbol represented, he answered as if everyone knew this—opposites that come together to bring wholeness, balance, and harmony. There is a common joke in Washington, D.C., about military intelligence being an oxymoron, but, clearly, this was no joke. Maybe because the concepts of balance and harmony are so universal, Jung wouldn't have been that surprised, after all—but I was.

Of Mountains and Water

In the fall of 1981, I was assigned to teach my first stress-management course at the University of Maryland. My predecessor had taught only "sound Western approaches," proven by Western science. He encouraged me to do the same. At a time when saying the word *echinacea* would garner a response of "Gesundheit," I felt that I was rather novel in teaching a holistic approach in what can best be described, at the time, as a very conservative discipline. Within my first week of teaching this course, a student who looked no older than seventeen walked up to me and said quite confidently, "You know, everything you have mentioned about stress management I have already heard before." Realizing that college kids can be hip and knowing how young he was, it occurred to me that he just might be lying. But I gave him the benefit of the doubt and inquired where he had come upon this wealth of knowledge. "In my tai chi class," he answered. In the back of my mind I could see Jung smiling.

"We just learned a proverb that I thought you might be interested in," he said. "It goes like this, 'Stand like mountain, move like water.'" He then smiled at me, said he enjoyed the course, shook my hand, and headed out the door. Upon first hearing this phrase, I have to admit that it resonated deep within me, and it has become a personal mantra ever since. Once again, I was reminded of the power of opposites and the message of balance. These six words contain a lot of power. To "stand like mountain" means to stand strong and tall in the midst of change. It means to be secure in your being and stable in your environment. Conversely, to "move like water" means to go with the flow with things you cannot control. It also speaks to the nature of taking the path of least resistance, rather than trying to budge an immovable object or change someone else's behavior. The metaphors of mountains and water have universal appeal. Thomas Jefferson once said, "In matters of style, swim with the current; in matters of principle, stand like a rock."

Balance is an inherent part of our constitution. Whether in our first attempts to walk upright or ride a bike or in our regular efforts to balance our checkbooks, it is the human condition—mind, body, spirit, and emotions—to continually strive for balance. Since first hearing this proverb, I have learned that almost every culture has a similar expression that speaks to the nature of living one's life in balance. The American version is a little longer than the Chinese axiom, but the message is the same, and Reinhold Neibuhr's "Serenity Prayer," a preamble to many twelve-step programs, is the best stress-management advice I've heard summed up in twenty-seven words: "God, grant me the serenity to accept the things I cannot change, the courage to change the things I can, and the wisdom to know the difference."

Stress and Spirituality

Anyone who has experienced a lot of stress lately will most likely tell you that his or her life is definitely out of balance. These same people, if asked, might say that stress and human spirituality don't belong in the same sentence, because these concepts are mutually exclusive. At a quick glance, stress and spirituality may seem like polar opposites of the human experience, but with the perspective of balance, like the yin/yang symbol, they are nothing less than partners in the dance of life, with each half taking a turn leading the dance.

In the first chapter, I highlighted several definitions of stress; however, the best definition I have come across in recent years states that stress "is a perceived disconnection from our divine source." Although the stress emotions, anger and fear, can be an asset in times of physical danger, they quickly become a liability when left unresolved for weeks, months, years—even decades. In simple terms, unresolved issues of fear and anger literally choke the life force of the human spirit. If they persist too long, they will ultimately wreak havoc on our bodies because there is no separation between body and spirit. You don't have to be the Pope, the Dalai Lama, or an Amazonian shaman to realize that every infraction of the moral code of humanity, whether it's lying, stealing, or murder, is based on unresolved issues of anger and fear.

In the Eastern culture, unresolved issues of fear and anger are often described as the "veils of illusion." In artwork, they are symbolically represented as clouds because they obscure our vision, our clear perspective. The result is a feeling of separation from our divine source, rather than a strong connection to it. Nothing could be further from the truth—we are *never* abandoned, separated, or disconnected from our divine source. There are no degrees of separation from God, although misperceptions give strength to these veils, adding layers and layers, to the point where, metaphorically speaking, darkness overcomes light. Perhaps it's no coincidence that this is typically how people describe states of depression, which is often called anger turned inward or, as the comedian Steven Wright says, "anger without the enthusiasm."

Our view of life can become rather myopic, a fact that has not gone unnoticed among optometrists. Studies show that the more stressed a person becomes, the greater the loss of peripheral vision. The phenomenon is known as "Streff syndrome," named for Dr. John Streff, who first observed the relationship between emotional stress and eyestrain. The implications of myopia go well beyond the practical to the metaphorical aspects of "vision." Perhaps the poet Maya Angelou said it best when she wrote, "I believe that Spirit is one and everywhere present. That it never leaves me. That in my ignorance I may withdraw from it, but I can realize its presence the instant I return to my senses. . . . I cannot separate what I conceive as spirit from my concept of God."

A Spiritual Hunger?

A disease is spreading across the country that has the potential to become a worldwide epidemic. The disease is called "affluenza," and the overriding symptom is a desire to buy and consume all kinds of goods and products, which in turn gives a sense of temporary contentment. Like an addiction, each purchase is a "fix" to soothe an insatiable desire for pleasure. The thrill doesn't last very long. So the next purchase is made to satisfy the threshold once again, and this cycle simply repeats itself. Collectively, this behavior may be great for the economy, but the result is a disaster for the human soul, because no amount of external goods can provide or sustain a sense of inner peace. The irony is that even though almost everyone knows this, we keep on shopping anyway, hoping that something will ultimately fill the spiritual void.

It is interesting to note that some people, known as the "cultural creatives," not only shop for material goods, they also shop around for ideologies to help govern their lives. People are no longer satisfied with answers derived from conventional wisdom to various issues in their lives. In an age of the Genome Project, cloning, planetary travel, and molecular microchips, humankind is taking on responsibilities that were once thought the domain of God, and the old wine skins cannot contain the new wine. As a result, people feel a deep-seated hunger to know more than the existing paradigms can possibly tell them. The term that describes this search for truth is *spiritual hunger*: the drive that answers the call to adventure. When stress is thrown into the equation, the hunger pangs become more noticeable, and thus the search intensifies. As such, people are seeking wisdom from sources that were inconceivable a generation or two ago, most notably from the Eastern philosophies such as Buddhism and Taoism. The Internet has certainly speeded up the process. Moreover, as the pressure of stress increases, so do the pangs of spiritual hunger.

In times of crises, people of every generation and every culture have been known to seek help from a divine source. In the past, they took spiritual refuge in their religious traditions. Although many still do, today many more seem disenchanted with standard religious practices, either for moral reasons or because these don't seem to provide answers to the problems looming on humanity's horizon. An article titled "Choosing My Religion" cites: "In 1958, for example, only 1 in 25 Americans had left the religious denomination of their upbringing. Today, more than one in three have left or switched. Most still believe in God, but now they are looking for a personal spiritual practice. According to a recent survey from the McArthur Foundation, seven out of ten Americans say they are religious and consider spirituality to be an important part of their lives. But about half attend religious services less than once a month or never."

In what is being called by some the postdenominational age, many people feel only a distant loyalty to their particular religious upbringing. Instead, they are seeking a host of sacred traditions, blending various practices to form their own spiritual paths. There are Catholics who practice Buddhist meditation, Jews who participate in Native American sweat lodges, and Methodists and Mormons who participate in Sufi dancing. Even hell has gotten a makeover, as the biblical conception of the most dreaded place in the universe moves from a literal to a figurative interpretation. Once it was described as eternal flames of death, but the Vatican now describes hell as being much like stress: "a state of those who freely and definitively separate themselves from God." Many people who claim to have already been to hell (on earth, that is), as well as those who have come close, are seeking a better understanding of God on a more intimate level.

Waking from a Spiritual Slumber

Once again, the expression used today is *spiritual hunger*, a term that describes a searching or a longing for truth that cannot be attained solely through one traditional religious practice. Another term used in conjunction with *spiritual hunger* is *spiritual bankruptcy*, a concept that suggests a sense of moral decay, perhaps due to an emptiness that cannot be filled with an abundance of material possessions, yet a strong element of human nature (the ego) encourages us to try anyway. We need only reflect on the 1999 shootings at Columbine High School in Colorado or other events like it to see that something is terribly amiss.

On the evening of December 31, 1999, Reverend Billy Graham was interviewed during the televised millennium celebration. Unlike others, Graham expressed words of caution: "I am afraid that people are losing their faith in God and replacing it with a faith in technology that will solve all our problems. They are being led down the wrong path. There must be a change in the human heart." The change Graham referred to is typically called a spiritual awakening (or remembering): moving from a motivation of fear to love, from an anxious heart to a fearless heart.

A third phrase commonly heard today is *spiritual dormancy*. It refers to people who, for one reason or another, choose not to recognize the importance of the spiritual dimension of health and well-being, at both an individual and a societal level. The result of such inaction often leads to a state of *dysfunction* (a term many now call our national adjective). Like a person who hits the snooze button on the alarm clock, falling asleep on the spiritual path can have real consequences, because, unaware, the individual is ill-equipped to deal with the problems at hand, as well as with potential problems down the road.

The Three Pillars of Human Spirituality

If you were to talk to the shamans, the healers, the sages, the mystics, and the wisdom keepers of all times and all languages throughout the history of humanity and ask them what aspects constitute the core of human spirituality, you would hear them unequivocally say the same three things, time and time again: relationships, values, and purpose in life—all of which lead one to a higher consciousness of the divine. Even with the understanding that human spirituality is extremely difficult to articulate (some say impossible), the unique alchemy of relationships (how we relate to ourselves and others), values (what we deem important in our lives), and purpose in life (why we are here in a mystical divine game plan) is understood to be at the heart of spirituality.

EXERCISE
The Spiritual Roots of Stress

Try taking this simple test. Make a current list of your top ten stressors: ten issues, concerns, problems, or dilemmas that you currently face. If you have forty-nine, please limit them to your top ten. If you have less than ten, consider yourself lucky and write down whatever comes to mind.

YOUR TOP TEN STRESSORS

1. _____   6. _____

2. _____   7. _____

3. _____   8. _____

4. _____   9. _____

5. _____   10. _____

Once your list is complete, place a checkmark by all the items that involve people or relationships. Next, place a checkmark next to each stressor that involves values or a values conflict, such as time, money, leisure, education, or privacy. Finally, place a checkmark next to any and all items that relate to a meaningful purpose in life (career, family, etc.). Now look once again at your list of stressors. If you are like most people, you will find that not only is everything checked off your list, some items may be checked off more than once. Stress and human spirituality are not mutually exclusive. They are inextricably linked. Ageless wisdom suggests that stress is an opportunity for spiritual growth, when we set aside the anxiety, the grief, and the frustrations that cloud our vision and learn from the situation at hand.

Spirits on a Human Path

During the many classes and workshops I've taught on stress management, people often ask me why, if they have followed all the rules, have they encountered such terrible circumstances? In essence, they are asking the perennial question "Why do bad things happen to good people?" When catastrophic things do happen, most people feel as if they are being punished, which leads us back to the idea of divine abandonment. The best answer I have heard to this question is from the renowned theologian and mystic Teilhard de Chardin, who once said, "We are not humans having a spiritual experience. Instead, we are spirits having a human experience." The Jungian analyst and author Jean Shinoda Bolen put it another way: "We are not humans on a spiritual path. Rather, we are spirits on a human path." These words strike a resonating chord in the soul of each individual who hears them because they bear the truth. Every time I share these words with an audience, I see reaffirming nods, which suggest to me that like the Ten Rules for Being Human, this is a nugget of innate wisdom that we tend to forget.

From the wisdom of Joseph Campbell and others, we learn that the divine source scattered itself like a multitude of seeds to the directions of the four winds in an adventure called the "human experience." In this urge to explore humanity from the inside out came the promise that all the scattered seeds would return home at some point, to share the multitude of life experiences: the good, the bad, and the ugly, and the meaning each one holds. This is what Campbell described as the quintessential human journey. It was Campbell who reminded us that only brave souls (heroes) walk the human path, because earthly existence is enshrouded in many veils of illusion. It is a brave soul on a noble adventure who attempts to lift these veils. In doing so, courageous souls are no strangers to stress on the Hero's Journey. Stress, we are reminded, thickens the plot.

True to the nature of the Tao, human spirituality reflects not only the dynamic peak experiences in life's expedition but the valleys as well. Human spirituality is as subtle as it is dynamic and as joyous as it is painful. Given the chance, moments of strife, conflict, boredom, and tension will offer unique spiritual nuggets of wisdom. In the midst of stress, though, the lessons offered may seem muddled in fear. Yet when viewed from the perspective of hindsight, the focus of soul consciousness is remarkably clear. With any sense of honesty, we will say to ourselves, "Oh, that's why that happened." More often than not, each stressor that appears like a thick cloud overhead turns out to have a magnificent silver lining—if we take the time to look. This, too, is the promise of the Tao: opposites are contained in the whole when we take the time to look for them.

If you see yourself as a human being on a spiritual path and something goes terribly wrong, you may feel as if you have been betrayed or abandoned by the divine force with which you are aligned. But if you recognize that you are indeed a spirit on a human path, then every situation that you encounter will be a learning experience. This is how consciousness evolves. Every lesson is based on the principles of love, in all its many manifestations.

Learning from experience is a choice that not everyone is willing to make because of the responsibility that goes with each lesson— it takes a significant conscious effort to ensure that each of our actions comes from a place of love, rather than of fear, when we cross each threshold of the journey. How long is the human journey, you ask? Ultimately, our destination cannot be measured in miles or years, nor can our success be measured in material wealth, though many have tried. Some say that it cannot be measured at all. I once heard a wisdom keeper say that the spiritual path is measured to be about twelve to fourteen inches—the distance from your head to your heart. The evolution of the soul (our spiritual growth) is gauged entirely by our capacity to love and receive love.

The Path and the Journey

Several years ago I took a trip to Switzerland with the intention of climbing the Matterhorn, one of the world's most dynamic mountains—a rugged peak that stands alone, majestic and proud. The town of Zermatt is itself a picturesque storybook town with narrow cobblestone streets and Tudor architecture: the quintessential Swiss Alpine village. When I arrived, I half expected to see Heidi running through the nearest meadow to greet me.

During my first night in town, I learned that the Matterhorn goes by several names, for it sits on the border of both Switzerland and Italy. The Italians call it Mounte Cervino, and if you say this with the right accent, it sounds kind of sexy. The French, being more dignified, refer to it as Mont Cervin. I am told that for several years, the British called it the Citadel. One mountain, four names. A powerful message.

Although not considered a difficult technical climb, the Matterhorn is renowned for being enshrouded in thunderclouds, which makes climbing extremely dangerous. The north face of the Matterhorn, which looks down on the village of Zermatt, Switzerland, has four distinct routes to the top and perhaps just as many on the Italian side. The morning I set out to reach the summit, the sky was a deep blue. Clouds were nowhere in sight. I made it three-quarters of the way up, before I was forced back down by bad weather. As I descended, I pondered the symbolism of the mountain's many names and the equal number of paths to the top. Like the metaphor it represented, the message was equally profound. (As a side note, I returned to the base to learn that the Matterhorn had been designated as an international peace park!)

One Destination, Many Paths

Ask any alpine hiker on a trek what his or her destination is, and the answer is nearly the same: the summit of some mountain.

Reaching the top is not merely a challenge; the height of a summit offers a vast, breathtaking view of the surroundings. Perhaps this explains the popularity of climbing Mt. Everest. Likewise, the drive that inspires the human journey is a desire to have this view of life—a clearer understanding of life's mystery and our role or purpose in it.

If our life's journey can be compared to a metaphorical expedition, then realizing our divine connection is analogous to reaching the mountain summit. In the words of Martin Luther King, "I have been to the mountain." To stand on a mountain peak with your arms stretched overhead in the familiar "Rocky pose" epitomizes the expression "I have touched the face of God." Ask any hiker about the best route up a mountain, and he or she will tell you that there is no one best path. Rather, several paths are available to reach the peak, each offering a different experience. If you were to ask any sage, mystic, or healer—someone who truly speaks from the heart—which is the best path to the divine source, this individual would smile and tell you that there is no one path, only the path that is best for you, according to where you are at this time. Carlos Castaneda became renowned the world over for his book *The Teachings of Don Juan*, which explored the further reaches of human spirituality. In it, he wrote, "Look at every path closely and deliberately. Try it as many times as you feel is necessary. Then ask yourself and yourself alone, one question. Does this path have a heart? If it does, it is good; if it doesn't, then it is of no use."

The path of human experience would be mighty crowded if everyone embarked at the same time. Therefore, it stands to reason that not only are there numerous paths, but we each move at a pace that's conducive for our own soul growth process. Like a college curriculum, no two paths are quite the same. Furthermore, if you glance around the spiritual landscape, you might notice that more often than not, it appears rather empty. Many times, the stressors we face make us feel isolated, forgotten, and lost. The good news is that as lonely as we may feel, it is impossible for us to get lost on the spiritual path, and we are never alone. The biggest problem is being immobilized by our own fears and frustrations.

As you focus on issues of the heart and the soul, your path will frequently align with, intersect, and parallel other trails over the course of your life. Although these words seem to contradict religious dogma, wisdom keepers agree that it matters not which path you take—Christianity, Judaism, Islam, Mother Earth Spirituality, or another—but only that you keep moving forward (growing) on the path you have chosen. Choosing to rest on the sidelines indefinitely is perhaps the greatest sin known to humanity (sin is derived from the word *inertia*), and this course of action serves no one. In addition, for a path to enhance the maturation or the evolution of your spiritual well-being, there are some recommended caveats. First, the spiritual path must be creative, not destructive. Next, it must be progressive, not regressive. It must stimulate and enhance, not stifle, the human spirit. Finally, true to the nature of any expedition, it is important for us to pack lightly, which means a minimum of emotional baggage. Remember, unlike a mountain trek in the Himalayas, there are no Sherpas on the Hero's Journey. As Frodo discovered in the *Lord of the Rings*, we each have to carry our own burden. Traveling light is great advice, but too often we become burdened by the additional weight of our thoughts and emotions, many of which no longer serve us.

If following a spiritual path were like coasting downhill, it might be fun at first, but sooner or later, it would be less than challenging. The spiritual path is anything but easy. Every journey will have its moments, and the spiritual quest is no different. You will be sure to encounter stressful moments because stress provides the resistance to strengthen the soul for what lies ahead. Gail Brook Burket once described it this way.

I do not ask to walk smooth paths
Nor bear an easy load.
I pray for strength and fortitude
To climb the rock strewn road.
Give me such courage and I can scale
The headiest peaks alone,
And transform every stumbling block
Into a stepping stone.

Profiles of Spirituality

Newspapers, magazines, and books are often filled with stories of remarkable human achievements, nothing less than grace under pressure. If they are well written, they portray the triumph of the human spirit, even if the protagonist's physical health is severely compromised. Take, for example, Marc Wellman, a man who became a paraplegic due to a climbing accident in 1982. Casting aside this limitation, he made it his goal to climb El Capitan Mountain in Yosemite National Park. In 1989 he did just that before a televised audience. Undaunted by the challenge, in 1991 Wellman climbed another of Yosemite's peaks, Half Dome.

A similar, but no less remarkable, story of grace under pressure is that of the former model Gari Carter. While driving on a country road one snowy afternoon in Virginia, Gari was hit head-on by a car whose driver lost control. Upon impact, her car spun in circles, then smashed into a side rail. Gari crashed through the windshield, and metal and glass destroyed her face. Medics were astonished to see that she was still alive. Completely immobilized and grossly marred, she was told that the damage to her facial structure was nearly irreparable. Gari was determined to come back strong, and that she did. I met Gari at a conference in Florida, where she explained that with incredible willpower and fortitude, she incorporated prayer, meditation, and a host of healing practices into her life, which have allowed her to return to normal.

One day while waiting to have my car serviced, I scanned a copy of *People* magazine and came across a story of a little girl who had survived a terrible fire. Her entire body had been engulfed in flames, with every inch brutally burned. She was horribly disfigured, so much so that she didn't even look human but resembled an insect or an alien. Yet if you glanced into her eyes, all doubt was removed. Within her eyes was a light, a sparkle of energy, an undeniable sense of the divine spirit within.

The Will of the Human Spirit

My father died of cancer in the fall of 1993. I flew to Florida to see him and stayed by his side for days, holding his hand until he took his last breath. As is common with people dying of a terminal illness, he waited until I arrived to explain several last-minute items he wished to have attended to. They seemed rather trivial to me, but to him, they were extremely important. Each day the hospice nurse visited and administered her special care. One day I walked her to her car and asked her point-blank how much longer my dad had to live. He hadn't eaten in well over a week and, from what I could tell, had taken no fluids either. Everything in my educational training suggested that a person couldn't live for more than three days without water, yet here he was going on five.

With a faint smile, she said, "It's hard to say, exactly. I know the scientists say you cannot go more than a few days without water, but I can tell you I've seen more than a few people hang on for weeks without taking anything. They are waiting . . . waiting for that son or daughter or perhaps a special someone to walk through that door, so they can say good-bye before they take their last breath. I've seen it too many times to know that it's very real." She gave me a hug, then got into her car to drive to the next patient. Before starting the car engine, she rolled down her window and motioned for me to come closer.

"There is an undeniable strength of the human spirit," she said. "It defies everything we understand rationally." With that, she waved and drove away.

Everyone in this earthly existence is forced to face the trials and the tribulations of the human journey. Although, on the surface, they look quite different, the lives of a Tibetan monk, an Irish musician, a Mexican housemaid, a New York stockbroker, a Korean schoolteacher, and a Peruvian farmer have more in common, in terms of human experiences, than the cultural or geographic differences that seem to separate them.

As the world of six billion people transforms from a collection of several hundred independent nations into a global village engaged in political commerce and economic trade, inundated with environmental toxins, and enthralled with digital communication, human spirituality and the evolution of human consciousness will take on greater roles as we pool our resources to help solve the problems that besiege our planet.

The Seasons of the Soul

In the course of my talks and lectures over the years on stress management, I often shared timeless insights that I call the "Seasons of the Soul." As if I were describing the search for the Holy Grail, the room always became very still and everyone was mesmerized by the allure of the message. One reason why this concept is so compelling is that we intuitively recognize the alchemy between humanity and divinity; perhaps the knowledge of this is even encoded in our DNA. Ironically, it's a message that is easily forgotten in the hustle and bustle of a twenty-first-century life, yet it begs to be heard again and again. Like a road map, this template of the soul's growth process gently and gracefully guides us toward the next stage of our own journey.

What is your favorite season? Spring, when the earth comes to life? Summer, with its oodles and oodles of sunlight and time to enjoy the outdoors with friends and family? Perhaps it's autumn, when the air is crisp and clean, or if you happen to reside in Colorado, as I do, you know that for some people who live to ski or snowboard, winter rules! We live on a special planet, one of the few known not only to revolve on its axis but at various times to tilt toward or away from the sun on its elliptical path, which gives us four distinct seasons. Like the planet we inhabit, so, too, does the human soul have four distinct seasons. The essence of these seasons is as old as the hills, and it can be found in stories, myths, and legends from all cultures and in every language. It is the mythic Hero's Journey so eloquently described by Joseph Campbell; it is the fourfold spiritual path outlined by the theologian Matthew Fox in his concept of creation spirituality; it is the template used by the American Indians in the vision quest; and it is the flow of the Tao, recounted by Lao Tzu many millennia ago. By all accounts, it is the human heart's yearning for wholeness.

We begin with the centering process (autumn), where we leave the known of the external world and enter the unknown depths of the mind. Next comes the emptying process (winter), a time of clearing and a cleansing of thoughts and feelings that no longer serve us; this may involve some grieving. As spring follows winter, so the grounding process follows the emptying process, a period in which new insights are gained to improve our quality of life. The fourth season is the connecting process (summer), where we come back home to share the wisdom we have learned and to celebrate the sacred connectedness of life.

Following is a more detailed look at each season. At the end of each section are meditation and journaling exercises to help you integrate these concepts, enhance your experience, and progress in whatever season you currently find yourself.

The Centering Process (Autumn)

One of the most glorious churches in all of Europe is the Chartres Cathedral about fifty miles west of Paris. Among the many features that make this place so sacred is its renowned labyrinth, a self-guided walking meditation that brings you to the heart of your soul. So popular is this labyrinth that its pattern has been replicated in churchyards and gardens all over the world. So profound is the experience that the memory of it will last a lifetime.

As you walk from the entrance of the circle's perimeter through a gentle maze of smaller concentric circles to the center, a divine stillness quiets the soul and a transformation takes place to prepare you, the student, so that the inner teacher will come. The word *center* actually contains the word *enter*. With this word, like the path of the labyrinth, is an implicit invitation to enter the heart. If the spiritual path is truly twelve to fourteen inches, from the head to the heart, then look no further than the centering process to get you there.

As we embark on our journey of self-exploration, we depart from a cacophonous external world of noise and distraction and enter into a less-familiar world that begs examination. This simple exercise becomes a version of the Hero's Journey all its own—from the known to the unknown (and back safely home). Ageless wisdom from all cultures reminds us that if we can calm the waters of the mind, we will see in the still reflection a depth of knowledge to help us solve our problems. The centering process is the first step to calming these waters.

The centering process is analogous to the fall season, where the tilt of the earth's axis decreases the amount of sunlight in the course of the day. As a consequence, people tend to head indoors and spend more time inside. The centering process also invites us to spend more time exploring the mind's inner landscape. In some circles, this is commonly known as soul-searching. Thus, we gain a sense of spiritual balance that is hard to come by any other way. The centering process underscores the wisdom of many luminaries, from Lao Tzu ("Be still and discover your center of peace") and Paramahansa Yogananda ("Calm the mind that without distortion it may mirror Omnipresence") to Psalms 46:10 ("Be still, and know that I am God").

Sensory Static Defeats a Quiet Mind

In the theme of balance, the time we spend with the five senses, searching externally, must be balanced with the time we spend going within, where sensory stimulation is first minimized, then eliminated, to reach the stillpoint of consciousness. Getting to this stillpoint isn't always easy. As in so many fables and myths where the hero is sidetracked, there are many distractions.

Current estimates suggest that the average person is bombarded with more than three thousand media messages a day. They range from television ads and billboards to World Wide Web banners and T-shirt logos, all serving one purpose—to get your attention and secure a safe place in your memory. When you add to this the information you take in and process from your job (e.g., staff meetings, proposals, customers, projects, readings, etc.), as well as personal and professional responsibilities and any bit of news on the radio you might catch while driving to and from work, it is easy to see that a tsunami of information hits the shores of our minds every day.

When we are not being bombarded with media messages, there are ever-increasing numbers of other distractions, ranging from cell phones and Palm Pilots to e-mail and voice mail. All of these gadgets have the ability to enhance the quality of life, but they can also distract us and disrupt our inner peace. Many people's attachment to these toys borders on addiction. Although eye candy (or any other type of sensory distraction) is nice, too much of a good thing is bad.

Among the many items posted on my office door is a Far Side cartoon that one of my students gave me—perhaps, with an ulterior motive. The cartoon shows a classroom with several students. One young man is waving his hand frantically in the air. The caption says, "Mr. Osborne, may I be excused? My brain is full." I think it is fair to say that at the end of each day, we could all say the same thing—too much information.

For as much as the mind loves to be entertained, it also craves and needs rest, regular periods of nonstimulation. The mind requires periods of peace and quiet. Research studies show that people who intentionally deprive themselves of adequate sleep exhibit signs that are similar to psychosis. Even with the recommended eight hours of sleep (which most people fail to achieve), to maintain mental stability in the face of the volumes of sensory stimulation we receive each day, we need an additional period of mental rest to balance the score. In the American culture, we are constantly encouraged to fine-tune our five senses to collect and process a vast array of stimuli. Sometimes we are even rewarded for doing this. Unfortunately, the same cannot be said for turning inward.

The Center of a Quiet Mind

You might not think that racquetball and the centering process have much in common, but Jon, a colleague of mine, does. Jon admits to having a pretty structured routine in the morning. He gets up around 5:30 A.M. and walks the dog. Then he comes home, takes a shower, fixes a cup of tea, and meditates for a half hour— sometimes less, sometimes more, but his daily routine is pretty much the same. "I have found that by centering every morning, I am a lot calmer throughout the day," he explained. "I used to do drugs in the sixties and seventies. This is so much better—and cheaper.

"About the same time I began meditating, I took up the sport of racquetball. I thought it was a good way to get exercise, but it also proved to reduce some stress. What I noticed was that to be good at racquetball, you need to play the center of the court. That's when it hit me. To be good at life, you need to be centered as well. So many people are out of balance in their lives because they don't take time to center." Then Jon added, "In racquetball, you grab the center position to dominate your opponent. In life, you center yourself so you don't get dominated by the stress others place on you—or you place on yourself. No matter how you look at it, centering is key."

Centering is the first step in the soul-searching process, in which we take inventory of our thoughts, feelings, perceptions, and attitudes. In doing so, we explore the vast landscape of the soul. It begins by simply sitting calmly in quiet contemplation. A friend of mine simply calls it "sitting."

When compared to the other seasons of the soul, the centering process may seem short in duration. What appears to be a small step is actually a mighty big leap in consciousness. The bottom line is that the real work of the soul cannot begin until this season starts.

Ways to Initiate and Enhance the Centering Process

First, there is no magic formula in practicing the art of centering, but some suggestions will help you get the greatest benefit out of the process. Keep in mind that it is best to try a variety of ways and see which one works best for you. When you find a routine that feels good, make it your own by incorporating it into your daily schedule. Here are some helpful hints to get going.

- Designate a specific spot in your house, apartment, office, or garden where you can be still for several moments. It is well known that by having a designated space, you specifically train your mind, body, and spirit for the task at hand.

- Select a specific time each day to engage in the centering process (e.g., 7:00 A.M.). Even if you don't practice it every day, by acknowledging that time period, you set your mind (like an alarm clock) to the training effect. Early mornings tend to work best.

- Begin small and build up to longer periods. Start by giving yourself about five to ten minutes of quality alone time without distractions—more, if you feel comfortable. For many people, initially, five minutes may seem like an eternity, so start small. If five minutes seems too long, try two or three minutes and build up from there.

- Eliminate distractions. Having good centering skills means having good boundaries. This means turning off the television, the radio, the cell phone, and whatever else can disturb the silence. Good boundaries also means asking others to honor them and not to disturb you at this time. Be firm about this, or you'll get walked all over.

- Some people find that playing soft instrumental music or burning candles or incense helps to create an ambiance that's conducive to centering. Although the sense of smell and sound are being used, these peaceful stimuli tend to redirect the mind's focus inward. In addition, some people find that holding a small object like a seashell or a tumble stone in one hand allows them to center better. Try whatever works.

- Focus your attention on the present moment. Centering means being present, not focusing on the past or the future. It's a given that the mind will surely wander, and this is okay. When you find yourself free associating, gently bring your attention back to the present moment by focusing on your breathing.

- Control mental overflow. Having a pad of paper and a pen nearby helps you to clear the mind and allows you to come back to important thoughts that bubble up in the course of centering and beg for attention. Once your distracting thoughts are placed on paper, you can let them go, knowing that you won't forget them.

The following is a centering/meditation exercise that will help you make the centering process a part of your daily routine.

EXERCISE

The Four-Chambered Heart Meditation

Every culture speaks of the heart as a sacred space. Both the anatomical heart and the symbolic heart are intertwined. Long before medical science learned of the heart's anatomy and physiology, the wisdom keepers spoke of a four-chambered heart. When four parts come together to form a whole, a sacred space is created. The mandala, a circular artwork with four quadrants, is a symbol of wholeness. Mandalas often depict the four directions; the four aspects of mind, body, spirit, and emotions; or any four components that unite to create wholeness, in which the whole is always greater than the sum of the parts. Your heart, in all its glory, is such a mandala of wholeness.

The first part of this meditation exercise, inspired by the anthropologist Angeles Arrien, invites you to go inward and focus on these four chambers of the symbolic heart: the full heart, the open heart, the strong heart, and the clear heart, all of which come together for wholeness.

But first, to begin, close your eyes, and once again focus on your breathing. Place all of your attention, all of your concentration on your breathing. If, by chance, any random thoughts come into your mind, very gently allow them to fade away, letting them go as you exhale, and then bring your full attention back to your breathing.

- Feel the air come into your nose or mouth and travel deep down into your lungs. As you do this, feel your stomach area extend out, then return as you exhale. As you repeat this cycle of conscious, slow, deep breathing, become aware of how relaxed your body is with each exhalation.

- Now, take a very slow, deep breath, as comfortably slow and as comfortably deep as you possibly can.

- Then, follow this breath with one more breath, and this time make the next breath even slower and even deeper than before.

- Next, place your attention on your heart space: the center of your upper chest. Using the power of your imagination, take one more slow, deep breath and feel the flow of air move through your entire body. As you exhale, feel a deep sense of relaxation in your heart space. Repeat this three times, making each breath comfortably slow and comfortably deep. With the exhalation of the fourth breath, bring to mind an image of a violet circle with four equal parts.

- Then, taking a slow, deep breath, allow the air you breathe to fill your entire heart space. As you exhale, imagine the air leaving your heart space (all four quadrants), as if you are inhaling and exhaling through your upper chest, rather than through your nose or mouth. As you focus on this symbolic image, fill each chamber with a deep breath until the entire mandala is complete.

The First Chamber: The Full Heart

A full heart is an inspired heart. Inspiration is the force that drives our destiny. Take a moment to search your soul and ask yourself what comes into your life that inspires you? What makes you artistic? What makes your mind clear and focused enough to be inspired? Sometimes, things block the flow of inspiration. These could be thoughts and feelings that take up space in the heart and actually diminish the sacred fullness—in essence, they inhibit inspiration. Bring to mind a thought or a feeling that diminishes your heart's full potential, and let it go as you exhale.

- In the heart space that you have provided, bring to mind one thing that inspires you, and place this thought and feeling in your heart space as you continue to breathe.

- Then, take several slow, deep breaths and, with each inhalation, allow the heart space to become full of inspiration and creative energy.

- On the last exhalation, feel a sense of wonderful fullness and inspiration in your heart space.

The Second Chamber: The Open Heart

Once again, take a slow, deep breath and fill your entire heart space. Remind yourself that an open heart, like an open mind, is one filled with acceptance and compassion. It's no secret that unresolved anger and fear close the door to an open heart. On your next breath, call to mind an issue or a problem that has placed a wedge in your heart space, leaving the heart's door nearly shut.

- Taking several slow, deep breaths and, with an air of acceptance, allow the heart space to open unconditionally with each inhalation. With each exhalation, give yourself permission to allow all thoughts of unresolved anger and fear that take up space in the heart to leave in a symbolic gesture of resolution. As you do this, fill this new space with a clean, deep breath of air to symbolize your open heart.

- On the last exhalation, feel a wonderful sense of openness and compassion in your heart space.

The Third Chamber: The Strong Heart

Once again, take a slow, deep breath and notice how relaxed your heart space is on the exhalation. A strong heart is a courageous heart. The word *courage* comes from two French words that mean "big heart." Many attributes constitute a strong heart, including a strong sense of confidence.

- Take five slow, deep breaths and reflect on the concept of courage and how you can increase the strength of your heart. A strong heart muscle pumps continuously to circulate fresh oxygenated blood throughout the body. A strong symbolic heart is one that is filled with confidence to aid you in the resolution of everyday struggles, as well as of major life issues. A strong heart is fortified with faith and optimism and holds the capacity to endure the greatest challenge.

- Taking several slow, deep breaths, feel with each exhalation the strength of a strong heart and the endurance to go the distance of the human journey.

- On the last exhalation, feel a wonderful sense of openness and courage in your heart space.

The Fourth Chamber: The Clear Heart

Once again, placing all of your attention on your heart space, take a long, slow, deep breath and clearly focus on the integrity of your heart. A clear heart is a heart unobstructed by negative thoughts. While it may be normal to have negative thoughts, it's neither normal nor healthy to harbor them. A clear heart is a clean heart that listens to the deep-seated wisdom of the soul.

- Using the breath as a metaphorical broom, allow your breath and your imagination to sweep clean your heart space with the next few breath cycles, releasing any mental chatter with each exhalation and thus giving a clearer focus to your life mission.

- On the last exhalation, feel a sense of clarity and peace in both your heart and your mind.

Pause now and take a moment to feel your heart space: full, open, strong, and clear. Sit still and be at peace with the vision you hold and the feeling you have created. Know that the power of the four-chamber heart has really taken hold.

EXERCISE
A Gift from the Sea (Journal Theme)

Not all centering exercises involve breathing. One of the best ways to center is to write in a journal. Sometimes, just getting something down on paper opens the mind to new thoughts. For some people, a blank piece of paper is all they need to start writing, while others need a little encouragement. For those who find a blank sheet of paper a little intimidating or who need a steppingstone, the following journal theme of self-exploration may help.

Individuals are so very different, yet we all share many common features, thoughts, even perceptions. Our makeup is so complex, yet similar, from one person to another. We all have qualities that we consider either strengths or weaknesses, and these vary from person to person. Strengths can be magnified to bolster self-esteem. Weaknesses, too, can be magnified and can become roadblocks to our human potential. The world is full of metaphors regarding the facets of our lives. For example, a seashell can be considered a metaphor, a symbol of ourselves.

After an extremely stressful event that changed the life of Anne Morrow Lindbergh and her husband, Charles, Anne took refuge on a secluded Hawaiian beach to find peace of mind and solace in her heart. In her book *Gift from the Sea*, Lindbergh shared her personal thoughts as she cradled different seashells in her hands and reflected on the images and the symbolism they suggested.

The following thoughts and questions, inspired by Lindbergh's book, will help you explore this metaphor. You don't need a seashell in hand to do this exercise, but often something tangible can open up your thoughts. If you happen to have a seashell collection or access to some seashells, select a shell that you are attracted to and use it as a centering device to enhance the self-reflection process.

1. Pick a shell from a collection (if available), and hold it in your hand for a moment. Close your eyes and really feel it. What

attracted you to this particular shell? Describe the shell you picked: its color, shape, texture, and size.

2. Many sea creatures have shells. Some are beautifully colored; some have incredible detail, with ridges, points, and curls. Some shells are quite small, and others are very big. Some are very fragile, while others seem like the epitome of strength. Like sea creatures, we, too, have shells, though ours are not quite as obvious. What is your shell like? Describe its shape, color, texture, and any other features that you wish to include, features that differentiate it from other shells.

3. Shells serve a purpose for sea creatures. They are a home, as well as a form of protection, a basis for security. Our shells also act as a means of protection. Our shells can offer a form of strength and security, but they can also overprotect. Does your shell overprotect, or is it a growing shell?

4. We all have strengths and weaknesses. Strengths are strong points of our personality or attributes that bring us favorable attention. Weaknesses, on the other hand, are what we perceive as our faults, our insecurities, or our attributes that have negative connotations. List your strengths and, beside this list, also write down your weaknesses. Now take a careful look at this list. Sometimes, strengths can actually be weaknesses, while some weaknesses can be disguised as our strong points. Take, for example, a person who is well organized. This could be considered a weakness if it spills over into perfectionism. Sometimes, what we consider our weaknesses, others see as our strengths, and these attributes may, in fact, be so. Many times, the perception makes the difference. Now look at your list again. Are any of your strengths potential weaknesses or vice versa?

5. Feel free to add any comments, feelings, and even memories to this journal entry.

From Falling Leaves to Snow Flurries
The centering process is perhaps the shortest season of the soul. Yet the duration of this season doesn't negate its importance, as all the other seasons depend on it. Once you make the time to go

within, you'll have some cleaning to do in the winter season, and then the fun begins.

The Emptying Process (Winter)

As the gentle winds of September become the strong gusty gales of November, and more than a hint of afternoon darkness is evident, an old adage reminds us that the trees sacrifice their leaves to allow more light into the hearts of humanity. The shedding of leaves is a wonderful metaphor for us letting go of things that we no longer need. This adage also provides a ray of hope in the depths of winter's darkness. As the cool winds of autumn usher in the harshness of winter, the human soul is constantly reminded to cleanse itself. In the words of Ecclesiastes, "There is a time for keeping and a time for throwing away."

This is what the emptying process is all about: letting go of something old so that you can make room for something new. To be sure, the emptying process is the hardest of the soul's four seasons because it requires the most work. As a rule, people do not like to let go of things, and the ego finds it really hard to relinquish control. For this reason, the emptying process (the winter season) is often called the "winter of discontent." It is also commonly known as the "dark night of the soul." Of the four seasons of the soul, this is the one people most often get stuck in. Some people call it "pure hell." Still others become depressed because it takes great strength to let go and move on. But it doesn't have to be this way. Winter is only one of four seasons, and every night is followed by a day.

Be in the World but Not Of It

The concept of emptying is not a new phenomenon, nor are the many ways in which to engage in it. Ancient Chinese, Greeks, Mayans, Christians, and Essenes all adopted the emptying process in their spiritual practices; their methods ranged from fasting and periods of silence to wilderness retreats. Each physical practice supports the spiritual essence of cleansing and releasing to make room for something new. Ironically, there are times when we are forced to release, let go, and cleanse, even when it seems like we are not ready to do so. Examples may include the death of a friend, the loss of a job, or the end of a marriage. At these times, it's important to remember this sage advice: "Be in the world but not of it." Jesus of Nazareth is often given credit for this expression; however, a recent search on the Internet to track the original source revealed that so important is this message, nearly every religion claims the sage advice as its own. It is the quintessential message of the emptying process.

Have you ever heard of the expression "nature abhors a vacuum"? Anyone who has ever planted a garden knows how true this is. The other side of this Taoist equation is that nature also abhors gluttony. In an effort to restore spiritual equilibrium, our lives will undoubtedly include many episodes of loss, balanced with wonderful gains. Although it may be hard to see in the midst of change, there is a higher purpose to letting go. The promise of the universe is that something of equal or greater value will always take its place.

To be in the world but not of it means to experience as many things as possible but not to get bogged down or attached to troubles that might impede our human journey. These troubles, which first slow and eventually deaden the pace, include everything from our overinflated egos to the material possessions we covet so much and a host of perceptions in-between. Traveling light isn't just good advice; it's essential wisdom, if we intend to go the full distance on the human journey in comfort and take in as many rich experiences as possible. This, by far, is the hardest challenge presented on the Hero's Journey.

The Womb of Creation

The emptying process is described by many as a dark void of nothingness—something to be avoided at all costs. Nothing could be further from the truth. The basic fear that once you go in, you'll never come out is a fallacy. Yet people often teeter on the precipice, looking over the edge, and then take a step back, hoping that maybe, just maybe, there is another way through it. The only way through the void is to let go completely and step into it with both feet. To let go is truly a leap of faith. To see the entire picture, we must remember that creating a space is essential for acquiring new insights. Empty spaces definitely serve a purpose, as Lao Tzu describes in the *Tao Te Ching*:

Thirty spokes share the center of one wheel;
Consider that the hole of the center is essential to
    wheel's function.

Craft a pot from earthen clay;
Consider that the space inside provides the pot's true function.

Cut a hole in the wall to make both window and door;
Consider that the space within four walls is essential for living.

Understand that the form and structure is most beneficial;
Consider also that the empty space within the form is
    most useful.

In terms of our human potential, Deng Ming-Dao, in his book *365 Tao*, describes it this way, "The concept of the void is central to many philosophies including the Tao. However, it seems so abstract at times. Here void has a functionary role. The pathway connecting the energy centers of the mind is like a long shaft beginning from the perineum and ending at the top of the head. If not for emptiness, or hollowness of this shaft, the sacred energy of the body could not be conducted."

Reaching the Stillpoint of Consciousness
If you talk to people who make their living by using the right sides of their brain (the imaginative side), they will tell you that it's not uncommon to go for stretches of time without inspiration. The "writer's block" and the "artist's cramp" are very real indeed. But these same people will tell you that the best time to tap into the vein of inspiration and imagination is what some call the "stillpoint of consciousness." It's what Deepak Chopra and Wayne Dyer call the gap: a point when the mind's slate has been wiped clean of expectations. The womb of creation is always ripe with possibilities, and it calls to us to step inside and make them happen. To reap the fullest effects of the emptying process, though, we must first surrender the control of the ego.

On the surface, stressors of biblical proportions may seem like spiritual breakdowns. Yet people who have been there will tell you that these are more accurately described as spiritual breakthroughs. Our moments of despair and resignation are the soul's attempt to take the first step into the void. People who have stepped into the abyss will tell you that it is actually quite liberating. Like jumping out of a plane with a parachute, it's scary as hell for the first few seconds, and then euphoria sets in. Remember, the dark night of the soul is meant to be only a night, not an eternity. There is an unwritten promise that you will emerge stronger and more confident than when you entered. Patrick Overton said it best this way: "When you come to the edge of all the light you have, and must take a step into the darkness of the unknown, believe that one of two things will happen; either there will be something solid for you to stand on, or you will be taught how to fly."

If you're still not convinced that the emptying process is a worthy destination, remember this thought: even the darkest night has bright stars!

Ways to Initiate the Emptying Process
There are several ways to engage in the emptying process. They range from traditional practices of fasting, periods of silence, and meditation, to more contemporary means of cleaning closets, journaling, and solitary walks. The premise of each method is to set a mental attitude of letting go of things that are no longer needed, to make room for new ideas, intuitive thoughts, or insights. Just as there is no one best way to engage in the centering process, there is also no one best way to initiate the emptying process. Try several techniques, and see which one works best for you. Following are two meditation exercises to help you in this.

EXERCISE
The Hot Air Balloon Meditation

Find a comfortable spot to sit or lie down, and begin by focusing your attention on your breathing. Take several slow, deep breaths and notice how you feel upon each exhalation. You may wish to mentally repeat the phrase "I am calm and relaxed." When you begin to feel completely relaxed, call upon your power of imagination to create an image where you find yourself standing comfortably in the basket of a hot air balloon. (You can also use an image of sitting near a river and watching logs float by.) Inside the basket are four sandbags on each wall. Each sandbag represents an issue, a concern, an unresolved emotion, or a perception that holds you down—in essence, immobilizing you so that you can't move freely in life. These can range from doubts and fears to frustrations and prejudices.

Lift one sandbag off the hook, and gently throw it on the ground. As you do this, feel the release of weight as it lifts the hot air balloon several feet off the ground. Before the sandbag reaches the ground, it dissolves into the air. With the balloon now untethered, call to mind one more thought or feeling, place that association on the next sandbag, and gently toss it over the edge, once again feeling the balloon rise as it loses the extra weight. As you feel the currents of air take you higher and higher, notice that your field of vision expands. Comb your mind for one or two more perceptions that you know in your heart it's time to let go of, and again, associating each perception with a sandbag, gently toss it over the edge of the basket and watch the bag slowly dissolve into thin air.

Take five slow, deep breaths and feel a sense of relaxation and liberation from the weight of those issues and concerns. When you feel ready, bring yourself back to the present surroundings, open your eyes, and appreciate your newfound freedom.

EXERCISE
The Silent Walk Meditation

This exercise became a popular morning routine for a runners' group I conducted several years ago. Basically, it involves making a temporary vow of silence during a fitness workout, such as a long walk in the company of friends. Although it works best when you are forced not to talk with anyone, it works quite well alone, whether during a walk, a jog, or a swim. Pick one issue you are dealing with at the present time, ponder the issue from all sides, and then ask yourself these questions before you actually set out to solve it.

What feelings arise when you think about the situation?

Why do you feel this way?

What benefit is there from hanging on to these feelings?

As you continue to walk, imagine your mind to be like a clean blackboard. What is the first thing that appears on your mind's board? When you come back, feel free to write down whatever solutions come to mind.

EXERCISE
A Grieving Celebration

At a cancer survivors' workshop, a woman approached me and asked point-blank how she should embark on the emptying process. After hearing her story, I made this suggestion: bring a sense of closure to this loss by creating a grieving celebration. Though the expression may sound like an oxymoron, what it really means is to consciously allow for time to grieve but, at the same time, get on with your life. Mark a day on your calendar as your "Day of Independence." Write down all of your thoughts and feelings on paper, and then have a cremation ceremony in the fireplace. Make a list of all the things that you used to really enjoy doing. Next to each activity, write down something new that you can do as an alternate activity to breathe fresh air into your life. Then set out to do these things. Celebrations don't have to be extravagant. Rearrange your bedroom closet, move the furniture around in your living room, plant a tree in the backyard, or rotate all the artwork in your house. Get the energy moving so that you don't feel stuck.

The Light at the End of the Tunnel
As a cautious reminder, you don't have to sell your condo, divorce your spouse, total your car, or renounce the world to begin the emptying process. It can be initiated quite simply through your will and desire in meditating, journaling, exercising, fasting, abiding in long moments of silence, or setting aside quality time that's dedicated to clearing your mind. There are many ways to engage in the emptying process, each one offering the promise to cleanse the

mind. The emptying process may seem like a dark void, but, true to the cliché of the dark tunnel, there is light at the end—not a train, either, but a glorious light.

Nature is loaded with examples of the emptying process, from the ebb of the evening tide to the waning of the full moon. In human terms, the body empties several times a day; the mind empties hourly, if not more, with thoughts slipping below the radar of the conscious mind. Catharsis (e.g., laughing, crying, etc.) is how emotional emptying takes place. These are all reminders that the spirit needs to cleanse as well. The way it does this is by letting go of thoughts, attitudes, and perceptions that at one time might have been useful but now no longer serve us. These include frustrations, fears, grudges, and so on, that actually hold us back— choking the spirit, so to speak. At the time these events occur, they seem like the epitome of life's crises, but in time, they offer life's greatest lessons, if (and it's a big *if*) we can learn from the experience. A Danish proverb reminds us of the same wisdom: "It is friction that causes the polished touch of the gemstone." The emptying process holds great promise, if we let it. By wiping the slate clean, we begin with a fresh outlook on life, and that is exactly what the next season of the soul does.

The Grounding Process (Spring)

In every culture since the dawn of humanity, there have been many occasions to seek the council of one's higher self, whether through moments of solitude, during periods of seclusion, or in an organized retreat. In a literal sense, *groundedness* means to be connected to the earth and to feel that you are indeed part of nature. In a figurative sense, to be grounded is the ability to feel comfortable in your surroundings, in your own environment, to achieve a sense of inner peace. Ask any teenager what it means to be grounded, and he or she will emphatically tell you that this is not a good thing. Ask any adult the same question, and this individual will most likely confide in you that he or she cannot get enough of it, for what was once a restriction now is a liberation. Semantics notwith-standing, what a difference a few years makes!

As the third season of the soul, the grounding process is a

designated time of gathering insights. To hear the voice of God; to receive a sign, a vision, a long-awaited epiphany, or a simple revelation reconnects us to that part of our divine essence and, in turn, provides a sense of security, a sense of stability on the path of the human journey. In times of need, we go looking for these insights. On rare occasions, they come looking for us, especially when we are distracted and not paying attention. The net result is a sense of insight and courage when we confront the winds of change.

You Cannot Demand Enlightenment

In simple terms, the grounding process is a time when we seek an answer, and the answer arrives, sometimes immediately or perhaps eventually, down the road a ways. In either case, the grounding process is a stage of reaping new ideas, insights, and intuitive thoughts to help you get from point A to point B on the next leg of your human journey. Please keep in mind that it cannot happen unless and until the emptying process has been fully engaged. You cannot take in new information until there is room to store it. An ancient Chinese proverb speaks to the very heart of the grounding process: "When the pupil is ready, the teacher will come." The wisdom of this proverb suggests that we are both the student and the teacher. When the mind is clear of mental chatter, true wisdom will bubble up deep from within the unconscious mind. The result is very reassuring. It gives us a sense of comfort and stability, and once again, this grounds us in the midst of the winds of change.

Specifically, the grounding process is a time of revelation and resolution with regard to your relationships, your values (and value conflicts), and, perhaps most important, your discovery of a meaningful purpose in your life. If the emptying process is like plowing a field, then the grounding process is like planting and harvesting the crop. Some people refer to the wisdom gained in the grounding process as fertilizer that feeds and deepens the roots of a tree to withstand the winds of change. Regardless of the metaphor used, please know that once a space has been made in the soul, the universe promises that something of equal or greater value will arrive to fill the space that was made available from the emptying process.

An Open Mind Is a Clear Mind

How do these nuggets of wisdom appear? They come in a great many ways, from intuitive thoughts and dreams to synchronistic events and recurring themes in conversations. Remember that like a seed ready to germinate, the seed of an idea will take root in your awareness only where there is fertile soil; in other words, a receptive mind is imperative. You can seek insights on the spiritual path, but you cannot order them on demand. You must be ready with an open heart and mind. Just as you cannot push water uphill, neither can you demand enlightenment. Discipline, patience, and receptivity are essential requirements for the grounding process.

Is there something magical about the number three, such as three wishes or three wise men? Many people think so, including Amy. "I go by the Rule of Threes," she explained to me one day. "If I hear of something three times, whether it's a book title, a recipe, or some concept floating through the air, it usually takes me three times to acknowledge it before it sinks in, and I act on it." She proceeded to explain how she had been very impatient with a job search. In the course of two days, she observed three people showing signs of tremendous patience, and then it dawned on her that there was a message in each encounter she observed. Amy continued, with a smile, "Life's getting short, and I am hoping to evolve to the point where I can graduate to the Rule of Twos."

Lowering Walls and Opening Doors

Only when the walls of the ego are lowered are we receptive to the divine whispers, insights, creative ideas, intuitive thoughts, and ageless wisdom that, at some level, we solicit and require for each situation we encounter. You don't have to strip naked and wander through the desert plains for days to receive a vision. The entrance to universal consciousness can be accessed just about anywhere, including in the privacy of your own home. The grounding process can occur in meditation, through dreams, or in moments of synchronicity—those wonderful coincidences that leave you scratching your head in amazement. As the saying goes, "A coincidence is merely God's way of remaining anonymous."

Artists, poets, authors, and songwriters will be the first to tell you that when the walls of the ego are lowered, the most amazing thoughts bubble to the surface. And they happen during the most unpredictable times: while washing dishes, driving home from work, walking the dog, or taking a bath. You must constantly be receptive. Receptivity to divine insight is groomed, not just by creating stillness in your mind but also through cultivating and refining of your thoughts, perceptions, and attitudes by lowering the walls of the ego. And although the flow of consciousness cannot be forced, it can be enticed. Relaxation and patience are the keys.

The Quest for a Vision

Perhaps nowhere is the idea of the grounding process more evident than in a ritual in the American Indian culture known as the vision quest. In this rite of passage, a person departs from his or her community and spends a number of days in the wilderness—alone. The vision quest begins with a reflective period of centering: turning within to address the soul. Next comes the emptying process, where no food is eaten and little, if any, clothing is worn, to reinforce the meaning of detachment. The vision quest is an intense period of searching the corridors of the mind, to connect with the divine source and come to an understanding of the meaning of life, with two basic questions: "Who am I?" and "Why am I here?" During this time, answers to these questions come—perhaps not always immediately, but they come. If the seeker has a keen inner ear, an insight or an intuitive thought process will lead the way out of metaphorical darkness into the light of life. Listening at this level requires a unique receptivity to hear, to open up, and to learn. But most important, we should not be afraid of the wisdom we might encounter through our thoughts, visions, or sensations. The standard joke that exaggerates this fear is the person who, upon asking God for advice, hears a response he doesn't like, pauses for a moment, and then, looking up to heaven in search of another God, asks for a second opinion.

Bite-Size Morsels of Wisdom

The nuggets of wisdom that cascade down through the layers of consciousness to our receptive mind are usually short in length, yet profound in wisdom. It may be a few words, a concept, a symbol, or an idea: a quantum particle of knowledge acting like a bridge over the abyss of stress that allows us to move on with our lives. In my own experiences, as well as in those others have shared with me, I have learned that insights come in small morsels, such as words or phrases, and not in big chunks like anthologies. The Higher Self, angels, or, for that matter, God doesn't speak in half-hour soliloquies. To the contrary, insights gained in the grounding process are distilled down to simple truths or clichés that, collectively, provide a road map to guide you in the right direction. Gentle whispers of patience, surrender, and forgiveness may fall upon your ears. Clichés and proverbs are examples of a type of wisdom that appears to give a subtle message when we most need to hear it.

The Wisdom of DNA

It's often been said that we have a wealth of knowledge inside us. What was once a poetic proverb now seems to be a surprising reality. As scientists explore the wonders of our DNA, they've found that the two spiraling strands of sugar and protein molecules contain a vast source of information that would make even the National Library of Congress envious.

Recently, I came across a compelling book, *The Cosmic Serpent*, and, I have to admit, I found it to be one of the most astonishing stories I have ever read. The book described one man's search for an understanding of life through his research into a drug used by Peruvian shamans, called Ayahuasca (eye-a-whas-qua). Jeremy Narby, an anthropologist by training, set out from his home in the Swiss Alps for Peru in 1985 to study the work of shamans—particularly, the hallucinogenic drug they used, its chemical properties, and what he calls "plant communication." He was amazed to discover that the wisdom (in this case, the medical properties of plants) the shamans brought back from their "trips" was identical to the scientific data revealed in research studies years later. What intrigued Narby most was that these shamans had virtually no formal educational training. Somehow, they were tapping into a deep-seated wisdom that science had yet to explore or explain. It wasn't long before Narby discovered that he was on the trail of something big.

In reviewing his research notes back home in Switzerland, Narby was puzzled by this mystery. He wrote, "They talk of a ladder, or a vine, a rope, a spiral staircase, a twisted rope ladder that connects heaven and earth, which they use to gain access to the world of spirits." Narby said that he began to trust the literal descriptions of his mentors, even though he didn't quite comprehend their source of knowledge. When he was told by one shaman to study the form, Narby's intuition stepped in, and he began to see a connection between the ladder, the pool of knowledge frequently accessed, and the DNA molecule. Could it be that these shamans used the drug Ayahuasca as a key to unlock the secrets stored in DNA?

Some Interesting Facts about DNA

Intrigued, Narby began to research what was known about the double helix of life. What he discovered helped him to connect the dots to form a new understanding of the human mystery. For instance,

- DNA, a double-strand molecule of twenty proteins and sugar, is a reservoir of immense data.

- DNA is referred to as both a chemical compound and a language of instructions. Narby goes so far as to say that DNA has consciousness.

- Whether one looks at animals, plants, or humans, DNA contains a code of four letters, A, G, C, T (which correspond to four chemical compounds: adenine, guanine, cytosine, and thymine).

- Only 3 percent of human DNA is deemed active, while 97 percent of it is labeled "junk" (it's not really junk, but, as Narby suggests, this is a stupid label given by arrogant scientists).

- Genes make up only 5 percent of our DNA.

- The smallest known bacteria genome contains 58,000 DNA letters, comparable to the information found in a city telephone book. The Human Genome Project to determine human DNA configurations is currently underway, with plans of full completion very soon.

- If a strand of DNA were stretched out end to end, it would be a two-yard-long thread that's only ten atoms wide.

- If all of the strands of DNA in your body were extended end to end, its length would reach 125 billion miles, enough to circle the earth five million times.

- DNA emits photons of light in the narrow band of visible light.

- DNA emits light like a laser with luminescent colors.

- DNA appears to be not only an information molecule but a text as well.

- DNA has crystalline properties, acting as both a transmitter and a receiver.

After distilling the information he collected, Narby came to the conclusion that these shamans carefully used sacred medicinal herbs as a means to access a source of information that he attributed to DNA. His presentation of facts is impressive. Equally impressive is his presentation of symbolic art from around the world that contains snakes as they relate to wisdom, from the serpent in the Garden of Eden on the tree of knowledge to the caduceus medical symbol. He even suggests that the yin/yang symbol could be interpreted as an aerial view of the DNA spiral.

There has long been an association between hallucinogenic drugs and nirvana. Narby contends that an active ingredient in various hallucinogenic compounds seems to allow one access to the wisdom found in DNA. However, he notes that access can occur *without* the aid of these compounds. Yogis and sages seem to do it through meditation and come back with remarkable wisdom. Yet you don't have to take a trip to Peru or be a Himalayan yogi to access this wisdom. Anybody can. It's as close as your next breath.

The word *sacral* comes from the same root word as *sacred*. The sacral area of the spine is consider sacred by people who are aware of the mystical energy in the body that's commonly known as kundalini. Kundalini energy, as described in the Hindu culture, is a serpent-type energy that rests in a coiled position at the base of the spine. People who meditate regularly often describe the movement of kundalini energy spiraling up the spine and emanating through the top of the head. Enlightenment is said to be reached when this occurs. Some people now correlate the inactive DNA to the inactive serpent energy, and others believe that this is where the next step of conscious evolution will occur. Yet others say, don't wait for this to happen. Although many people debate what enlightenment is, the consensus among those who walk the talk is that it's best described as compassion in action, putting your heart into everything you do.

EXERCISE
The DNA Meditation

The beauty of the grounding process is that you never know just how or when new insights may appear on the horizon. To keep your mind sharp and focused, the following exercises might help. I'm delighted when I hear that people try various exercises and gain great insight into solving a problem. This exercise and the next are two that people have found very helpful.

Research indicates that we use only 3 percent of our DNA; the rest seems to be inactive. Like a string of lightbulbs that has not been plugged into a socket and is therefore assumed to be useless, it appears that our DNA needs some attention to become activated or, as mystics described, to be awakened. Some scientists say that so-called junk DNA is more akin to a blank tape. One could use this metaphor to record a new program on the blank tape. Select whatever metaphor best suits your imagination.

This meditation is an exploration into the wonders of DNA. Again, it requires the use of your vivid imagination; please feel free to change these suggestions to make the exercise most comfortable for you.

1. Sit in a comfortable position with your back straight and your eyes closed. Take a few deep breaths and, as you exhale, remind yourself that you are becoming more calm and relaxed.

2. Now, imagine that you have the ability to look within your heart muscle. Travel to your heart and focus on one specific cell, then enlarge the cell so that the image is directly in front of you.

3. Next, look deep into the cell and find its nucleus. Focus your attention on the nucleus. Then enlarge the nucleus so that this cell structure is directly in front of you. Once you have an image, find the double helix, the spiral strand of DNA within the nucleus.

4. Focusing all your attention on the DNA, enlarge the image of this structure so that it is directly in front of you. Depending on your perspective, the strand of DNA may look like a ladder or a twisted bridge. From an aerial view, it may even resemble the Taoist yin/yang symbol. Take a moment to look at this DNA strand from every possible angle, watching it rotate in motion.

5. As you study this double helix and all its many complexities, imagine that like a string of lights with a hundred bulbs, only a few (three) are actually lit. Using your imagination, create a light switch that, when turned on, makes all the lights shine. Not only does each bulb radiate brilliant brightness, but, upon closer examination of the double-stranded helix, there appears to be a beam of light that the two strands surround and actually embrace. The light from the DNA emanates out to the edge of the nucleus and then continues toward the cell membrane itself.

6. Again using your imagination, think that as one cell contains this vibrating DNA of light, so do all cells. Just as pixels on a computer screen emit light, every cell in the body now contains a double helix of DNA that emanates light, with all the parts active.

7. Surround yourself with the glow of the light and put forth a question to which you seek an answer. Take a deep breath and pause, knowing that the wisdom of the DNA will broadcast a message to you when you are most receptive to hear it.

8. Now allow this image to fade from your mind's eye, but retain the feeling of light. Pay attention to the wisdom that comes to your conscious mind as you travel through the course of your day. Remember, the repeated use of this visualization will enhance your ability to access the deep-seated wisdom within.

JOURNAL EXERCISE
The Vision Quest

Our lives are a series of events strung together through the spirit of each breath and heartbeat. Some events are more significant than others, marking powerful changes in our growth and development. In cultures that go back to the dawn of humankind, these events of change, these transitions from one life stage to another, were called rites of passage. The rites often included a ceremony of celebration. Today, they frequently take other forms, such as bar mitzvahs, weddings, baby showers, and funerals. In modern American culture, the importance of personal rites of passage has been deemphasized or forgotten. Attention is placed on the ceremony, without our retaining the recognition of its purpose. In reality, we undergo many of our major life events alone, with no supportive guidance, no community involvement, and no celebration. Modern technology has also replaced our sense of origin, leaving us uncentered and ungrounded. This often leaves individuals unable to deal effectively with the stress produced from life crises or too immature to progress through life.

In the tradition of the American Indian, a vision quest marks a significant rite of passage. It is a wilderness retreat, in which one reflects on one's inner resources and reaffirms one's centeredness and connection to Mother Earth. In a vision quest, you seek a vision of a meaningful purpose in life, to gain a greater understanding of who you are as a person. This concept has been adopted as a cornerstone in the nation's Outward Bound program: self-reliance through introspection in nature. A vision quest marks a major life transition. People who undertake this quest are seeking a vision to guide them through a transitional period of change. Although, in the truest sense, a vision quest is done in the solitude of the wilderness, you can undergo this process anywhere. The following three questions are provided to lead you on the first steps of your vision quest.

1. What significant events to date would you consider to be the rites of passage in your life? Why do you consider these your rites of passage?

2. Ask yourself, what life event are you in the midst of? What dragons are you battling right now? What life passage are you entering or emerging from? Rites of passage are thought to have three distinct phases. As you ponder these questions, follow these phases of the vision quest.

a. Severance—A separation or a departure from old ways or familiar lifestyle habits, perhaps even from people, to the unfamiliar and the unknown.

b. Threshold—The actual quest, a search for a vision or an understanding of this transition. This will include an inventory of your inner resources and external surroundings to provide guidance through the transition period. The threshold may also contain a series of trials to test these inner resources.

c. Incorporation—A return home from the quest, with new insights and the ability to apply the knowledge from this experience as you progress through your life.

3. In the Native American culture, during a vision quest one receives the gift of a name—not one that you give yourself but one that is given to you by Mother Earth through the elements of creation and her creatures. What name does the wind whisper in your ears? Your name can also be a positive affirmation statement, a phrase to keep you grounded or to boost your self-esteem, or a personal thought to give you inspiration.

The Breath That Refreshes

Mountains are symbols of strength, stability, and resilience. We, too, become strong, stable, and resilient to the winds of change that stressors bring to our lives when we listen to the deep-seated wisdom of the soul. The image of mountains towering above the clouds conveys to many people the mirror image of their own divine consciousness. For just as the mountain rises above the clouds, so, too, it connects to the very core of the earth, and that is the epitome of groundedness. Breathing air on a mountaintop is truly invigorating. Mountaintops are known the world over as a symbol of clarity and insight. Many legends, fables, and stories, from Moses' receiving the Ten Commandments on Mount Sinai to Sir Edmund Hillary scaling Mt. Everest, have become a part of the human psyche. We climb the metaphorical mountain to gain a better view of the world, to glean insight, to peek into the heavens. Once again, to see the light is akin to kissing the face of God. But the journey never ends on top of a mountain. Eventually, we must descend from the peak, all the while savoring the taste of exhilaration, so that we can share what we learned so that others may benefit as well.

The Connecting Process (Summer)

Standing on top of Mount Antero, one of Colorado's highest peaks, I raised my arms in the now-familiar Rocky pose and said a silent prayer of gratitude. The view was positively breathtaking, without a cloud in the sky. It was no exaggeration to say that you could see more than a hundred miles in every direction. A clear sky feeds a hungry mind. Anyone who has ascended to the top of a mountain knows the glory of looking out over the world. There is a feeling of both humbleness and exaltation. Balance strikes again. I took a deep breath and reminded myself that I had completed only half of the journey.

Without a doubt, reaching the summit of any mountain is a noble adventure, but as any mountain climber knows, the summit is only the halfway point. As nice as it is to be on top of the world, at some point, you have to come back down. Whether the mountaintop is an hour-long mediation, a vacation, a retreat, a vision quest, or even a soulful conference, the connecting process calls us to emerge from the cocoon of solitude and reunite with members of our community.

When we come down off the proverbial mountain, when we emerge from the solitude of the soul, glowing with inspiration, we have an obligation to share what we have learned, encountered, or experienced with friends, family, colleagues, and peers. Balance is derived from both receiving and giving. This is the expectation of the universe because greed is *not* a spiritual value. In the spirit of the connecting process, our mission is to build bridges, not walls; to offer a hand in guidance, rather than turn our backs away in indifference. In reality, the connection we hold between all people already exists. The only request we are given, as we consciously initiate the connecting process, is to acknowledge, sustain, nurture, and honor this connection. In the words of Mother Teresa, "There is no such thing as great acts, only small acts performed with great love."

The Bonds of Love

Call to mind the activities that you engage in during the summer months: barbecues, parties, picnics, and family reunions. The summer is a time of gathering and celebration. This is what the connecting process is all about: sharing and caring. Metaphorically speaking, this is the time of coming together to watch beautiful sunsets and hug warm, fuzzy puppies. As great as the experience is, it is so much better when it is shared. And by far, this is what most people think about when they speak of human spirituality: the "Disney World" effect, sharing exhilarating moments of euphoric joy and happiness with people you love. Poets and mystics agree that love is the glue that holds the universe together. The connecting process is a metaphor for love.

Haven Trevino writes in his book *The Tao of Healing*, "People seek love. This is what makes us great. People abide on the Earth. Earth abides in the Heavens, the Heavens abide in Love. Love abides in us all. This is what makes us One."

Alan is a Lakota Sioux from South Dakota. I met him at a workshop several years ago, and over lunch, we shared some thoughts about spiritual hunger in America. The topic of the vision quest came up, and Alan explained to me that in many ways, it was quite similar to a retreat but a lot more powerful. Then he explained that a vision quest isn't over when a wave of inspiration hits. The end of the vision quest comes when the person returns to his or her community and shares with everyone the insights gained from the experience. This way, the whole community benefits from the wisdom. He described in detail his most recent experience in the Black Hills of South Dakota. "Doing a vision quest is like detoxing from all the negative stuff in society," he said. "It gives you great perspective. I have learned a whole lot, but I also learned I needed to unlearn some things that were impeding my own personal growth."

Alan then revealed that although he had completed his medical degree with the intention of returning to his tribe and helping to improve the quality of health care, something was missing. In the course of his vision quest, he got a clear message that while Western medicine was good, it wasn't enough, and he needed to incorporate the traditional ways of healing to really be effective. "I got a real clear message for my calling, not to change it, but to strengthen it, and it's really exciting," he said.

So, what are some ways that people can share their insights after coming down from a mountaintop? It could be as simple as sharing the title of a good book with colleagues over the water cooler or perhaps starting a community garden. The possibilities are endless. The gestures don't have to be huge in scope, just genuine and sincere.

Being a Conduit of Love

Many engaging stories illustrate the spontaneous altruistic acts of the connecting process. In my opinion, we can never hear enough of them. The connecting process is really twofold; it's a combination of both receiving and sharing love in all the ways that love becomes manifest. This is one of my favorite stories.

During my tenure as a professor at American University, I taught a course called Humor and Health. Rather than assign a term paper, as most professors do, I decided to take a more creative approach. I invited the students to create a tickler notebook, a personal collection of jokes, cartoons, photographs, birthday cards, funny Dear Abby letters, Dave Barry columns, and anything else they thought would lighten their hearts. Selfishly, I knew that I would have fun reading through these, but I had an ulterior motive. Knowing the importance of comic relief and the absence of it in most hospital settings, I wanted these students to be well prepared in the event that they found themselves incapacitated for any length of time.

As part of the course, I brought in several guest speakers, including some stand-up comedians, musicians, political satirists such as Art Buchwald, the renowned physician Patch Adams, and from a local hospital, an oncology nurse, Christine Flanagan, who had written a grant to establish a humor program in her department. With the money she received, Christine created a humor cart that was brought from room to room for patients who sought a diversion or relief from their illness. The cart, she explained, was filled with comedy CDs, videos, books, and cartoon books (the *Far Side*, *Calvin & Hobbes*, etc.). Although humor didn't cure anyone of cancer, Christine explained, the entire oncology ward became a more healthful place to work because patients were given permission to laugh. Something the nurse said that night created a spark in the souls of several students, and the magic of the connecting process had begun.

On the last night of class before a review for the final exam, the students gathered around me and asked to have a few moments of my time. Unbeknownst to me, in the last few weeks of the semester, they had pooled together the best of their own tickler notebooks and created an impressive comic relief compendium, which they presented to me as a donation to the oncology ward's humor cart, in what can best be called a true random act of kindness.

All of Life Connects

Several years ago, I toyed with the idea of writing a screenplay. The name of the movie was to be called *Jung/Einstein*, and like the movie titled *My Dinner with Andre*, this, too, would be a dinner conversation, this time among two giants in the field of consciousness. About a year after I came up with this idea, I learned that Carl Jung and Albert Einstein actually did sit down over lunch to discuss matters of the universe. Jung was fascinated with Einstein's Theory of Relativity and his Unified Field Theory. Einstein explained that beyond the speed of light, time and space don't play by the same rules. He postulated that something beyond nuclear energy, electromagnetic particles, and gravitational forces held the universe together. My favorite quote of Einstein's (and he is known for many profound observations) is this: "Gravity cannot be responsible for people falling in love." In essence, he explained, everything is mysteriously connected.

Jung, who was formulating his own theories of psychology at the time, was, to put it bluntly, deeply enthralled. In his explorations of the human mind, Jung had also found that both time and space, particularly in the dream state, did not play by the same rules. He later admitted that Einstein's theories inspired his own idea of the collective unconscious, which, simply stated, suggests that at the deepest level of the unconscious mind—the divine aspect of consciousness—everyone connects. Jung used his theory to explain everything from intuitive insights and clairvoyancy to synchronicity. With Einstein's influence on Jung, even the fields of physics and psychology were now connected. The "collective unconscious" is a unified field.

Einstein's work gave rise to the field of quantum mechanics. The subtleties of quantum theory suggest that everything is made of energy, with particles and waves moving freely in the universe. What, to the naked eye, looks like individual or separate objects is really an illusion because, energetically speaking, everything connects. Everything is one. Of course, physicists weren't the first to discover this fact (most likely, they were the last). Wisdom keepers the world over have said this for millennia. Poets, philosophers, and a few liberal physicists tell us that indeed, it is love that holds the universe together. The connecting process is all about love, which is why this season of the soul (the Disney World effect) is the most sought after. Everybody wants to be loved. The connecting process isn't about building bonds of connection; it's about nurturing the bonds that are already there.

There is a short, wonderful American Indian prayer that speaks to the nature of the connecting process. It goes like this: "Mitakuye Oyasin," which means, "All my relations." The wisdom of this prayer refers to the web of life, where all the strands of the earth's fabric, from the people we meet, to the air we breathe, to the ground we walk on, are woven together in a unique tapestry. The connecting process is all about relationships: cultivating, nurturing, and sustaining relationships. Our interactions with family, friends, colleagues, acquaintances, and even strangers are a small fraction of the elaborate network of universal life. We are continually in relationship with everything and everybody (seen and unseen), even when we are unaware of this profound association. For this reason, we are never alone, never disconnected from our divine source, despite the ego's best attempt to convince us otherwise.

The aspect of connectedness did not escape the wisdom of Lao Tzu, either. In what Taoist scholars call the Principle of Oneness, Taoism honors that which connects all life as one. Separateness is clearly an illusion. Taoist wisdom encourages us to transcend the limitations of the ego, so that our highest potential can be realized. Moreover, from a Taoist vantage point, when we see ourselves as superior to nature or ignore the whole by focusing only on the pieces, we not only weaken our inherent link to nature, we isolate ourselves from other people as well. In turn, this separateness weakens our human spirit. If a connection is not reestablished, our very essence will suffocate. The nature of the Tao reminds us that the whole is always greater than the sum of the parts, and we are forever part of the whole.

The Healing Power of Friends

In stress-management circles, the "buffer theory" is central to the theme of connectedness. It's loosely based on the idea that misery likes company, but it's so much more powerful than that. Quite simply, it says that when people can come together and share their thoughts and feelings, their stress is greatly reduced. In some cases, a community of friends can even prolong your life. This is the whole basis for support groups, from A.A. to those for cancer survivors, which offer unique forums for people to come together and share their innermost thoughts and feelings in a safe environment. The bottom line is that having friends who support you in times of need tend to soften the hard blow that stress can bring. The result is not only an improved quality of life but a longer life as well.

This was made quite clear in 1989 by Dr. David Spiegel, who conducted a study at Stanford University School of Medicine to determine the effects of support groups on women who suffered from breast cancer. He learned that women who attended a support group lived, on average, five years longer than those who didn't. Further studies have yielded similar results. There was a time when families served as the primary support group, but social dynamics have changed dramatically over the last several decades, and this has diluted the power of connectedness. The 2000 census reports that fewer than 25 percent of all households in America consist of married couples with children. Moreover, more than 27 million Americans live alone. And while living alone is not the same thing as being lonely, scores of people confide that they are indeed very lonely and depressed. This is why many people spend afternoons at a Starbucks or a Borders Bookstore Café, simply to be near and possibly meet other people. Experts agree that "community" is now more important than ever and will become even more so in the coming decades, as technology invades more aspects of our lives.

E X E R C I S E
Building and Nurturing Connections

It is human nature to socialize, but in an increasingly fragmented society, it takes greater and greater efforts to find the right people, as well as the quality time to spend with them. It's no secret that while the global village becomes smaller, there is a greater sense of alienation among many people. For this reason, the connecting process becomes more important. To make the connecting process powerful, time must be spent in the other seasons of the soul as well. So, here is a suggestion: make it your goal to find a new friend this season. Open your heart to the possibilities of meeting someone new.

One Person, Many Seasons

What makes life complicated, yet equally exciting, is that like the planet itself, we, too, have many seasons occurring at one time. In our personal lives, we can be going through the connecting process (the marriage of a daughter or a son), while at the same time, in our professional lives, we might be in the middle of the emptying process (a corporate merger and a downsizing). To make matters more complex, our spouses, kids, or friends may be in one season, while we are in another altogether. When we feel that no one understands what we are going through, we can feel emotionally isolated, which tends to perpetuate stress.

The cycle of seasons revolves many times in one's life. There will be many periods of emptying, yet, true to the nature of the Tao, there will be an equal number of times to connect. It is interesting to note that only the connecting process is done in the company of others, whereas we enter the first three seasons alone. This, too, is part of the balance. While each season is unique unto itself, it is important to remember the rhythm and flow of the seasons and not intentionally stay too long in any one place. As powerful as one season may be, remember this piece of ageless wisdom: the whole is always greater than the sum of the parts.

EXERCISE
The Heart-to-Heart Meditation

We all know how important the heart is. It is considered crucial to the human anatomy. However, with the anatomical heart comes certain problems. There is no doubt that heart disease is the number-one killer in the country, taking the life of one person every thirty seconds. The association between clogged arteries and heart disease is well proven, but, in addition to cholesterol buildup, the consequence of hardened arteries is, in essence, a *hardened heart*.

Before we knew about the dynamics of anatomy and physiology, we trusted our body wisdom, which told us about feelings from the heart. As it turns out, every part of our gross anatomy also has a symbolic aspect. Placed over our physical heart is a symbolic heart. In Eastern cultures, this is called the *heart chakra*, a spinning wheel of energy that allows energy to flow into and out of the anatomical heart. Ancient wisdom tells us that our emotions are closely tied to the heart chakra, with an expansion of energy occurring through love and compassion and a constriction or a closed chakra in times of fear and anger.

We have all heard the expression "a hardened heart." We use it to signify being mean, nasty, hateful, rude, aggressive, stoic, inconsiderate, or indifferent. Symbolic messages can have very real consequences in our physiology. Stress—unresolved feelings of anger and fear—is now thought to be the single most important risk factor for coronary heart disease. Recently, the cardiologist Dean Ornish discovered that when cardiac patients were introduced to meditation, there was clear evidence of a reversal of the blockage of the coronary arteries. Ornish, who spent time studying in India, is no stranger to the concept of the heart chakra. The expression of love through the heart is the strongest healing power known. And we each have the ability to receive, share, and be an instrument for this love. Opening the symbolic heart, the heart chakra, comes from the depths of ageless wisdom, and its message is one that we must put into daily practice.

1. Sit quietly for several minutes and focus on your breathing. Feel the air come into your nose or mouth, down into your lungs, and feel your stomach begin to expand, only to contract as you start your exhalation. Repeat this seven times, and as you exhale, repeat the phrase "My body is calm and relaxed" to yourself.

2. After the seventh breath, focus your attention on the center of your upper chest, the area over your heart. If you desire, you can imagine that over this area is an image of a heart, a flower, or whatever symbol you associate with love and compassion. If you use a flower, imagine that the flower is opened up fully toward the sun (e.g., lotus, rose, chrysanthemum, etc.).

3. For the next seven breaths, imagine that you are breathing air into your lungs through your symbolic heart. Follow each inhalation with an exhalation back out through the symbolic heart.

4. Using your imagination, picture someone whom you care about in front of you, and visualize a rainbow of light, a beam of light, or some other manifestation of loving energy flowing from your heart to the heart of this person.

5. It is important that you not only think thoughts of love, compassion, and bliss, but that you actually *feel* them as well. Feel the feeling of love in every cell of your body, and then express the intention and the desire to share this feeling with the person whom you have chosen to connect with.

6. Sending love to people whom we feel a sense of fondness toward is easy. Sending feelings of love and compassion to people whom we dislike, whom we feel violated by, whom we are not at peace with is a much greater challenge, but it's not impossible. Using your imagination, recreate a beam of light, a rainbow of love, shining from your heart to this person's heart. If this seems too hard at first, then merely place an image of this person(s) in front of you and send a message acknowledging the individual's

human spirit, for even though we may not like the person's behavior, the divine presence in him or her is a reflection of the divine presence in ourselves as well.

7. Continue this meditation by refocusing on the image of a dear friend or a family member with whom you wish to communicate a bond of compassion. Take seven breaths, each time renewing the thought and the feeling of love and compassion as you focus on this image.

8. Close with one final, slow, deep breath, sending a ray of loving light to yourself.

On Being a Good Mystic

A fourth pillar of human spirituality often stands in the shadows of relationships, values, and a meaningful purpose in life. Some people say that it is the foundation on which the other three are situated. Others say that it is an aspect all unto itself. This component of spirituality is best described as mystical, and it encompasses all things that can never be fully explained, even by the best means of scientific scrutiny. For a number of reasons, the mystical aspect often takes a backseat in discussions about human spirituality, due in large part to our inability to understand the unique alchemy of humanity between divinity, not to mention our obvious desire to avoid looking stupid because there is no way to validate or prove it.

The mystical side of spirituality includes all the experiences and happenings that defy rational explanation in the human mind, yet we know they really happened because we experienced them. People with a strong sense of faith may categorize these synchronistic moments or unexplained healings as miracles. Those with a more logical approach to life call these events "unexplained anomalies" and either dismiss them or simply forget that they ever happened.

Carl Jung was not only intrigued by these events, he actually studied them. It was Jung, after all, who coined the word *synchronicity*. Jung was often ostracized for his explorations in this aspect of human psychology, but that didn't stop him. Ever the good mystic,

Jung explained the rational mind this way: "The conscious mind rejects that which it does not understand," and he chose not to reject it. Just because we don't understand something does not give us license to dismiss it, yet that's what happens, perhaps because to accept it would threaten our current worldview. Who wants to look gullible or be embarrassed?

St. Augustine, himself no stranger to the divine mystery, is quoted as saying this: "Miracles do not happen in contradiction to nature, but in contradiction to what we know about nature." By all measures, human spirituality is inclusive, not exclusive. To ignore the mystical side would not only paint an incomplete picture, it would also be a gross injustice to the entire topic.

History is punctuated with mystical happenings, from Moses' parting of the Red Sea and St. Teresa of Avila, who levitated when she prayed, to the apparitions of the Virgin Mary that recently appeared in Medjugorje. In every age and in every culture, mystical experiences are about as common as the cycles of the moon. I recall my first mystical experience as a child: a psychic dream that foretold an event that actually happened days later. Not only has my life been filled with mystical experiences, but I have encountered hundreds of people who have told similar stories, some of them looking for validation, yet most just wanting to share the wonder of the moment. M. Scott Peck described this process of searching for cosmic clues as the fourth and final stage of the path of spiritual development: the Mystic Communal. In this stage, he explained, you thrive on looking for clues to the mysteries of life, yet you know that you will never come close to finding all the pieces of the big picture.

Experiences that are mystical in nature are not restricted to a chosen few. Rather, these moments—some people call them "holy moments"—are available for everyone, but you need an open mind to be receptive to their meaning. Being a good mystic doesn't mean that you can perform miracles or use supernatural powers. To appreciate the divine mystery, you merely need to view the world with an open mind. Being a good mystic means seeing the supernatural as natural and the ordinary as extraordinary. In other words, you simply appreciate the mystery of life without needing to fully know the hows and the whys of the universe.

A Final Thought on Mountains and Water

If you have never been to the Tetons, here is a suggestion: the best time to go is in the autumn, when the aspen leaves turn gold. With a blue sky and the majestic mountains as a backdrop, the place is nothing less than magical. Almost every September I go to Jackson, Wyoming, to get away, to renew, and, if I am lucky, to shoot some photographs. On one particular trip, I rented a cabin in the national park for three days. Usually, I have good luck with the weather, but this time as I drove into Jackson Hole, thick clouds began to form around the mountains. As it turned out, I never actually saw the Tetons during this trip because it rained cats and dogs the entire time I was there. Sitting on my bed in the cabin, hearing the raindrops bounce off the roof, I decided to open my journal and do some writing. I had written a poem to open a book I was working on, about balance and inner peace. Suddenly, it dawned on me that the back of the book needed a poem to balance out the poem at the front. The proverb "stand like mountain, flow like water" quickly came to mind, and I found the following words spilling from my pen to the paper. Because I now close each presentation with this poem, it has become my signature trademark. I thought it was a nice way to round out this chapter.

Stand Like Mountain, Flow Like Water

To walk the human path is hard,
To stay put is not an option.
At times my head is filled with doubt,
I pause, uncertain and insecure,
Then I hear these words aloud,
Stand like mountain, flow like water.

I walk each step in search of truth,
My quest brings both joy and sorrow.
Light and dark dance unified,
Yes! Balance is the key to life,
Again I hear the words aloud,
Stand like mountain, flow like water.

We come to earth to learn to love,
A lesson we all must master.
To know and serve the will of God,
Is not a task for a chosen few,
We must each answer the call to love,
Stand like mountain, flow like water.

The Call to Love

Like the call to adventure, the call to love comes in many ways, for there are many colors in love's rainbow. It is love, in the name of faith, that transports us over the water's surface, and it is love, in the name of courage, that allows us to either stand like a mountain or move one, when the situation calls for it. With love, truly all things are possible.

4

Move a Mountain,
Walk on Water

We are all visitors to this time and place.

We are just passing through.

Our purpose here is to observe, to learn,

to grow, to love, then we return home.

—ABORIGINAL SAYING

A Leap of Faith

It's rather hard to accurately describe a South African accent to someone who has never heard it before. To the naïve ear, it sounds a bit British. There is a relaxed sound to the vowels, yet it isn't the laid-back drawl of people who hail from Australia or New Zealand—both places that I visited years ago. Perhaps because of the Dutch influence, the South African accent lulls you in by familiarity then captures your imagination with nuances of dialect in each phrase. Such was the case when I was introduced to my pilot instructor, after arranging to paraglide off Aspen Mountain in the summer of 2000. I was about to jump off a cliff, which some people might consider insane, but the excitement of this adventure was heightened by hearing my pilot's accent and seeing his air of confidence and infectious smile.

"Hi, my name is Pine Pienaar, and I will be your instructor. I'll be right behind you the whole way. When I tap on your shoulder, I want you to run as fast as you can. Don't hold back. The parachute will take us straight up. Any questions?"

Looking him square in the eye, I shook my head no. Then I stepped into the harness that would hold me suspended in midair for the next hour and fastened the belts really tight. Double-checking my harness, Pine shook my hand and said, "Let's go." I glanced down at the firm earth directly beneath my feet, then out at the mountains that lay on the other side of a valley thousands of feet below. I took a deep breath. Before I had a moment to reflect on the symbolic meaning of jumping off a cliff, I felt a slap on my shoulder, and we were off and up in less time than it takes to say "Pretoria."

I didn't expect a conversation on the nature of God and the meaning of life, as we hung effortlessly in the air several thousand feet above the ground. Perhaps I should have. Given the magic of aerodynamics, combined with the spectacular mountain scenery, I should have expected nothing less.

"I found the secret of life," Pine said, after making sure that I was seated firmly in the harness. Absorbing the exhilarating experience through each of my five senses, I nodded for him to continue.

With a tug of the right string and the help of a thermal lift, we ascended several hundred feet and he said, "For so many years I was living a life of other people's expectations. I would have died a quick death in Johannesburg, had I conformed to mediocrity. I was reading a book at the time, contemplating what really to do with my life. There was this one passage that has become the compass of my life journey ever since."

"What did it say?" I yelled, hoping the wind would carry my words back to him.

"It said love is the greatest force in the universe. Love can move mountains, yet so many people are paralyzed by fear." He paused for a moment to check the drafts. "Each time we let fear rule our lives, the soul dies just a little bit. Truly, this is no way to live." As he paused once more to read the wind, we glided like a bald eagle over Aspen valley, with a bird's eye view extending at least fifty miles in every direction. Banking on a left turn toward the sun, he picked up the conversation again.

"So I stopped living in fear. I began to take risks, calculated risks. I made a list of things I wanted to do in my life and started doing them, like travel and cooking, learning to sail, and paraglide. I started taking guitar lessons, and I learned to surf. Every time I cross off one more item, I end up adding four more. I make sure each experience is an adventure!" I thought of something that a friend often says, "If you're not living on the edge, you're taking up too much room. . . . Life is short, but it's wide!" To show my agreement, I gave him a thumbs-up.

"Now, take paragliding," he said nonchalantly. "To jump off a mountain and do it gracefully, you need faith to know you're going to land safely, but at the same time you need confidence to take that first step. Intuition is critical to knowing how to read the wind and, of course, humbleness to take it all in and enjoy the immensity of it all."

"What's the longest you have ever been in the air?" I asked.

"Eight and a half hours," he replied. "Simply heaven!"

As Pine spoke, we sailed in a circle that was at least a half-mile in radius. "Jumping off a mountain is the proverbial leap of faith," he said. "Sometimes to move mountains you have to fly over them." We both laughed at the wisdom of these words. I realized that moving mountains is neither impossible nor entirely difficult. With a little distance behind you, the experience can also be exhilarating.

Mountain Movers

Lance Armstrong, a cancer survivor and the winner of six consecutive Tour de France's, said this of his near-fatal battle with cancer: "At the time, I thought it was the worst thing that could ever happen to me, but in hindsight, it has become the best thing that has ever happened to me." As strange as it may be to hear these words, they are commonly used by people, both famous and unknown, who have encountered the "stress from hell" and have emerged from the circumstance gracefully. We call these people heroes. Joseph Campbell certainly would have. They left their comfort zones and became the masters of two worlds. They appear to have moved mountains or walked on water because they have overcome insurmountable odds. By moving mountains, they have not created an illusion. They have made the impossible possible. The actor Laurence Olivier once said, "Legends are made of ordinary people who do extraordinary deeds." Legends are not limited to sports heroes and celebrities. We all have the potential to be legends. Whether we know it or not, we are all on a Hero's Journey.

Simply put, there are two ways to emerge from a stressful situation. The first and most common is in the role of a victim. Traveling on this path, people milk a difficult situation for all it's worth by cleverly begging for sympathy and pity. They bitch, moan, and whine until the cows come home about some personal injustice, and just when you think that everything that could possibly be said has been hashed out, they start all over again. After a while, they sound like a broken record, except that because they have the victim mind-set, they always seem to find something new to complain about. Hence, the cycle is repeated again and again. Victims are everywhere. Listen closely to the next conversation you have with acquaintances, friends, and family members, and you will see how common the role of victim truly is. To go one step further, listen to yourself speak and see whether you notice similar behavior.

The second way to emerge (note that *emerge* is the root word of *emergency*) is to move through any given situation gracefully, meaning with no lingering trace of resentment, animosity, or bitterness. People who do this shine. They glow. These are the people whom you really want to hang around because they are fun to be with. Now, keep in mind that these people are quite human, and they, too, have their moments of anger and resentment. But unlike the proverbial victim, who wallows in the mind-set of victim consciousness, the victor works through a problem and then quickly moves on. In the resolution process, not only does this person come out stronger in spirit, she or he glows. I call these individuals "transcenders" because they don't get stuck in the muck, but, like butterflies, they rise above their problems.

Transcenders often echo the words of Lance Armstrong, by saying that what at the time seemed like a curse of biblical proportions is now nothing less than a blessing—the best thing that ever happened to them. While many things distinguish a victor from a victim, perhaps the most notable is the ability to learn whatever lesson is offered from each situation. In doing so, the person's rough edges—both big and small—get polished, so that this metaphorical gemstone becomes smooth and irresistible to the touch.

High on a Mountaintop

In his study of several hundred remarkable people, the renowned psychologist Abraham Maslow searched for personality traits that culminated in what he called the "self-actualized" person. He described these individuals as being able to rise above the stressors of everyday life and reach their highest human potential to enjoy peak experiences. In his search for what made these people tick, he discovered a host of attributes that formed the foundation of self-actualization. He learned that humor, creativity, patience, and faith acted as buffers for the torments of life's stressful moments. In recent years, the term *hardy personality* (a character type that embodies three traits: challenge, commitment, and control) has been used to describe people who deal effectively with life's ups and downs in today's ever-changing workforce. Although the attributes of a hardy personality work well for a media sound bite, I think it's fair to speculate that the human treasure chest has more than three tools in it.

Humanistic psychologists suggest that we most likely use only a fraction of our innate talents. Like our DNA, of which scientists have determined that we use only 3 percent, we have barely tapped into our human potential. It has often been said that if we, as a human species, were to employ all of our inner resources at any given time, we would not only amaze ourselves, we would probably appear superhuman, perhaps unrecognizable. We see glimpses of remarkable humans who do this during the Olympics or in cata-strophic circumstances that require heroic degrees of strength and internal fortitude. We glimpse these feats often enough to know that they are indeed possible. Yet good news seems to quickly evaporate from human consciousness. We forget that not only are these achievements possible for others, but that we, too, can accomplish them.

In the course of my life, I have encountered many people who have not only made lemonade from lemons, they have transformed the lives of nearly everyone they came in contact with. I meet these people on airplanes, at rock concerts, in ski chair lifts, or in grocery store aisles. Some are college students, others are workshop participants, but most of them are everyday people, strangers who become friends, unassuming people who most likely will never make front-page headlines. Perhaps I consciously seek them out, but even when I think I am not looking, I still meet them. They begin by sharing their stories, much like Lance Armstrong's—the hero with a thousand faces. I know immediately that these people are not victims, because they radiate a vibrant energy that I can only describe as loving compassion.

Curious, I always ask what helped them get through their horrible ordeals. As if they had all gotten together to conspire on one answer, they begin by mentioning an inner resource. For some, it was humor; for others, it was faith; for still others, it was forgiveness. And although they might begin with one attribute, before long, they have included several more. When I hear these inner resources mentioned, I think, these are not gifts for a chosen few; they are everyone's birthright. Humor, faith, patience, forgiveness, creativity, persistence, humbleness, and compassion are just a few of the gems in the crown of human potential. There are many, many more. I call these inner resources the "muscles of the soul," because they act like a guiding force to help us overcome the obstacles we face on life's journey. In many ways, they are akin to the spiritual aids that Campbell mentioned, which appear on the road of trials. Similar to our physical muscles, these attributes never disappear; however, they will certainly atrophy with disuse.

Every day we are called upon to use these muscles, sometimes many of them at the same time. These are the tools of the human spirit that help dismantle roadblocks on the road of life. They are skills that help us circumnavigate, deflate, or transcend the problems in our lives so that we can keep moving on the human journey. And the beauty of these inner resources is that they are always available, no matter what the size of the problem, whether it's some guy in the grocery store with seventeen items in his shopping cart when the sign above his head reads TEN ITEMS OR LESS, or the angel of death comes knocking on your door. Metaphorically speaking, these inner resources make you strong enough to move a mountain or light enough to walk on water. The muscles of the soul are grounded in inner peace. In the sage words of Thich Nhat Hanh, "People say that walking on water is a miracle, but to me, walking peacefully on earth is the real miracle."

The Muscles of the Soul

The colorful list of attributes that comprises the "muscles of the soul" is as long as it is impressive. These inner resources typically begin with more obvious ones, such as faith and humor, but tucked away among these sinuous fibers are the equally important traces of persistence, integrity, patience, imagination, tolerance, and resiliency—characteristics that the researchers heading up the Human Genome Project most likely will never find in the double helix code of our DNA. Metaphorically speaking, these are the colors of love's rainbow. When loved is looked at from this perspective, the wisdom imparted from Jesus of Nazareth to "love your neighbor" becomes more possible. All aspects of our human potential quickly gain our attention when the odds are stacked against us. Similarly, these same muscles of the soul are equally as powerful when we deal with smaller annoyances in life, like the man who neglects to use his turn signal or the daughter who insists she needs a new pair of jeans when you just bought her a pair last week. Described here are some of the more commonly used muscles. In the spirit of Joseph Campbell, several stories are woven around these muscles, stories of common, yet uncommon, everyday heroes who learned the lesson of not getting stuck. Through these stories, the promise of our human birthright is revealed. Like fables, myths, and legends of long ago, they awaken our souls to the promise of our highest potential, so that grace under pressure prevails. At the end of each story is a small section titled "Testing Your Spiritual Potential," where questions are posed to help you exercise the same muscles.

Patience: The Virtue That Counts

Clifford was diagnosed with type 1 (juvenile) diabetes three days before his eleventh birthday. At an age when his friends could make forts and go off in the woods to hunt mythical dragons, Clifford led a more cautious life. Although he would admit that his life was pretty normal, the constant monitoring of his blood-sugar level before and after each meal was a clear sign that Clifford was indeed different. For the rest of his life, the insulin kit would always be within arm's reach.

"When I was first diagnosed, there were no insulin kits. Blood sugar was measured through urine tests. I remember the days when we had to boil the syringes before each insulin injection," he said.

In 1971, when he proposed marriage to Kathi, his high school sweetheart, he promised her that their life together would be wonderful, but he couldn't guarantee that he would be there by her side in the retirement years. Diabetes is the third leading cause of death in the United States, and life expectancy is about twenty years shorter than for nondiabetics. Regardless of how well a person monitors his or her sugar levels, nerve damage occurs in the eyes and the extremities. There are numerous complications with the heart, the kidneys, and other organs as well. Diabetes can be a very cruel disease.

When Clifford was first diagnosed, medical science had not even conducted the first heart transplant, so any thought of a pancreatic transplant was nothing more than science fiction. With the advances of medical science today, organ transplants have become almost commonplace. Clifford was forty-seven when he first heard of a chance for a pancreatic transplant. Knowing what was in store for his health status, he immediately pictured his name on the list of potential recipients. The only problem was that time was not on his side. Time and patience can either be our best friends or our mortal enemies, depending on our perception. He decided to make time and patience his best allies, hoping that one day, he would find himself at the top of the donor list. Biding his time, Clifford took up a few new hobbies, including car restoration and repair.

"The doctors told me that after age fifty, the complications become too great, so they conduct transplants only with younger patients. I'm forty-nine, and although I am in good shape, the clock is ticking and it's not in my favor," he explained. "Not only that, but you basically are waiting for some poor guy to die, so you can live. Then on top of that, assuming you do get the transplant, there is no guarantee that your body will accept the organ. It's a very strange ordeal to go through."

Clifford will admit that patience was never his strongest card, but his attitude changed when his name was placed on the donor list. It had to. For nearly three years he waited for a healthy pancreas. For nearly three years he waited for the phone to ring with a voice telling him that he had a new lease on life. Patience isn't just waiting for what you want to happen. Patience is waiting with dignity and humbleness, even if what you are waiting for never comes. It is the realization that the timing of your desires is not always in sync with the universal clock. There is always a bigger picture to consider. Fear can act like blinders to our worldview. The result is often a hurried pace that is out of step with the grand picture. Perhaps nowhere is this more evident than in the American lifestyle, where fast-food convenience and drive-up window service support a lifestyle built on immediate gratification. Sometimes fear can obliterate patience altogether.

On April 3, 2000, Clifford got a call from his surgeon to drive down to Yale, New Haven Hospital. His name had been at the top of the list for the last three months, and every time the phone rang in the house, he and Kathi both held their breath. When he arrived for surgery that afternoon, shaved, scrubbed, and prepped to go under the knife, the physician told him it wasn't a good match and he should get dressed, go back home, and wait. Patience was called upon again. Some people might have gotten mad. Clifford smiled graciously and headed back home. Patience is like a lighthouse beacon that never dims. Two days later, the hospital called again.

"My son had just come home from a date. The phone rings at 1:30 A.M., and Matthew yells upstairs, 'Hey, Dad, you got your pancreas!' I was so nervous, I knew I couldn't drive, so I asked a good friend to drive us to the hospital. Surgery was scheduled for 6:00 A.M. Then, for some reason, they told me it was rescheduled for 1:00 P.M. that afternoon, and again I had to wait."

Indeed, a new pancreas sat in an iced cooler, waiting for Clifford's freshly scrubbed and shaved body. This time, it was deemed a good match. The waiting game was over. By the time Clifford arrived in postop, his whole family had gathered around his bed in support. I talked to Clifford a few days after his seven-hour surgery. "I am not out of the woods yet," he said to me. "But I have to tell you, I have never felt this good in my life. You know what the first words were out of my mouth in the transplant recovery room?" he asked with a huge smile. "Hey, Dad, I'm not a diabetic anymore!"

In these times of fast food, drive-up bank tellers, and instant messaging, patience is a rare commodity. We would all do well to follow Clifford's lead and employ the skill of patience at every possible moment. As Clifford will tell you, patience offers its own rewards.

TESTING YOUR SPIRITUAL POTENTIAL: Are you a patient person? What undermines your sense of patience in times of stress? Humbleness and patience go hand in hand. How humble are you in times of stress?

Faith: Trust without Reservation

Nearly every person I have met who is on the rebound from a trip to hell speaks of faith as a crucial tool in his or her journey home, regardless of the individual's religious orientation or lack thereof. These transcenders may not list faith as the first muscle they flex, but it always seems to find its way into the story at some point. Faith isn't a belief in something that might be; it is a knowing of what truly is. In a world crowded with six billion people and counting, it is easy to think that we are very insignificant and obscured from God's view. In a sound bite, faith can best be described as a deep-seated knowing that as insignificant as we might seem in the vast cosmos, we are *essential* to the grand design of the universe. Faith is the seat of that knowing, an undeniable awareness of our connection to the divine source. Like the fairy tale hero who gets distracted from his or her destination, it is easy to forget this divine connection. Yet like a trusty compass, faith is the act of remembering that brings us safely back home.

To help pay my tuition in graduate school, I taught beginning swim lessons to undergraduate students. Having swum competitively in high school and college, I consider pools my second home. On the first day of each semester, it was my job to make my students as comfortable in the water as I was. My third semester proved no different than the rest. Students shuffled onto the pool deck with towels draped around their necks like life vests. As I finished taking attendance, a black woman walked out of the locker room with a towel in hand and introduced herself as Lawanda. At first glance, it was no exaggeration to say that Lawanda weighed over three hundred pounds. She dwarfed everyone in class, including me. Most of us were half her body weight. Yet as big as she was in stature, she was the epitome of timidness. This woman was deathly afraid of the water. As the students jumped in, Lawanda perched herself delicately on the edge of the pool, barely dipping her big toe in. The next few classes proved even more challenging, because this young coed simply refused to get her face wet. To pass the course, each student had to jump off the high board into the deep end and swim to the edge unassisted. I looked at this human bundle of nerves and could tell it was going to be a long semester.

Within a few weeks, however, things got better. Lawanda soon realized that her weight was an asset in the water. She floated beautifully. With a little confidence under her belt, she learned to swim on her back relatively easy, as long as no water got into her eyes or nose. From there, we worked on the freestyle and the breaststroke. All the while, the high board at the deep end of the pool waited, like a hungry great white shark lurking just yards off the coast. When the day came to jump off the high board, Lawanda was mysteriously absent. In a way, I was rather surprised, because over the last few weeks, she seemed to have really taken a liking to the water. When she showed up the next day, she was more nervous than any student I have ever taught. I explained to her that she already knew how to swim; jumping from a few extra feet above the edge wouldn't matter that much. Tears rolled down her checks.

After a very long pause, Lawanda stepped up on the diving board and walked with painstaking slowness toward the edge. In what seemed like an eternity, she just stood there and looked down. I got in the water to coax her, to no avail. Twenty minutes later the class ended, and Lawanda never even got wet. During the next class period, Lawanda perched at the edge of the high dive and remained in that position the entire time. Nothing I said or could have said would give her any comfort. She was frozen with fear. When we met again as a class, Lawanda failed to even show up that day. With only two more class periods remaining, Lawanda's fate—specifically, her graduation—was in question. I walked out of the pool office and began picking up kick-boards and was surprised to see Lawanda sitting poolside. "I'm ready today," she said. "Can I go over to the deep end?" Not wanting to dampen her enthusiasm, I nodded. Other students walked onto the pool deck but kept their distance, so as not to intimidate her.

There are ten steps leading to the top of the high dive. Lawanda paused at each one, as if to say a prayer. As she made her way toward the edge of the board, I quietly slipped into the water and swam a few feet, gently talking to her, coaching her the whole time. "Will you promise to catch me if I jump in?" she yelled, looking up toward the ceiling.

"I promise!" I yelled back. But before I finished speaking those two words, she leaped high in the air and splashed feet first into the water. In less than a nanosecond, Lawanda surfaced. Her face was beaming. She quickly reached for my hand but then turned on her back and sculled toward the pool edge. As she climbed out, she was met by a thunderous round of applause from the other students. She turned to me and said, "I want to do it again!" And sure enough, she did, several more times that hour.

When class was over, she walked up and gave me a hug, saying, "I woke up this morning and had me a little talk with God. I was told in no uncertain terms that this was a test of faith, and with my attitude, I was not passing. God said, 'Let go of fear, and I'll catch you.' I was using you as a backup, but I didn't really need you." She paused for a second to reflect on the concept of faith. I cannot remember her exact words, but they reminded me of Nelson Mandala's eloquent wisdom: "Faith is not belief without proof, but trust without reservation." Lawanda smiled and winked at me, then headed into the women's locker room. For her, walking on water was no different than swimming beneath it.

TESTING YOUR SPIRITUAL POTENTIAL: How strong is your faith in times of stress? What holds you back when faith calls you to move forward?

Forgiveness: Moving On

Stress has many balls and chains, but the heaviest one that keeps people tethered to the ground is unresolved anger in the form of grudges. If unresolved anger is a toxin to the spirit, then forgiveness is the antidote; and where anger is a roadblock, forgiveness is a ladder to climb over and transcend the experience. For forgiveness to be complete and unconditional, though, you must be willing to let go of all feelings of resentment, anger, and animosity. Sweet forgiveness cannot hold any aftertaste of bitterness, as these emotions are mutually exclusive.

Feeling victimized is common when one encounters stressors in the form of another person's behavior. When we sense that our human rights have been violated, our feelings of rage can quickly turn into resentment. Left unresolved, these toxins can taint the way we treat ourselves and others. To forgive those who we feel have wronged us is not an easy task. Often it's a process, and at times it's a very arduous process. Yet turning the other cheek does not mean that you have to let others walk all over you. And forgiveness is not a surrender of your self-esteem, nor is it a compromise of your integrity. Forgiveness is not the same as restitution, so don't go looking for an apology. When fully engaged, forgiveness can turn a hardened heart into an open passageway, in which we move gracefully through a difficult situation.

The drive from Jackson Hole to Boulder is a little more than eight hours. The majestic view of the Rockies at either end is breathtaking. It's no secret that the Tetons in October are simply stunning. The trip in-between Jackson Hole and Boulder, however, is much less exciting. The wide-open spaces of Wyoming are often monotonous. In the late afternoon I approached Laramie. It's normally a quiet little town, but I noticed police sirens in the distance, and for a moment my attention was distracted. Sometimes I stop in Laramie to refuel, but I thought that I had enough gas to reach Fort Collins and decided to keep driving. Hours after I got home, I heard on the news that a young man had been found beaten and tied to a rail fence a few miles from Laramie's city limits. Barely alive and in a coma, he was brought to a hospital in Fort Collins. His name was Matthew Shepard. The local news media followed his story closely, as did the national news. Brutal murders like this just didn't happen out West. The next day it was reported that he died, and the search was on for his killers. Soon the whole world descended on the sleepy little town of Laramie. It seemed that the murder of Matthew Shepard had become the hate crime of the decade. Within a few days, the police had their suspects and a trial was underway.

Ask any parent, and he or she will tell you that the hardest thing to go through in life is the death of your own child. Such was the case for Judy and Dennis Shepard. The fact that Matthew had been murdered and the story was now national headline news only magnified an already difficult personal crisis. But as tough as it was, they both held their heads high. Perhaps most remarkable, during the year that it took the trial to be completed, was Judy Shepard's ability to forgive the convicted murderers of her son. The two men faced the death penalty, but due to Judy's efforts, their lives were spared. Rather than death, she lobbied for mercy. Her efforts were successful. When the trial was over, she explained that if she held contempt for the murderers, she could never get on with her life. And she needed to move on. In Dennis's words, "Now is a time for healing."

About the same week that Matthew Shepherd was brutally murdered, another life was extinguished all too early just eighty miles south of Laramie. Again the seeds of forgiveness were sown to take root. At the age of twenty-one, Benjamin Shank was looking to transfer to Goddard College in Vermont. Music had become a deep-seated passion for Ben, and just months earlier, he had recorded his first musical. Music, he felt, was a way to make the world a better place in which to live. He decided to stay in Colorado during the fall and work on the final editing of his project. One night, however, while he was driving through Boulder, Benjamin's car was struck by a drunk driver, and he never returned home.

"When a mother loses a son, it is devastating," explained Rose Shank. "When the phone rang at four in the morning on Sunday, October 4, my life changed in a way that I could not have imagined. In addition to mourning the loss of Ben, I have had to learn how to best help three teenagers mourn the loss of their brother."

I first met Rose at a stress-management workshop nearly a decade ago. The instant I met her, I felt a strong presence of peace. With her feet well anchored and her spirit soaring like a kite, it became obvious to me that Rose was a woman of great faith. Yet, as she explained, the path of faith is not an easy road. Faith is continually tested in many ways. Forgiveness became the challenge of her faith. Years later, I learned of her son's death through my personal assistant, who mentioned that her own son had attended school with Ben. I took the liberty to call Rose and express my condolences. We agreed to meet for lunch and catch up on our lives. There, I learned firsthand how powerful the act of forgiveness can be.

Rose told me that she had attended the sentencing of the young man accused of drunk driving and manslaughter. She had stood up in front of the judge and read her statement:

My family and I have come to a decision. I ask you for leniency in terms of time sentenced to prison. I feel that time in prison would harm the defendant more than it would help him change his decision-making process. Believe me, it is very difficult to do this. By stating our feelings publicly, I risk judgment, criticism, derision, and also the risk of feeling unheard in the courtroom. There are many people with me in the courtroom today who have come here, not only to offer us support but to make a statement by their presence. They, too, believe in a compassionate life and are willing to make this public. Compassion doesn't lessen the pain caused by our loss, but it gives us freedom from anger that would prevent us from living our lives fully. We feel blessed in that we truly have no room in our hearts for vengeance. It's true, there is nothing that will bring Ben back to us. So, once again, we look at what we think might produce some good from this tragedy, which is why I stand before you requesting leniency for the defendant. We have spent many hours in reflection, discussion, and discernment. In the spirit of Ben, who was a compassionate, generous, and caring human being, we continue to live our lives in a way that makes this world a better place to live.

Forgiveness is a powerful antidote to anger.

TESTING YOUR SPIRITUAL POTENTIAL: List two people whom you feel have violated you in some way. Ask yourself, How long have I been carrying a grudge against each person? Then pick one person and begin the forgiveness process, so that you can leave the person behind and move on to the next individual, doing the same thing. This will enable you to really start moving on with your life.

Willpower: Connecting to the Source

Willpower is one of the most desired muscles working the engine of the human spirit. It provides the energy not only to set things in motion but to keep them moving as well. We call a lack of willpower laziness, but it's really more than that. Indolence is a conscious decision to turn against the divine tide and even try to buck it. Willpower is a source of strength, but it is not merely a strength that resides within us. Anyone who describes his or her use of willpower will tell you that it's a team effort, of sorts. Such is the case of Lance and his remarkable ability to harness his willpower. I first met Lance at the pool where I work out. He's a lifeguard. One day as I walked back into the locker room, we struck up a conversation about the Christmas holidays. As it turns out, we were both going to the Hawaiian Islands. Lance was going to his sister's wedding, but, as he explained it to me, it wasn't his first trip to the South Pacific. The first time was not exactly a vacation. Later, over steamed rice and wontons, he gave me the inside scoop on that very first trip.

Picture this: you're asleep in bed, only to awaken and find three federal marshals in uniforms, surrounding you. They tell you to get up and put your hands behind your back. They have handcuffs and they mean business. Before you can register what is going on, you're basically being kidnapped and being hauled out of the house and into a car. Within forty-eight hours, you find yourself on a plane to a South Pacific island, Samoa, and although the place is called Paradise Cove, this isn't paradise. It's the furthest thing from it. It's a boot camp for teenage drug addicts, and the suggested length of stay is one year. This was the initial experience Lance found himself in one night in 1996. Some stressful situations you walk into blindly; however, this was not the case for Lance. He himself had laid the groundwork for this experience by dealing drugs at age fifteen, and now he takes full responsibility for his actions.

Like so many kids who experiment with drugs, Lance had tried nearly everything: pot, mushrooms, crack, amphetamines, and acid, to name a few. His rebellious behavior very quickly turned to a serious addiction. He may have been looking for acceptance or perhaps felt anger directed at his estranged dad, now divorced; perhaps he was just driven by plain curiosity, which got out of control. No matter what the direct cause, now he was in deep trouble. His mother realized that not only was he on a downhill slope, he had practically booked himself a one-way ticket to prison. So she did the only thing she knew that would work. She arranged to have him picked up and delivered to the world-renowned Paradise Cove drug and alcohol rehabilitation program for teenagers. Lance was anything but impressed with this token of generosity. In fact, he was furious at her when he learned that she'd arranged the whole thing. Given the chance to call home, he flatly refused. When the number was dialed for him, he could barely utter a word.

"It was the day before my seventeenth birthday. I couldn't believe what was happening. First, they ship you off to Brightway Rehab Center in St. George, Utah. They shave your head, give you a uniform, and keep you up all night, I suppose to disorient you. You get one phone call home, which turns out to be the last phone call you'll make for about six months. From that point, there is absolutely no contact with your family. There is no contact with anybody. You are stripped of everything. It's rough, really rough," Lance said.

But it turned out that it only got rougher. The Paradise Cove rehab center is spartan at best, in terms of food (rice and mutton), clothing (standard issue T-shirt and shorts), and lodging (barracks with no showers). To get an accurate picture, imagine the exact opposite of Club Med—a never-ending boot camp with as many as two hundred kids all in the same situation. And all for the same reason: a lack of willpower.

"The hardest part of being there was knowing that no one was going to do it for me. Nobody was going to rescue me. I had to do it myself. I had to change within to set myself free. What did it take to do this? Coming to terms with who I was as a person. Dealing with a lot of anger. I had to learn to like myself. I never felt that before. That was really hard."

If the shock of being hauled off to Samoa for twelve months wasn't hard enough, there was another shock: coming back home. Lance no longer had anything in common with the friends with whom he once associated—nor did he want to. To make matters worse, not only did he have one year of high school to finish, he had to make up the difference in the work he'd missed while he was away. In other words, the end of hell didn't mean the beginning of paradise. Lance was now back in the environment he had initially left, but unlike the situation in Paradise Cove, drugs, alcohol, and sex were readily available. Lance admits that many things have helped him and continue to help him cope with life's challenges, the most important of which is willpower.

"Being at Paradise Cove, you begin to realize rather quickly that you aren't going to get any help, but at the same time you're not alone. For those who were inclined, there was a focus on the higher self: God. I tend to see willpower as collaboration with the higher will. It's what gives you strength. It's what gives me strength. Toward the end of my stay, a kid said to me, 'Man, you are so strong!' At first, I thought he was speaking about my character. But what he really meant was that my willpower was being fed from a higher source. I truly understand that now," he explained.

"Every day is a challenge, but I have put all that behind me now. You've got to! You've got to move on," Lance said.

TESTING YOUR SPIRITUAL POTENTIAL: The strength of your willpower depends on the situation at hand. It is also tightly intertwined with your values. Willpower isn't moving away from something, as much as it is moving toward something else. What issue are you tackling that requires willpower? What value is associated with it? What are you moving toward?

Acceptance: The Final Step

Palm Springs, California, is a very hot place in the summer, as temperatures can reach well above 110 degrees. I was attending a conference, giving a presentation on stress and human spirituality. In contrast to the scorching heat outside, the room was comfortably cool. Typically, I provide handouts and place them on the chairs so that people who come in early can glance through the material and become familiar with it. With the handouts distributed, I headed toward the slide projector with my slide carousel but was intercepted by a man wishing to chitchat.

"I looked over your list of muscles of the soul. Good list, but you forgot one," he said.

"Oh, really. Which one?" I inquired, knowing fully well that my list was incomplete.

"Acceptance," he answered. He looked down at the ground for a moment, then raised his head to make eye contact and spoke again.

"My granddaughter was murdered last year. It was a terrible loss to my son and daughter-in-law, as you can imagine. It was a terrible loss to us all. I think I had to employ nearly every muscle you have listed, but it came to a point where I knew I also had to accept the situation. There was a lot of anger and a lot of unanswered questions, but after a while the resentment really drains you."

He explained that acceptance isn't a one-step process. It is a long journey.

"Just when you think it's all behind you, something surfaces, perhaps a memory, perhaps a news story, and there it is, all back in your face again. You can try to fight it, but in the end you'll lose, so acceptance is the only thing that gives your heart peace."

Acceptance is perhaps the most important muscle of the soul to exercise, particularly with things we have absolutely no control over.

TESTING YOUR SPIRITUAL POTENTIAL: Is there an issue you feel conflicted about that has been draining your energy? Without compromising your integrity, pick an issue that begs for acceptance and work toward its resolution.

Time to Flex Your Muscles

Just as a circle is a universal symbol of wholeness, the butterfly is a symbol of wholeness. The Greek word for butterfly means "soul." Given the fact that butterflies, unlike the lowly caterpillar, have wings, they are also considered a symbol of transformation. They can rise above what was once considered a limiting existence. There is a story of a boy who, upon seeing a young butterfly trying to emerge from its chrysalis, tried to help by pulling apart the paper cocoon that housed the metamorphosis. The boy's mother quickly stopped him, explaining that the butterfly strengthens its young wings by pushing through the walls of the cocoon. In doing so, its wings become strong enough to allow the creature to fly. When we strengthen our muscles of the soul, we do the same.

EXERCISE
The Human Butterfly

If you were to talk with people who have emerged gracefully from a difficult situation, they would mostly likely tell you that the muscles they used to break through their barrier(s) included patience, humor, forgiveness, optimism, humbleness, creativity, persistence, courage, willpower, and love. These are the muscles we use to dismantle, circumnavigate, and transcend the roadblocks and the obstacles in life. Like physical muscles, these muscles will never disappear; however, they will atrophy with disuse. We are given ample opportunity to exercise these muscles, yet not everyone does.

Using the butterfly illustration on the next page, write in the wings the attributes, inner resources, and muscles of the soul that help you get through the tough times—with grace and dignity, rather than feeling victimized. If you wish to include other traits to augment the health of your human spirit, yet you feel they aren't quite there, write them outside the wings, and draw an arrow into the wings, giving your soul a message that you wish to include (strengthen) these as well. Finally, if you have a box of crayons or pastels, color in the wings of your butterfly. Then hang it up on the fridge or the bathroom mirror—someplace where you can see it regularly, to remind yourself of your spiritual health and your innate ability to transcend life's problems, big and small.

Butterflies need the balance of two wings to fly properly. As Lao Tzu correctly observed, balance is an inherent quality found in all of nature, including the human species, despite our recent ignorance of it. Like the butterfly, each person requires balance to ensure progress on the human journey. Not only do many aspects of the mind, the body, and the spirit necessitate balance, there are many ways to achieve and maintain balance as well. The muscles of the soul provide the means to assist you in this process.

PART III

Life in
the Balance

In every hero's tale, the hero must first learn to find his or her center of gravity and then master one or more skills to accomplish the task at hand—skills to regain and sustain a sense of balance so that progress can be made to ensure a safe passage home. The Taoist influence suggests that behind every weakness is an undiscovered strength, yet every strength can also become a weakness, if overused. Balance is the key. This part offers an abundance of insights, skills, and how-to advice to help you maintain or regain your sense of balance, turn your weaknesses into strengths, and stand strong against the winds of change as you progress on your path.

5

The Human Equinox

Six Ways to Bring Balance into Your Life

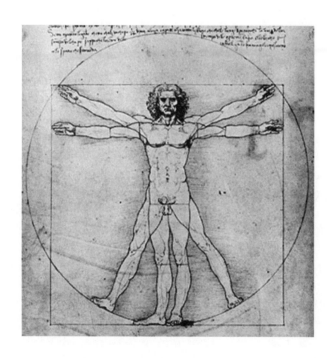

*B*e humble, for you are made of earth.

Be noble, for you are made of stars.

—SERBIAN PROVERB

Second to the *Mona Lisa*, Leonardo da Vinci's most familiar work of art is a sketch of a naked man, his arms and legs outstretched within the confines of a perfect circle and a square: the *Vitruvian Man*, as it is more commonly known. The configuration of these shapes forms a mandala, and this now-famous icon speaks, both implicitly and explicitly, to the nature of balance. Da Vinci drew this sketch as a representation of what was understood at the time to be "Divine Proportion," nature's ubiquitous architectural blueprint with a proportion scale that was always equal to the mathematical number phi. By inserting the man into a circle, Da Vinci also paid homage to the balance of male and female energies, a concept he felt was imperative to the integrity of each individual.

Da Vinci's sketch of the *Vitruvian Man* has been studied by a multitude of art historians, and the coded symbol of wholeness that Da Vinci sketched out, as well as the concept of Divine Proportion, appears to have many layers of meaning. The circle is a universal symbol of wholeness, where all parts come together to form a whole. The words *whole* and *holy* share a common root, and implicit in this symbol is the message that the whole is always greater than the sum of the parts. The ageless wisdom of wholeness, as represented by a circle, can be found in nearly all cultures, from the Taoist yin/yang symbol, Stonehenge, Tibetan mandalas, and the American Indian medicine wheel to the peace symbol, the labyrinth, and the Christmas wreath. So impressed was Thomas Jefferson with the power of the symbolic circle that he designed his home, Monticello, with this in mind.

If you have ever doubted the depth of your wholeness or the

idea that you hold the spark of divine essence within your own being, all you need do is look into the mirror (and if no mirror is available, look into the face of anyone you meet). Within each eye is not one, but two, symbols of wholeness: the pupil centered in a remarkably colorful iris, a perpetual reminder that we are indeed a segment of the divinely proportional universe. Perhaps Shakespeare knew more than he let on when he wrote that the "eyes are the windows of the soul." Humans are innately whole.

The idea of wholeness can be expressed in many ways, such as inner peace, homeostasis, and balance. The concept of balance, as explained by Lao Tzu, is as inherent to the human condition as it is in nature itself. Yet in this day of rapid change, it becomes quite easy to get knocked off balance. Moreover, by not acknowledging and consciously integrating the spiritual aspect of our lives, we find equilibrium even harder to maintain.

Balance doesn't necessarily mean a 50/50 ratio with whatever sits on either side of the scale. Rather, it might be proportional to a 60/40 or a 30/70 split. Only you will know, in the scales of your mind, what the key to balance is each time you find yourself weighing all the factors of your life. Moreover, the complexity of life suggests that the human condition is comprised of not one but rather several hundred sets of scales, with each striving to maintain equilibrium. Not only are these scales delicate, they are extremely complex and interconnected. Consider this: one aspect of your life, such as your marriage can be well balanced, yet there may be significant problems at work, which over time may affect your marriage. Even when things come to a place of balance, new life experiences and the growing pains that accompany them can once again throw things out of whack. The flow of life suggests that periods of balance are followed by brief interludes of imbalance. The Taoist scholar Deng Ming-Dao said it best this way, "No matter how extreme the situation is, it will change. Natural events balance themselves out by seeking their opposites, and this process of balance is the heart of all healing. Without these slight imbalances, there could be no movement to life." Therefore, balance isn't an end to the means, but rather a means unto itself.

Does it seem that under a confluence of stressors, coming back to a point of balance remains ever elusive? For as inherently natural as balance may be, the concept of the human equinox becomes more like the human paradox when things fail to return to equilibrium. It would be nice if there was a rationale to explain this, if for no other reason than to attempt to correct the situation. The lack of a simple answer suggests, once again, the complexity of the human condition. Ageless wisdom suggests that perpetual imbalance is the result of a controlling ego that clings to things, rather than letting go. Thus, if we do the math, it becomes clear that the equation of balance involves not just addition but subtraction as well.

The Rules of Subtraction

Once a good friend who was trying to reclaim the balance in her life told me point-blank that she needed to "edit her life." She explained that her entire life was just too cluttered; many things needed to be "thrown out," including some useless relationships. I smiled upon first hearing this explanation, and since that time, I have taken a liking to the concept of subtracting by "editing one's life," because it speaks to the nature of consciously bringing things back into balance. All things being equal, balance is inherent in the human condition; however, in this day and age, all things are not equal, hence balance becomes a conscious choice. To some extent, we are still hunters and gatherers, only now we gather everything from knick-knacks and clothes to scores and scores of information. It's enough to give everyone attention deficit disorder. The rules of subtraction (like the emptying process) suggest that to find balance, one must release and let go of things on a regular basis.

The following sections highlight six significant aspects of the human condition, which only begin to constitute this set of delicate scales that constantly needs our attention and some occasional fine-tuning (including subtraction), so that our minds and spirits are clear to make good choices.

1. Work Life Balanced with Personal Life

In one of my first job interviews after college, I was asked about the last book I had read for pleasure. I can recall the answer I gave that day: *The Dove*, by Robin Lee Graham. It was an autobiography of the youngest man (age sixteen) to circumnavigate the globe. I love to travel, but when my wings are clipped, I like to read about other people's worldly adventures. Graham's book gave me a phenomenal round-trip ticket. As it turned out, my future boss had asked this question (and several others) to determine how well rounded I was. It was clear that he wanted to hire someone who had lived a well-balanced life.

Reading books for pleasure isn't the only indication of a well-balanced life, but it's a good start. Since I entered the job market in the early eighties, not only have I seen a dramatic change in the workplace setting; with few exceptions, I have yet to be asked that same question, even among most friends. The most stressful environment I lived in was Washington, D.C., where it was not uncommon to hear people brag (or sometimes whine) about putting in twelve- to fourteen-hour workdays. Perhaps the saddest comments I heard (on many occasions, no less) were from people who had forfeited their vacation time to show company loyalty, only to be let go several months later in a restructuring effort, with nothing to fall back on. The advice given in the investment trade is equally important for personal success: diversify your assets. If you see yourself only as your job (or your paycheck) and your job crumbles, then all the other dominos in your life will fall as well.

The Art of Priorities

Every morning I walk my dog around the lake near my home. Most days, relatively few people are up at 6:00 A.M. so the walk typically becomes a meditative practice. Every now and then I meet up with a fellow dog lover, and we chitchat for a while. Jack is one such dog lover. I came to learn that Jack is newly retired and walks many miles daily to keep in shape. Several years ago, he suffered a heart attack, which became a wake-up call of sorts that prompted him to rearrange the priorities in how he was living his life. His previous myopic focus on work, before the heart attack, had now become a grand perspective on the true quality-of-life issues.

One day he told me that he found it odd that Americans have so little vacation time each year (two weeks, if they're lucky). "The Germans, the French, the Australians, now they have their priorities straight—they've got over a month of vacation time," he said.

Jack paused for a moment to observe a blue heron swallow a fish, then continued, "I used to be the kind of person who would put in a few extra hours each day, trying to get things done. After working nearly three decades, I finally learned something. No matter how much work you accomplish in the course of a day, there is always something more to do. It never ends! When I had that realization, I made the habit of leaving for home on time, regardless of what was still left to do. I became a much happier person because of it," he said.

Strolling through a bookstore one day, my eye caught the clever title of a book, *Affluenza*. Based on a PBS series with the same name, the book described Americans' addiction to consumerism and the desire to be rich: a disease aptly termed *affluenza*. The authors noted an interesting phenomenon about the etiology of this disease. Before the advent of television and well into the first few decades of this public utility, people's view of materialism was restricted to the neighborhood or the region in which they lived. "Keeping up with the Joneses" was an expression used to describe envy of your neighbor's goods. More recently, though, ads on television have not been the only thing sold during prime time. At a more subtle, perhaps unconscious, level, what's being sold is a lifestyle, a rich and comfortable lifestyle that exceeds the grasp of most middle-class citizens—that is, until the advent of the credit card. Perhaps you see where this is leading. To keep up with this elusive lifestyle, we easily rationalize the excuse to work a few more hours, and thus the time spent for personal enrichment is greatly compromised. By the time we get home, there's no passion to fix dinner, only to order out. After that, there's just enough energy to crawl into bed before the whole process starts all over again (*Groundhog Day* revisited).

Let there be no doubt, the Puritan ethic (worth equals work) is alive and well in the Western hemisphere, particularly in the United States. As of 2001, Americans have outpaced the Japanese in terms of hours per week worked. Sadly, Americans also outrank all other nations in personal debt and score quite low on the index of personal happiness. As the expression goes, something doesn't add up here.

Why do people spend so much time at work? There may be several reasons, but, for the most part, people identify with their work. First and foremost, they see themselves as their job, more so than any other relationship. In fact, it's not uncommon when people first meet to ask each other, "What do you do for a living?" as if their jobs are everything and nothing else really seems to matter. Personally, I prefer the question "What is your life's passion?" Initially, you may get some strange looks with this question, but the answers prove to be a lot more interesting.

Is there an imbalance between your professional life and your personal life? If the answer is yes, consider yourself in good company. Perhaps a more pertinent question is "Do you have a life?" Judging from the conversations I hear, most people claim not to. Instead, they insist their lives are nothing more than a few recurring panels from a *Dilbert* or a *Cathy* cartoon strip. Creating a balance between one's professional life and one's personal life begins with identifying and honoring clear boundaries in terms of work hours, as well as cultivating the aspects of your personal life that crave attention.

EXERCISE
The Call to Balance

One reason why people's personal lives are often eclipsed by their professional careers is that many aspects of the personal life are not well defined. If your personal life has been neglected so long that you're not sure where to begin, try asking yourself one of the following questions: What would I do for work if my profession didn't exist? What would I do tonight if watching television wasn't an option? What would I do if I were only seventeen years old? What would I do right now if I lived a hundred years ago or a hundred years from now? Whom can I invite over for a spontaneous potluck dinner tonight? What are the top three countries I would like to visit on my next vacation? Do I have a passport, and if so, is it still valid? What musical instrument would I like to learn to play? Currently, what are my top three hobbies, and when was the last time I was actively engaged in any one of them?

Once you have defined various aspects of your personal life that you wish to devote more time to, then comes the task of enforcing clear boundaries at work, so that you have a better chance of achieving your personal goals. Referring back to da Vinci's sketch, think of the circle that surrounds the *Vitruvian Man* as a cell membrane, a necessary boundary that regulates and balances our internal and external worlds. How good is the circle that separates and regulates your two worlds. Is it too porous? Remember, it is often fear that motivates a person to work extra hours or to rationalize bringing work home. Finding balance between work and home also requires letting go of the fear that you are solely your job or your paycheck.

On a final note, as a graduation present to his son who was heading off to college, H. Jackson Brown Jr. wrote him a book called *Life's Little Instruction Book*. Among the many pearls of wisdom found within the covers is this gem: "Get your priorities straight. No one ever said on his death bed, 'Gee, if I'd only spent more time at the office.'" We would all do well to follow this advice.

2. Freedom Balanced with Discipline

Of the many great insights shared in Victor Frankl's classic book *Man's Search for Meaning*, I was taken by his keen observation regarding the imbalance of American values. In the course of his career as a psychologist, Frankl made frequent trips to the United States until his death in 1997. Here, he gathered these insights.

Freedom, expressed as liberty, is one of the most famous lines quoted in the Declaration of Independence ("life, liberty and the pursuit of happiness"). It is also the hallmark of the Bill of Rights. Freedom is undoubtedly one of the most precious gifts bestowed on humanity. Freedom, however, is one face of a two-sided coin. The other side, which rarely sees the light of day, is responsibility.

Frankl noted that one of his earliest fond memories of coming to the United States was of viewing the Statue of Liberty: the quintessential symbol of freedom. Noting that freedom and responsibility go hand in hand, he tossed out a suggestion that perhaps what this country needed for moral balance is a "Statue of Responsibility" on the West Coast (he even hinted that the

San Francisco Bay area would be a nice location). To the best of my knowledge, no one has taken him up on the suggestion. More important is the ever-growing abyss between these two values, since his book was first published in 1959.

It is often said that responsibility is the ability to respond. Although responsibility and discipline are not the same thing, it's fair to say that responsibility requires discipline—in fact, great discipline. It takes discipline to practice the piano or the guitar, just as it requires discipline to empty the trash or mow the lawn when you would really rather do something else. Discipline also requires willpower, a skill we all have within us, but one that is often under-utilized. Moreover, both responsibility and discipline involve a higher level of consciousness than that of merely reacting to the situation at hand. If you look around, you'll notice that there are a lot of knee-jerk reactions to problems that require a higher level of consciousness. Freedom, in and of itself, necessitates calculated restraint; in this case, the restraint is discipline.

There is an old joke about a young man walking the streets of New York City, with a violin case under his arm. After failing to find the desired address on his own, he stops and asks the first person he sees for directions. "How do I get to Carnegie Hall?" he inquires.

Without blinking an eye, the other man replies, "Practice, my dear man, practice." Discipline is a skill that requires lots and lots of practice. To be sure, mistakes will be made at the initial stage of learning any skill, until the wisdom of experience begins to guide one's conscience. Yet to make mistakes, one has to practice.

We live in a dominant culture that is strong on freedom, yet weak on responsibility and perhaps weaker still on discipline. These two values are tested every time we go shopping, sit down to eat, sit in front of the television, surf on the Internet, or order drinks at happy hour. Like opposite sides of the yin/yang symbol, freedom and responsibility balance each other; yet when discipline is eclipsed by freedom, problems are bound to ensue.

An old adage states, "Control without power is stifling; power without control is reckless." It could as easily have stated, "Discipline without freedom is suffocating; freedom without discipline is irre-sponsible." In his book *Power vs. Force*, David Hawkins shares his insights from years of research on the nuances of energy patterns created by our ego that ultimately determine our behavior. Therefore, the first step toward acquiring discipline is to control the ego, which typically uses force against the power of the mind itself.

How, exactly, is discipline implemented? Here are some examples. Discipline is the commitment to get up a half hour early to meditate or go for a quiet walk. Discipline is the self-imposed limit of watching *60 Minutes* and then turning off the television for the night. Discipline means refraining from swearing in casual conversation. Discipline means having the willpower to stay home and cook dinner, rather than eating out and charging the expenses on a credit card. Ultimately, discipline means reclaiming your personal sovereignty. This takes work, but it's not impossible.

It's easy to lose sight of the fact that freedom is a privilege in a world where many people still have little or no freedom. The practice of discipline is a healthy reminder not to take freedom for granted. While it is important to live in the present moment, discipline throws a cautionary glance toward the future, ensuring that our ability to engage in life freely is not compromised.

As we mature, we learn that life is not a hundred-meter sprint. If anything, the human journey is an ultra-endurance event that includes a well-measured amount of pacing. Pacing requires discipline, so that we don't shoot our wad of energy too quickly and burn out. Burnout is often thought of as "being overworked," but burnout can also occur as a result of unbridled freedom. There is a lot of burnout today. The consequences of too much liberty can show up months or years later, as a serious illness or a chronic disease. Once again referring to da Vinci's sketch, in this case, the *Vitruvian Man* is lying facedown in the circle, passed out.

EXERCISE
Healthy Boundaries

The real issue behind the balance of freedom and discipline is, once again, healthy boundaries. By and large, people today have very inadequate personal boundaries. Ask yourself this: what areas of your life are loaded with freedom, yet lack the restraint of discipline? List them here. Once you have identified at least three areas, consider what changes you can make to bring these three aspects back into balance.

POOR BOUNDARIES   WAYS TO IMPROVE YOUR BOUNDARIES

1. _____   _____

2. _____   _____

3. _____   _____

3. Mental Stimulation Balanced with Quietness

From the moment we wake up each morning until the second we fall asleep each night, like a thirsty sponge, we are rapidly absorbing information through our five senses. Some estimates suggest that as many as forty thousand bits of information are processed through each person's brain every day. This is likely a conservative estimate. Most of the information, about 70 percent, comes into the brain from our eyes. Our sense of sound pulls in another 20 percent, and at any given point, the remaining 10 percent fluctuates among the remaining three senses: taste, touch, and smell. In the course of our normal waking hours, our brain is inundated with sensory information, sometimes to the point that we cannot think straight. This phenomenon was once described as "sensory overload." Today, coupled with the skill of multitasking, it's called "mental fatigue" or simply "burnout."

These days, voices from the adjoining work cubicles crying, "Too much information," are quite valid. If predictions from futurists are to be believed, then fasten your seat belt, because the pace of change, expressed through information decimation, is approaching warp speed. Given this fact, we have a couple of choices: either we can strap ourselves in for a light-speed ride, as we are hurled through a packed universe of information, or we can periodically exit the turnpike of broadband sensory stimulation and give our minds a much-needed rest. Balance, through inner peace, is achieved quite simply by temporarily turning off the five senses to quiet the mind. Because our society does not encourage us to do so, most people are not aware that they have this option, but they do. At the risk of becoming roadkill on the information super-highway, it behooves you to periodically unplug from the world and take the time to calm the waters of your mind—in essence, to reconnect to your deepest self, which quietly begs for attention. Practice the art of centering, a topic that was covered in detail in chapter 3.

Despite advances in civilization since the time of Rene Descartes and the European Renaissance, there is still a division of understanding regarding the mind and the brain. Hard-core scientists are committed to the paradigm that the mind is merely a consequence of brain physiology, with a host of neurochemicals responsible for each and every thought and feeling. Advances in the study of consciousness (discussed in chapter 3), however, reveal that the mind and consciousness are independent of the brain. The mind simply uses the brain as its primary organ of choice, and the latest developments suggest that every cell in your body has consciousness, too. Regardless which side of the fence you sit on with this issue, everyone agrees that too much sensory stimulation leads to poor concentration, mental fatigue, poor decision making, and poor communication skills, all of which promote stress. Without frequent pauses, this becomes a never-ending cycle of burnout.

Using an apt metaphor, the mind is like a radio receiver, with each of the five senses acting like specific radio stations on the dial. Too much information entering the brain becomes nothing less than mental static, which, under the best conditions, distorts our thinking abilities. Under the worst conditions, it can compromise our best thoughts and behaviors. At these times, you can hear Jay Leno's voice in the back of your head, saying, "What were you thinking?"

To seek balance between the world of information at the peak of the information age and the calm world of inner peace, we need to enter the world of stillness with regularity (e.g., every day). Again, creating healthy boundaries, combined with having the will to enforce these boundaries, comes into play. Quietness requires setting aside a small block of time each day to unplug from the high-tech world. This means turning off the television, the radio, the stereo, the cell phone, and the computer. In doing so, please realize that for five or ten minutes, the world is not going to come to an end without you. Taking time to quiet the mind (through meditation, centering, or just sitting) is analogous to deleting old e-mails from your computer, thus allowing more space for incoming information. If you have ever let your e-mails accumulate, you know that at some point, the mailbox reaches maximum capacity.

The Art of Empty Spaces

Not long ago, the Taoist concept of empty space became a topic of discussion with a friend of mine. Over lunch, Kelly explained an idea that he was working on, with regard to an engineering project. "I call this the Theory of Complementary Space," he said. "People think that space has to be filled, but the truth of the matter is that empty space is important. Take a sculpture, for example. The spaces of the eyes are usually empty, to make them look more real. Empty space is the yin of the yin/yang. As an engineer, the concept of empty space is rarely considered, but the implications go far beyond art or engineering, they run the gamut for all of life."

In terms of mental stability, the implications for empty space are obvious; without a clear space for new thoughts and ideas, the mind shows signs of fatigue and stress. Let there be no mistake, sensory stimulation is enticing. In fact, for a great many people it's addictive. (How many times a day do you check your e-mail? Do you turn the TV on the instant you come home?) Sociologists have also noted that technology offers an illusion, of sorts. While you may feel like you are more connected to the world, in truth, the reliance on technology has the tendency to sow the seeds of alienation. Alienation has long been recognized as another symptom of stress (specifically, depression). Making the time in each day for empty or complementary space is essential for health and well-being. The wisdom of empty space reinforces the concept of subtraction, rather than addition, as the means to achieve balance.

4. Right-Brain Thinking Balanced with Left-Brain Thinking

Several years ago I attended a creativity workshop for educators. After introducing herself and the concept of creativity to the audience, the speaker reviewed the concepts of right-brain and left-brain thinking processes by first writing down left-brain skills on one side of a flip chart. Then she added the corresponding right-brain skills across the vertical line that symbolically separated the two cerebral hemispheres. As she was writing this, the person sitting next to me said under her breath, "The left side is how Americans think; the right side is how Asians see the world." Within a few moments, I heard the person on my other side mention that the left side represented the conscious mind, while the right side represented the unconscious mind. Clearly, the information being shared that day wore many faces. In fact, both comments that I heard are quite accurate.

Since the compelling data presented by the Nobel Laureate Roger Sperry several decades ago on split-brain research, it has come to light that each hemisphere of the brain is indeed gifted with a host of specific talents. The left hemisphere is well versed in logical, analytical, rational, linear, and judgmental thinking, while the right hemisphere has become renowned for its abilities of intuition, nonlinear thinking, global awareness, imagination, and acceptance. Neither side of the brain holds a monopoly on intelligence, and each side needs the other to complete the full realm of consciousness. The combined package of these two masses of gray matter is nothing less than astonishing, and it has yet to be equaled by the most sophisticated computer technology.

Using only one side of your brain is akin to sleepwalking. Perhaps you know people like this. They are clueless! Although some Americans are not left-brain dominant, it is fair to say that most of them are. As a nation, first and foremost we are very judgmental, analytical, and rational thinkers. By and large, our whole education system is built on the foundation of left-brain critical-thinking skills. Furthermore, under conditions of chronic stress, the left hemisphere of the brain is the side that's most active. Virtually all of the mental processing skills of the left brain are highly utilized in a state of stress, if for no other reason than for physical survival. Given that these same skills are crucial in times of fight or flight, this can only be a good thing. The problem, however, arises when the modus operandi of chronic stress becomes the dominant mode of thinking, rather than the exception. Over time, chronic stress conditions cause the left brain to become muscle-bound, while the much-needed right-brain skills atrophy due to neglect. In simple terms, we never think outside "the box."

The creative process is a great example of utilizing the skills of both the right and the left hemispheres of the brain. Creativity is a systematic process of imagination (ideas) and logistical organization (making the best ideas become reality). Many people have incredible ideas but lack the ability to make them happen. Conversely, far more people can make things happen but lack the ingenuity to come up with original ideas. Both skills are housed under the roof of the same brain, meaning that we have access to both hemispheres to help us with creative problem solving. We just need to cultivate and use them.

Like the attempt to cut open the goose that laid the golden egg, the topic of creativity has undergone much investigation over the last twenty-five years. Unlike the goose, though, the creative process wasn't killed; it was enhanced. My favorite work is that of Roger von Oech, whose books include *A Whack on the Side of the Head* and *A Kick in the Seat of the Pants*. In no uncertain terms, the creative process begins in the right hemisphere. Here, ideas are formulated, then incubated, giving birth to a whole host of possibilities. Once all the possibilities have been brought to the table for consideration, the left hemisphere of the brain steps in, first judging all the ideas for the best outcome and then championing the cause to make the best idea come to fruition. The danger arises when these specific steps of the creative process are reshuffled by the ego, so that judgment takes place before all the ideas are assembled. This course of action always leads to disaster. Although judgment is a crucial part of creativity, as often happens, it can lead to disaster when it initiates the creative process. In the words of the French philosopher Emile Chartier, "Nothing is more dangerous than an idea when it's the only one you have."

The Art of Creativity

There are several ways to engage the right side of the brain, to first initiate and then achieve a greater sense of cerebral homeostasis. Listening to instrumental music is one example (e.g., the Mozart Effect). Using your nondominant hand for a day is another (e.g., try moving the computer mouse and the pad to the opposite side of your keyboard. Once you get past the frustration of relearning this skill, it becomes fun). Flexing the muscles of the right hemisphere not only means thinking outside "the box"; it means learning to be comfortable roaming outside the box for days on end.

If you are looking for inspiration to step outside the box, look no further than the creator of the *Vitruvian Man* himself: Mr. Leonardo da Vinci. That's what Michael Gelb did. He was so impressed with the workings of da Vinci's mind, he wrote a book to help everyone think like the quintessential Renaissance man. In *How to Think Like da Vinci*, which outlines seven steps to unifying the powers of both hemispheres, Gelb writes, "You are gifted with virtually unlimited potential for learning and creativity." He's right.

Creativity and humor often go hand in hand, as anyone who glances at the supermarket tabloids knows. I don't know if da Vinci had a sense of humor, but a friend of mine who read the book did. When he was stopped by a policeman for speeding, the officer said, "Man, I've been waiting all day for you."

Doing his best to think like da Vinci, my friend answered, "Hey, I got here as fast as I could." Hearing that response, the officer laughed so hard, he only issued a warning.

In these turbulent times, I see creativity and the creative process as essential for both personal stress and global crises. I am not alone in this mind-set. Nearly six decades ago, during the stressful events of World War II, Einstein said, "Creativity is more powerful than knowledge." Ever the pacifist, he also said, "No problem can be solved from the same consciousness that created it," meaning that we need to step outside the box of dominant thinking and explore new options. Given the rapid changes in the world today and how each life is affected by change, his insightful words are as significant now as they were when he first spoke them half a century ago.

5. Technology Balanced with Nature

If you are old enough to have watched the original episodes of *Star Trek* in the sixties, then perhaps you are also old enough to remember a host of magazine articles and television documentaries regarding the future of technology and the promise it held for more leisure time. Remember those claims? If you do, you're probably smirking right now, because if you are like most people, you probably have less leisure time, not more of it.

It's true; the advances in technology over the last three decades are nothing less than astonishing. And while they might not have increased the hours of leisure per week, it would appear, on the surface, that they have definitely made some aspects of life more convenient, with inventions such as word processors (remember typewriters?), CD players (vinyl used to scratch easily), electronic garage door openers, photocopiers, and even laser surgery. What is good for short-term convenience, however, is not always good for long-term health and well-being. Through our love affair with technology, we have grown fat, lazy, and out of touch with the natural world, with which we are inextricably linked.

Up until about a hundred years ago, the average person was quite intimately linked to the natural world. Family farms and gardens produced well over half of people's dietary intake. Sadly, today most people don't even go outside enough to get adequate amounts of natural sunlight. Moreover, most people have lost a healthy relationship with the food they eat. Rather than picking fruit off trees or plucking vegetables from the ground, we now grab boxes of processed foods, infused with preservatives and chemicals, off the grocery shelf, not even knowing the product's original source. With the horrendous state of processed food today, saying grace before a meal takes on a whole new meaning. Currently, estimates suggest that most processed food is transported over 1,500 miles from its point of origin to the final destination: to your local grocery store. This is a far cry from your backyard garden or the nearest local farm.

In and of itself, technology is not bad. Ultimately, it is the use of technology that can have good or bad consequences. Sociologists who keep their fingers on the pulse of humanity confide that the human heart is approaching tachycardia with not only the proliferation but also the constant use of microchip gadgets. Things are becoming so out of balance that the *Vitruvian Man*, with throbbing temples, is standing on his head. This is not to say that you should renounce the high-tech world and become Amish (although some people think this is not a bad idea). What it does mean is that you need to learn to use technology to help run your life, not run it for you.

The Art of Star Gazing
Several years ago I picked up a book titled *Handbook for the Soul,* a collection of essays written by several contemporary luminaries in the field of psychology. Each author was asked to share his or her thoughts on the soul-growth process. Perhaps it's no surprise that the majority of contributors made reference to the importance of taking time to reconnect with nature: walks in the woods, strolling through a park, gazing at the stars, sitting on the beach, working in the garden, or strolling in a primeval forest. Moreover, nature holds a special sacredness that man cannot replicate but can only appreciate. Ageless wisdom reminds us that reconnecting to nature is essential to the health of the human spirit; after all, we are earthlings, not techlings.

At the onset, immersing yourself in nature does two things. First, when you step outside and look around, you cannot help but be aware of the wonders of creation, the varieties of species, the majesty of the mountains, and the vastness of the ocean. When you stop to think about it, nature is simply amazing! No matter how great virtual technology is, it will never equal the simplicity, the complexity, or the beauty of the natural world. Nor will a steady diet of the Discovery Channel or Animal Planet equal quality time outdoors. Second, reconnecting with nature gives us a powerful sense of perspective and of our humble, yet essential, place in the world. All problems are reduced to their correct proportion. Furthermore, if we look close enough, we are reminded of the balance of nature and the flow of earth's seasons. With this comes a subtle promise that no matter how bad any situation is, it, too, shall pass.

Being in balance with nature means more than mowing the lawn or planting flowers in your garden each spring. It means recognizing that you are a part of the natural environment, not separate from it, and it is a part of you. Research in the field of circadian rhythms reveals that like the earth itself, our bodies operate on a twenty-four-to-twenty-five-hour clock. Our physiology is genetically programmed to the earth, the sun, and the moon. We cannot deny this. Nature isn't something to dominate or ignore. Rather, it is a dynamic force with which to connect. Reconnecting with nature includes everything from getting out in the woods (preferably, without the cell phone) as often as possible, to knowing what phase the moon is in at any given time of the month. In essence, it means living in rhythm with the seasons.

For thousands of years, humans lived in balance with nature. Sadly, today many people have lost this vital connection. We now know that inadequate amounts of sunlight affect not only mood but cholesterol levels and bone density as well. Nowadays, people armed with sunscreen and bug repellent seem afraid to be in nature. It doesn't have to be this way. Finding a balance between technology and nature comes down to learning to pace yourself. This means taking time to unplug from the computers, the cell phones, and so on, and spend adequate periods of time in the beautiful world of nature.

6. Ego Balanced with Soul

I turned on the radio one day to catch the last few minutes of NPR's *New Dimensions* program and heard the show's guest speak about various aspects of human potential. She posed a final question to the listening audience: "Is the strength of your ego superior to the will of your soul?" This profound inquiry speaks of the perpetual need to balance the ego and the soul, two intangible constructs of the human condition that are rarely in equilibrium.

Rest assured, behind every unresolved personal drama lies an overactive ego trying to control, manipulate, or dominate whatever it can. Many failed marriages are like this. Take a look at news headlines on any given day, and whether it's politics, sports, or entertainment, you can see just how pervasive (individually or collectively) the strength of the ego really is. Ironically, it is the ego that signals the stress alarm in times of physical danger, yet the ego pulls the alarm for nonphysical dangers as well. On the surface, it seems that we are a little too tightly wired for stress. Perhaps this "mis-wiring" is a genetic flaw in the DNA's code (a theory I am still working on). Be that as it may, what is designed as a means of protection often sabotages our highest potential.

Freud's theory of the ego has withstood the test of time. Perhaps he became a bit jaded by his clientele in that era, because his view of humanity was anything but optimistic. He was of the opinion that the ego operates continuously below the radar of the conscious mind, controlling all aspects of behavior through the use of denial, rationalization, and other ploys. The ego, he postulated, holds the potential to undermine any given situation. Usually, it does.

Long before Freud coined the term *ego*, the bodyguard for the soul was referred to as the "little self" or the "false self" by a host of indigenous global cultures. Conversely, the big "Self" or the "true self" was the name given to the essential sacred aspect of each individual (what we might commonly call the soul). Like a cat or a dog that must first be house-trained before being allowed to roam freely indoors, we, too, must domesticate the ego or run the risk of finding poop all over the place. Domesticating the ego involves a conscious effort to serve, not be served; to offer protection, but surrender control. Curbing the ego means finding humor in self-deprecating moments without compromising our self-esteem. Surrendering the ego means really appreciating all the things we have, rather than becoming envious about the things we don't. Ultimately, domesticating the ego means making a transition in consciousness, from a motivation of fear to a motivation of love and altruism. This is no small task, but it's not impossible. Balancing the ego with the soul also means knowing when to use the strength of self-reliance and when to ask for divine guidance.

If for no other reason, the ego is essential for survival as the means to trigger the fight-or-flight response for physical stressors. At its most rudimentary level, the ego is the bodyguard for the soul, to serve in the role of protector. The problem comes when the bodyguard forgets its primary position, eclipsing the soul's splendor, to dictate a policy of human behavior. A big ego is yet another expression of an imbalance between the ego and the soul. When this happens, the only thing that can be seen in the *Vitruvian Man* sketch is a large head. It fills the entire circle! Remember that the ego's primary job is to ring the bell for fight or flight when there is physical danger.

Regardless of whether we are overly impatient, arrogant, insecure, or rude, each of these characteristics (and many more) describes the ego being stuck in the stress response, acting out of fear. A good soul-searching habit to get into, to cultivate your conscience, is to ask yourself in every situation, "Am I coming from a place of fear or compassion with this decision?" Remember, the ego reacts; the soul responds. Moreover, true soul-searching requires that we not only look at our soul-growth process, but we also scrutinize the role that the ego plays in either inhibiting or supporting our highest potential. A large part of soul-searching requires ego watching. A previously mentioned Serbian proverb bears repeating, as it speaks to this delicate balance: "Be humble, for you are made of earth; be noble, for you are made of stars."

Domesticating the Ego
A wonderful story has been passed down through the wisdom of the Cherokee Indian culture regarding the imbalance of the ego and the soul. It goes like this: One day the grandfather of an adolescent boy caught him stealing from another boy. The grandfather asked why he had done this, but the grandson refused to answer. The grandfather inquired again, but this time he asked the boy why fear had entered his heart to commit this act.

"I am not afraid of anything," the boy replied defiantly.

"Surely, you must be," the grandfather said, "for stealing and lying are the hands of fear's work." The boy looked at his grand-father and began to wipe away tears that had welled up in his eyes. The man pulled his grandson onto his lap and drew a sketch of a wolf in the sand.

"The wolf is a mighty animal. Each person holds the essence of not one, but two wolves inside him. The first wolf is the spirit of compassion, exhibited through faith, humility, kindness, honesty, peace, forgiveness, patience, and love. The second wolf survives on fear, envy, anger, resentment, arrogance, and greed. There is an inherent tension between these two spirits. These wolves fight daily within the heart of every man, including yours," the old man explained.

"Grandfather, which wolf will win the fight?" the boy asked nervously.

"The wolf that wins the fight is the one that you feed," he replied.

This story begs the question, which side do we favor, consciously or unconsciously? Which wolf do we feed? Many of us unwillingly feed the ego with fear-based scraps from our thoughts and actions, never realizing just how powerful this wolf has become until it leaves a path of destruction.

The Human Equinox Realized

How does one create balance between the ego and the soul? Perhaps we need look no further than the sage advice of St. Francis of Assisi. Each of his suggestions guides us to shift our consciousness from a motivation of fear to the inspiration of love and compassion. It takes a conscious effort to do this. If you ask any wisdom keeper or almost anyone who has had a near-death experience, the individual will tell you that above all else, this is the reason we are here: to love and be loved.

Following is an adaptation of St. Francis's timeless suggestions for becoming an instrument of peace.

Where there are weeds of hatred in your heart, instead sow the seeds of compassion,

Where there is injury in your heart, express forgiveness first to yourself, then others,

Where there is doubt and fear in the unknown, demonstrate faith that you are never alone,

Where there is despair in future events, learn to express hope in your own potential,

Where there is intolerance toward others, extend the hand of patience and sympathy,

Where there is apathy in your spirit, learn to cultivate and express inspiration,

And where there is undue sadness and grief in your heart, remember the joy in simple pleasures.

Once the legendary actress Audrey Hepburn was asked if she would share what she considered to be her secrets for lifelong beauty. Her favorite reply was a passage written by her close friend Sam Levenson. This text contains the secret to achieving balance between the ego and the soul. As a tribute to his mother, Audrey's son, Sean Hepburn Ferrer, recited this passage at her memorial service on January 21, 1993.

Beauty Poem

For attractive lips, speak words of kindness.

For lovely eyes, seek out the good in people.

For a slim figure, share your food with the hungry.

For beautiful hair, let a child run his fingers through it once a day.

For poise, walk with the knowledge that you never walk alone.

We leave you a tradition with a future. The tender loving care of human beings will never become obsolete. People, even more than things, have to be restored, renewed, revived, reclaimed, and redeemed; never throw out anyone.

Remember, if you ever need a helping hand, you will find one at the end of each of your arms.

As you grow older, you will discover that you have two hands: one for helping yourself, and the other for helping others.

Many people consider the delicate balance between the ego and the soul to be the foundation upon which all other aspects of the human condition rest, suggesting that this is one area of life that needs constant attention. Some say that the real Hero's Journey is the struggle between the ego and the soul. Just as the soul cannot and should not be neglected, neither can the human spirit, the life force of energy that feeds both the ego and the soul. Every good stress-management program begins by honoring the health of the human spirit.

6

The Health of the Human Spirit

Twenty-one Strategies for Letting Go of Stress

*T*o *know and not to do*

is not to know!

—ANONYMOUS

A Healthy Spirit Means
Letting the Chi Flow

While I was lying on the massage table, the acupuncturist, Mary Ellen, reached for my wrist to read my pulse, then she carefully placed a tiny needle in my chest on the acupuncture point known as the "spirit storehouse." The practice of acupuncture dates back several thousand years to ancient China. The overall premise is to restore balance to the body's flow of chi. It's very likely that Lao Tzu was treated in much the same way I was, perhaps at one time even on the same acupunture point. Eastern culture describes the life force of universal energy as chi, as honored in the practice of tai chi. It is also known as qi, as in qi gong; or ki, as in Reiki or aikido. In other parts of Asia it is known as pranayama, and in the West we might associate this with a divine essence of the human spirit.

Chi circulates around and permeates through the body in rivers of energy known as meridians. In classical acupuncture, a holistic approach based on the concept of five elements suggests that unresolved thoughts and emotions (stress) can block or congest the flow of energy. The human spirit is also composed of free-flowing energy and like chi, it, too, can be blocked by stress—specifically, by prolonged issues of anger and fear. Left unresolved, anger, fear, and all emotions associated with them can literally choke the human spirit. My gaze shifted from the tiny needle in my chest to a cute Chinese proverb that Mary Ellen had framed on the wall behind her desk. Addressing the nature of assertiveness and the subtle aspect of chi, it read: "That birds fly overhead, this you cannot stop. That birds build a nest in your hair, this you can prevent." Regardless of Eastern or Western philosophy, this tenet of ageless wisdom reveals that to stay vibrant, our river of energy, called the human spirit, must continually move freely, unobstructed by the rocks of human emotions.

As I drove home from my appointment in time to prepare for a radio interview, this metaphor came to mind: every effective technique for stress management, like an acupuncture needle, is a means to allow a clear flow of energy through mind, body, and spirit.

The voice over the phone was tense. On the other end of the line was a radio talk show host. "Okay, good, we got him," he said, as he patched me through to the studio. I was about to speak to a national audience from my living room, and I caught myself marveling at the technology in communications. The connection on the other end was so clear, you would have thought I was sitting in the studio a thousand miles away. "This interview could not have come at a better time," the show's host said, panting. "I have had the worst day of my life. Okay, we're on in thirty seconds."

I was a guest on the *Northern Lights* show, and the whole hour was dedicated to the topic of stress. Typically, with an hour-long format, the talk show host begins by building up interest with introductions and stories, leaving the "how to" information for the last segment. The purpose, of course, is to keep listeners tuned for the whole show. This was not to be the case tonight. The host jumped right to the meat of the interview with the very first question: "Dr. Seaward, what is the best way to deal with stress?"

I was ready, because this is the most commonly asked question I hear today. However, I always pause first when I hear the question, because I know that many people are looking for a quick solution to a very difficult situation or perhaps a simple answer to a confluence of stressful moments. Unfortunately, there is no one simple answer. There are, however, countless viable options, proactive steps we can take to strengthen our personal integrity. Each option, each strategy in this chapter is designed to do one thing: bring you back to a sense of balance and, in doing so, restore a sense of inner peace.

The simple truth is that there are hundreds of ways to deal effectively with stress, all of which honor the ageless wisdom of a healthy, vibrant spirit. Some strategies deal specifically with attitudes, while others are more action-oriented. Some techniques focus on the mind; other skills are directed toward the emotions, the body, or the health of the human spirit itself. Every technique addresses the aspect of balance, self-renewal, and harmony of life. All of these strategies have great potential, but the secret of success is to see each strategy as a means to keep the energy of your life force moving evenly, not getting blocked, congested, or distorted by the ploys of the ego. As you read through this list, consider them all, but focus your attention on a select few to see which ones might work best for you. As you read through this collection of ideas, many of which you have probably heard before, take a moment to experience each strategy a couple of times and see if there is a good match. Once you find a good fit, the next step is to incorporate these strategies as part of your daily or weekly routine.

These suggestions, based on content from the previous chapters, invite you to change or modify any behaviors that you feel promote stress and replace them with behaviors that not only return you to a point of balance but enhance your highest human potential as well. As a rule, most people choose not to change their thoughts, attitudes, beliefs, or behaviors until they have hit rock bottom and are forced to take a different course of action. Remember, avoidance is the number-one ineffective coping technique for stress. So, in these times of turbulent change, sage advice is a course of prevention: a personal strategy to change your course before you come close to hitting any rocks. The suggestions in this chapter are the spiritual equivalent of feng shu'ing your house. At the end of each strategy is a suggested action plan to help you incorporate this skill into your lifestyle.

Coping skills are like any other skills. If they are to serve you well, you must engage in them many times until you become extremely proficient. Practicing these skills is just that: practice. Practice alone, however, is not enough. Once you feel a sense of proficiency, you must employ these skills in the hour of need. Walking the path of the Tao is not an exercise in perfection. Rather, it is a collection of experiences that culminates in a greater appreciation of life. Appreciation comes with experience. To repeat another bit of sage advice, "To know and not to do is not to know!"

1. A Bird's Eye View: Keeping Everything in Perspective

A popular adage says, "I felt bad because I had no shoes until I met a man who had no feet." No matter how bad our troubles may be, there is always someone who has it worse. In essence, Einstein was right; everything is relative. When we become stressed, it is very easy to lose perspective, particularly to keep in mind how good we really have it. Our view of life can become rather myopic, as mentioned earlier—a fact that has not gone unnoticed among optometrists. The implications of limited sight go well beyond the metaphorical aspects of "vision" to the literal aspects of vision.

A few days after the terrorist attacks in New York and Washington, D.C., when the shock of what had happened began to wear off, the dust had settled, and people were trying really hard to get back into a routine of sorts, I heard several people share their personal dramas. Within seconds of explaining their personal strife, they paused, then caught themselves and added that in comparison with the terrorists' victims and the victims' families, they actually had it pretty darn good. How easy it is to lose perspective. Here is another story that I often share about the importance of perspective.

In my office I have a large poster of the Milky Way Galaxy. Toward the end of one of the spirals of stars and planets is a tiny yellow arrow, with a small sign that reads: YOU ARE HERE. The poster is an obvious reminder to keep things in perspective. A student named Susan gave me this poster several years ago. Whenever I talk about ways to cope with stress, I always emphasize the importance of keeping things in perspective. Perspective is one of the hallmark themes of stress-management wisdom, and that poster offers a symbol of great wisdom. Some of my best teachers are my students. Susan was one such teacher.

To describe Susan as a worrywart was no exaggeration. In her mind, simple everyday issues became neurotic obsessions. To other people, small problems are typically viewed as molehills, yet to Susan, every concern became one more mountain to traverse in the Himalayan range. From rush hour traffic and the lack of available parking spaces to unanswered voice-mail messages and missed breakfasts, her petty fears obscured her view of the bigger picture of life—specifically, the joys and the smiles that also constitute the balance of life's journey.

One day while shopping in downtown Chicago, Susan met a high school friend, now in a wheelchair, crippled from a devastating car accident. The ensuing conversation felt like a wet towel across Susan's face—a shocking revelation that quickly brought perspective to her own life. All of a sudden, the problems she carried with her faded away. In their place she began to store thoughts of gratitude, compassion, and faith. Later that day, she came across the poster of the Milky Way Galaxy. She bought two. The first one she had framed and hung in her office. The second she gave to me. Some of life's best lessons may be introduced in the classroom, but the real learning occurs in everyday life situations.

ACTION PLAN 1:   When you find yourself focusing on the foreground of an issue, a problem, or a crisis, make a habit of taking a step back (detaching) and pausing to look at the big picture. Perspective helps us to keep things in balance.

2. Flexing the Funny Bone: Comic Relief

One afternoon a friend in Boulder invited me out to dinner. John worked as a ski instructor in the winter and was a self-proclaimed Dirtbag Executive the rest of the year. If there was one thing John had, it was an eye for bargains. He had invited some friends to get together for an all-you-can-eat spaghetti dinner that a local restaurant hosted every third Wednesday of the month. As I recall, I was not in the best of moods that night and almost stayed home. I am so glad I didn't. By the time I showed up, eleven guys were sitting down at a huge table. I pulled up a chair, and as if on cue, John started telling a joke—one of those jokes that begins as a story. The punch line had the whole restaurant laughing. Without missing a beat, someone else at our table continued the momentum, by saying, "Later that day in the same bar . . ." What began as a spaghetti feast night turned into a jokefest. I nearly choked on my marinara sauce five times, I was laughing so hard, and I am not kidding when I say I saw milk coming from some kid's nose at least twice. Speaking of milk, here's one joke that I remember:

The wise old Mother Superior was dying. The nuns gathered around her bed to comfort her in her remaining moments. As a last request, she asked for a little warm milk to sip. A young nun ran downstairs to the kitchen to warm some milk in the microwave. While it was heating up, she remembered a bottle of whiskey she had received as a gift the previous Christmas and searched the cabinet until she found it. Then she opened the bottle and poured a generous amount into the warm cup of milk, stirred it a few times with a spoon, and ran back upstairs. Mother Superior drank a little, then a little more, and before they knew it, she had drunk the whole glass down. She even used her tongue to reach the last drop.

"Mother, Mother," the nuns cried. "Give us some wisdom before you die!"

The Mother Superior raised herself up in bed with a pious look on her face and, pointing out the window, said, "Don't sell that cow!"

ACTION PLAN 2:   It has been said that humor is the best medicine. That night at dinner it surely was. I know many people who agree that humor is their saving grace. Here are a few more ideas to tickle your funny bone.

- Start a joke file, consisting of good jokes from the Internet. Cut and paste them from your e-mail box to a separate file. Then at the end of each week or month, print the file and read them before you go to bed.

- Check out the birthday card selection at the nearest greeting card store. Don't go with an expectation of buying any of them (although you might). Consider this a one-hour therapy session.

- Pick up a *Calvin & Hobbes* or a Bizarro Anthology, rent a comedy video, or start reading a Tom Robbins novel (I highly recommend *Still Life with Woodpecker*).

- Subscribe to the *Funny Times*, a monthly newspaper with cartoons and satirical essays to brighten your day. Unlike the *Washington Post* or the *New York Times*, this paper contains only good news, and it is well worth the laughs. Call (888) 386-6984 to subscribe.

3. Physical Exercise: Flushing Out the Stress Hormones

Your body is an amazing creation that was designed for survival. Under pressure, it knows how to prepare for danger without a second thought. In times of physical peril, the fight-or-flight response is your ticket to safety. But what happens if you choose not to fight or flee? Answer: the body still prepares for survival, in the event that you might change your mind at any moment and decide to head for the hills. During the stress response, a flood of hormones is synthesized and released in an amazing orchestration of metabolic processes. The catecholamines epinephrine and norepinephrine are released immediately, while a host of hormones (vasopressin, aldosterone, thyroxine, and cortisol) each stagger their release in a coordinated effort for physical survival. The bottom line is that what is designed to be a very efficient survival system becomes very inefficient when no action is taken, such as sitting at your computer terminal for hours on end. To say that an excess of stress hormones becomes toxic to the body cannot be overstated. Ultimately, this is how stress kills.

In his book *The Best Alternative Medicine*, Kenneth Pelletier states that of over six hundred different healing modalities labeled "alternative" or "complementary," physical exercise is without a doubt *the* most beneficial means of restoring optimal health. And he says that unlike the majority of modalities, there is a ton of research on the beneficial effects of physical exercise. He's right. Any search on the Internet or in a library will confirm that the data show that regular physical exercise is imperative for good health.

In simplest terms, engaging in any form of rhythmic exercise (e.g., walking, jogging, swimming, bicycling, etc.) that gets and keeps the heart pumping moderately for an extended time (usually thirty minutes) uses the stress hormones for their intended metabolic purpose and then flushes out the remains, so that they don't cause a problem. What happens if you choose to stay put? Well, for starters, the hormone cortisol tends to destroy white blood cells, compromising your immune system. The consequences range from the common cold to cancer and everything in-between.

To be sure, physical exercise itself is a type of stress, but in this case, it is good stress, and the payoff ensures a greater level of overall health. Like a homeopathic remedy, a little bit of exercise creates the symptoms of physical stress, yet the rebound from exercise returns the body to a greater level of homeostasis. In scientific jargon, it's called the "parasympathetic rebound." Regardless of its name, it means resiliency in the course of your waking day and a restful sleep each night.

Regular physical exercise does more than just flush out stress hormones; it sets in motion a series of metabolic processes that help to keep the body's physiological processes in balance, from calcium absorption in the bones to optimal blood-sugar levels (this is why exercise is good for people with type 2 diabetes).

ACTION PLAN 3:   Research shows that the metabolic effects of exercise can last up to thirty-six hours. You don't have to start training for the Olympics to get the benefits of physical exercise. All it takes is getting outside three or four times a week for about twenty to thirty minutes each time. Walking is the ideal exercise. Losing weight through activity may be a goal for many, but the *best* reason for regular physical movement is to keep the body's physiological systems in check, by flushing out the stress hormones. If exercising by yourself seems like a daunting chore, find a friend to join you and make it a social event.

4. Decompression: The Art of Calm

If you have ever been caught in a downpour, you know the relief that comes when you can finally take off the heavy, soaking-wet clothes. This is decompression: a feeling of unloading anything and everything that's clinging to you: physically, mentally, emotionally, or spiritually. Deep-sea divers decompress. Released hostages decompress. Police and firemen decompress. Astronauts decompress. Situations that place people under stress require decompression, and if you are stressed, you need to decompress, too.

In simplest terms, decompression means the cessation of sensory intake to regain a sense of homeostasis. "Home" is the operative word here: a place of comfort and security, in which to return safely. Hostages and astronauts may take weeks, sometimes months, to decompress. The more intense the stressful episode, obviously, the longer decompression takes. If you make a daily habit of including decompression in your life, then it doesn't take anywhere near as long. In some cases, it can be done in as little as five minutes a day, and we all have five minutes.

Compression can result from a number of things, but in this day and age, it comes primarily from information overload. You take in a massive amount of information through your five senses—primarily, your eyes and ears. As you no doubt have noticed at times, too much information can suffocate you. Like the wet clothes that bog you down, information, in all the ways you encounter it, can deflate your daily momentum and most certainly overload your mental and emotional circuits. Decompression is another way of centering and emptying.

Just as you take in information through the five senses to get a bearing on your situation, you can also use your five senses to direct relaxing stimuli to the mind and the body. That's what the art of calm is all about: using your five senses to reprogram your mind and body for total rest and relaxation. In terms of pleasurable relaxing stimulation, no one way works best for everyone. In fact, there are literally hundreds of ways, yet they fall into one of five categories: sight, sound, taste, touch, and smell.

ACTION PLAN 4:   Here is a simple challenge: come up with five ways to decompress for each of the five senses, and assemble these into your own relaxation survival kit. A relaxation survival kit is like your personal first-aid kit for stress. Keep it well stocked with things that nurture or sustain your personal sense of homeostasis—in this case, homeostasis that comes from pleasing one or all of the five senses. To help inspire your thought process, here are some ideas to get you into this mind-set. When you come up with your own ideas, consider which ones best fit into your relaxation survival kit.

Sight: Closing your eyes might sound like the best option, but if that doesn't work, there are computer screen savers and color posters of nature scenes. If you are home, a good lightning storm in the distance is a sight to behold, and there is always the work of impressionist artists like Monet and Seurat in museums. Don't forget gazing at the celestial heavens on a cloudless night. If you are stuck indoors, pull out a *Far Side* or a *Calvin & Hobbes* collection (this counts double for the sense of humor, too!).

Sound: Ocean waves are a perennial favorite, as is the sound of children laughing. A good, long thunderstorm works, too, if you're under the covers. When all else fails, you can place a small water fountain indoors to calm your nerves.

Taste: Food is a great pacifier, and some foods are nothing less than heavenly. Chocolate comes to mind. Fresh succulent strawberries or hot buttered popcorn works in a pinch, and, of course, there is always ice cream therapy.

Touch: Without a doubt, at the top of this list is massage. Muscle tension is the number-one symptom of stress, and a good massage works every time. Hot tubs are a close second, and petting a cat or a dog is not far behind. There are many advantages to owning a pet. Kids who make these kits love to include bubble wrap for touch.

Smell: Sloan Kettering Hospital uses the scent of vanilla for people who are scared to have an MRI. Lavender is used in maternity wards to relax soon-to-be mothers when they deliver, and companies in Japan spray mint into the air ducts to relax their employees. It might be chocolate, grandma's kitchen, spice tea, or the scent of your lover that relaxes you, but it's important to know what these scents are and keep them around so that you can use them. Several aromas bring a sense of calm to the mind, body, and spirit. Let your nose guide the way.

Just as you would with a first-aid kit, please be sure to replace any items that have been used—like chocolate (taste)—so that in the event of another personal disaster or day from hell, you can pull out your kit and put yourself back on the path toward inner peace. To start this process, begin by making a list of the items you wish to include in your relaxation kit, and then use this list as a means of keeping inventory.

MY PERSONAL RELAXATION SURVIVAL KIT

Sight

1. _____

2. _____

Sound

1. _____

2. _____

Taste

1. _____

2. _____

Touch

1. _____

2. _____

Smell

1. _____

2. _____

Additional Items

1. _____

2. _____

5. Do Not Enter: Establishing Healthy Boundaries

It may seem rather ironic that at the same time you are trying to dismantle roadblocks and move on with your life, a suggestion comes along that says, "Start putting up barricades." There is no mixed message with this sage advice. Healthy boundaries are crucial to healthy living because they offer a sense of protection and security but only when they are honored.

In this high-speed world, our personal boundaries are eroding and crumbling daily. The most common example is where work responsibilities are done at home, and home problems interrupt work schedules, making home and work nearly inseparable. Where personal boundaries are weak or nonexistent, havoc ensues. Responsibilities seem to multiply as personal energy is quickly depleted. There are two kinds of unhealthy boundaries: those that erode and offer no protection, and those that are so tall and rigid, they end up eclipsing any light that may provide personal sustenance. Ideally, balance lies somewhere in the middle.

Rivers have boundaries. Human cells have boundaries. Countries have boundaries. Even layers of the earth's stratosphere have boundaries. These all exist for a reason: to keep some things out that aren't supposed to get in and other things in that are not supposed to leave. Boundaries also provide a sense of order in a potentially chaotic world.

So what, exactly, are healthy boundaries? Healthy boundaries are constructs we create in our lives to give support to our personal integrity. In terms of behaviors, healthy boundaries used to be considered part of personal etiquette, such as knocking on office doors before entering or identifying yourself on the phone when you make a call. Today, they include guidelines by which to successfully live our lives. Healthy boundaries also include good communication skills so that you can explain to others what your expectations are. An example might be letting your friends and colleagues know that it's not appropriate to call your home after 9:00 P.M. Remember, boundaries that are routinely broken lead to feelings of victimization.

Parents try to teach healthy boundaries by explaining what is appropriate versus inappropriate behavior to their children. As we move from childhood to the teenage years, our natural inclination is to rebel against these boundaries because we see them as a deterrent to our personal freedoms. Yet as we mature into adulthood (and perhaps have kids of our own), we see the need for boundaries. Establishing healthy boundaries is much easier than honoring them, and that's where willpower (also known as assertiveness) comes in.

ACTION PLAN 5:   Here is a thought to reflect on. What boundaries do you have in place to provide a sense of organization in your life? Make a short list of your personal boundaries. Then ask yourself, "What boundaries do I have in place that I slip, by letting people in, only to feel trespassed against?" Next, identify the value associated with the new healthy boundary you wish to adopt. Finally, ask yourself, "What can I do to honor the boundaries I have set in place?" Start making a list right now. This is your action plan. The only thing left to do is put it into play.

NEW HEALTHY BOUNDARIES	ASSOCIATED VALUE	STEPS TO HONOR THEM
1. _____	_____	_____
2. _____	_____	_____
3. _____	_____	_____

6. Respond, Don't React: Taming That Ego

Perhaps it's instinctual that when things don't go as planned, you head directly into the fight-or-flight mode. In times of grave danger, this is certainly a good idea. Most likely, it will save your life. But reacting to situations that are not life-threatening can cause more harm than good. The classic example would be yelling at your boss. Without a doubt, stress instincts can get us in trouble when not used properly. Instincts, however, can be overridden. A conscience, we are told, is what separates humans from the rest of the animal kingdom. And it's your conscience that needs to be called upon to respond, not react, in times when you're stressed, but your life is not in immediate danger.

One of my favorite stories about how not to react involves a man named Jim, who became infected with the road rage virus when an approaching car tried to cut him off from an exit ramp. So he flipped the bird to the driver behind him. He admitted to yelling several choice words, but because the windows were up, he was rather certain that the guy couldn't hear them. At that point, he decided to use sign language. What he didn't expect was that the guy behind him, who himself was now infected with the road rage virus, began to follow Jim home. Ten miles off the freeway, Jim realized that things were serious. Moving from fight to fright, with beads of sweat pouring down his face, Jim decided that it was best to get help. So he pulled into the nearest Dunkin' Donuts, where two police cars were parked, and yelled for assistance. Jim learned a valuable lesson that day: respond, don't react.

We can learn that lesson, too. Whether it means counting to ten, taking several deep breaths, leaving the room to get a drink of water, or doing nothing until we gain our emotional equilibrium, there are several initial steps to responding appropriately. In moments of stress, we are responsible for how we respond; we do not need to lose our heads in the midst of chaos. Responding means surveying all the viable options, combining intuition and judgment, and then selecting the best course of action. Initially, responding may seem as if it takes more work—specifically, more mental preparation—but ask anyone who has reacted inappropriately, and that person will tell you there is always a big mess to clean up afterward.

ACTION PLAN 6: Here is a suggestion: observe your behavior in situations that provoke stress, and note what your first course of action tends to be. Are you someone who reacts or who responds? If you find yourself reacting to things that might better be served by a response, get in the habit of pausing first, before doing or saying anything, and then coming up with two viable responses. Try the best of the two. Lao Tzu often talked about doing nothing, which can be interpreted here to mean simply waiting. In this case, his advice might be well worth adhering to.

7. Seeking a Balance: Complexity versus Simplicity

One reason why it is so easy to get stuck on the road of life's journey is that it's human nature to assume more responsibilities than we can comfortably handle. Nowhere is this more apparent than at the worksite, where Americans now hold the dubious honor of the most hours spent at work per week. When family responsibilities are added to the load, the weight can seem unbearable. The typical mind-set is to act before thinking things through—saying *yes*, when *no* might be more appropriate. Not only can the weight of looming responsibilities slow things down, it can cause resentment to build up, which in turn brings on feelings of victimization, hence making the task even more grueling.

One of the great pleasures of being human is having free will, the ability to make choices in all aspects of our lives. But as we all know, the flip side of free will is responsibility: accepting responsibility for the choices we make. Common sense would dictate that we might think through our choices a little more carefully, but it's no secret to say that this doesn't always happen. When hastily made decisions go bad, resentment is not far behind. Thinking things through doesn't have to take a lot of time, and the time and emotional energy it can save are immeasurable.

There is wisdom in taking the path of least resistance, particularly when your load is already heavy. While some types of resistance can certainly build character, other situations can instill fear, guilt, and frustration. In an age of codependency, where approval-seeking super-achievers burn out quickly, the path of least resistance is the preferred path.

Some choices require more information than others; answers to the questions who, what, when, where, and how are always good to know. One of the most common coping techniques for stress management is called "information seeking": getting all the facts before jumping headfirst into a situation. While unforeseen aspects always crop up in any given situation, being well prepared by knowing what there is to know can save you an immense amount of time. How can you begin to gather and process information to take advantage of the situation?

ACTION PLAN 7:   Ask yourself this simple question as you consider taking on new responsibilities, whether big or small: will this task complicate or simplify my life? By thinking ahead, you may save yourself a lot of time and frustration. Make a habit of asking yourself this question regularly, as a proactive step in the organization of your life.

8. Good Vibrations I: Turning Off the TV

The television, as we know it, was patented in 1930. By 1953, one out of every two homes in the United States had a television in the living room. Today, almost every room in the house has one; some households have more TVs than occupants. Perhaps it's ironic that the two guys who independently invented the television (Philo Farnsworth and Vladimir Zworykin) refused to allow this device into their homes or let their kids ever watch it. They knew something. Television has become human kryptonite. If Karl Marx were alive today, he would say that TV, not religion, is the opiate of the masses.

While most people say that there are surely some good programs on television (usually, they cite shows on PBS or the Discovery Channel), the average person will admit that there really isn't much on that's worth watching, even with more than a hundred channels running twenty-four hours a day. Few people realize the link between stress and prolonged television viewing, but there certainly is one. Here's why: a mild stress response is triggered by constant visual stimulation. To keep the viewer's attention, most television programming is now produced with three- to five-second camera angle changes. Consequently, health experts agree that the number-one addiction in this country isn't alcohol, cigarettes, or even drugs. It's television. People have a really hard time taking their eyes off the screen. Research reveals that on average, you can watch several murders, numerous accidents, and countless acts of violence each night. While some people say they merely become numb to it, the truth is that these scenes are picked up by the unconscious mind, where the toxic effects are played over and over again throughout the mind, body, and spirit.

Anyone who watched the television coverage of the terrorists' attack on the World Trade Center saw as many as one hundred replays of the second plane crashing into the north tower. Some estimates suggest that it was in the thousands. Several studies have shown that people can go into the fight-or-flight response merely by watching a scary movie. So imagine if you have had a bad day at the office, got caught in the traffic from hell on the way home, and then proceed to sit and watch up to four to six hours of television. Yikes! In the Academy Award–winning documentary *Bowling for Columbine*, Michael Moore concluded his film by saying that the reason there is so much violence on the news and in entertainment programming is that fear boosts Nielson ratings, thus garnering more advertising dollars. The bottom line is that whether it's politics or the economy, fear sells. Don't buy into it!

Andy Weil, M.D., is the author of the book *Spontaneous Healing*. In his list of recommendations to augment one's health, he suggests a "fast" from watching the news, particularly while eating dinner. He notes, quite accurately, that there will still be fighting in the Middle East, some politician will be involved with a sex scandal, and jitters will continue on Wall Street. You can walk away from the news for days at a time and step back a week later without missing a whole lot. The names may change, but the headlines are basically the same. In essence, he says that the negative news coverage is nothing more than negative vibrations. These bad vibrations certainly affect your health, especially if you're stressed, because, consciously or unconsciously, they add to your stress.

ACTION PLAN 8:   On the Hawaiian island of Kauai, citizens have banned together to proclaim a "turn off the television week" in December. They say that aside from the violence aspect of television, it has broken down the family structure. Other towns across the country are starting similar programs. You can do it, too. In fact, you can do it for longer than one week. Consider getting rid of it altogether.

Is there a chance that you may be addicted to television? Here is a way to find out. Successful rehabilitation programs are based on the thirty-day abstinence model. Can you give up television for a whole month? Just as in other rehab programs, family members need to be involved, or it won't work. So, here is a suggestion: gather the family or the people you live with together and suggest that the television be off limits for the next month. Unplug it and store it in a nearby closet. If you are like most people, you will be surprised at the following: you'll gradually feel less tension and more peace, you'll sleep better and wake up more rested, and you'll find an abundance of time to do other projects and have improved quality time with your loved ones. Give it a try.

9. Good Vibrations II: Music That Soothes the Savage Breast

What does deodorant have to do with music, you ask? The answer is a little more complex than humming with a can of Arid under your arm. It seems that several years ago, the makers of Mitchum deodorant did an exhaustive study to find out what makes people sweat. While the researchers were at it, they looked at a number of things related to stress. What they came up with was most interesting.

As it turns out, they learned that the number-one technique that's used to settle the nerves is listening to music. Some call it music therapy, others call it the Mozart Effect, although Bach and Brahms are no second fiddles. Scientists have proven that the old adage about music soothing a savage breast is right. Heart rate, blood pressure, muscle tension, and a whole list of physical parameters are significantly influenced by a good melody and a gentle rhythm.

It is also interesting and perhaps not a coincidence to learn that many of the terms used to describe stress (e.g., dissonance and tension) and relaxation (e.g., sympathetic resonance, resolution, and harmony) are the same words used to describe similar aspects of music theory. As of yet, no one theory can explain why music can soothe a savage breast—or beast, for that matter. Some researchers suggest this has to do with how the eardrum translates vibrations into biochemical properties. Others note a particular effect of vibrations through entrainment, and then there are people who suggest that music is the language of the gods. After all, the word *music* comes to us from the word *muse*, the angelic beings who taught Apollo to play the lute so many millennia ago.

It is hard to say which type of music is the most relaxing because everyone has specific individual tastes, but the consensus among people who study music therapy is that instrumental music (without lyrics) seems to work best. The reason is that the mind (specifically, the left hemisphere of the brain) is not distracted by words. The choice of effective music ranges from classical to jazz to New Age. Throw in some Celtic music or Tibetan chanting, and the list is extremely diverse. Whether it's George Winston playing piano solos or Enya singing etheric melodies, the range of relaxing music to choose from has never been greater. So, turn on the CD player, lower the lights, hit the play button, and let your mind coast along for the ride. You will be pleasantly surprised. And here's an idea, if you haven't already done it: make a mix of relaxing music that you can play in your car or at home after a rough day at work.

ACTION PLAN 9: I am often asked to recommend selections of relaxing music. These ten CDs are what I (and many others) consider to be the classics to soothe the savage beast, breast, or anything else that's stressed in your house. If you don't find these CDs in your favorite music store, they can be special ordered. You can also order them online. Consider making your own compilation as your personal music prescription.

ARTIST	CD TITLE	INSTRUMENTATION
Eversound Series	*One Quiet Night**	Various instruments
Jim Wilson	*Northern Seascape*	Solo piano
Michael Hoppé	*The Poet*	Solo cello
Michael Hoppé	*The Dreamer*	Solo flute
Secret Garden	*White Stones*	Violin and piano
Bruce Becvar	*Forever Blue Sky*	Solo guitar
David Lanz	*Christophori's Dream*	Solo piano
Chris Spheeris	*Eros*	Solo guitar
Yanni	*In My Time*	Solo piano
Sean Harkness	*Aloft*	Solo guitar

One Quiet Night is a compilation from the Eversound Music collection that I was invited to put together in conjunction with this book.

A final note on music: not all relaxing music has to come from a CD. Live concerts are excellent. There are also the musical sounds of nature. About a year ago, I attended a conference on the topic of holistic healing. One of the presenters was the noted music therapist Steven Halpern. Rather than speak from behind a podium, he walked to the center of the stage and stood next to a large rhododendron. Then he attached an electrode to a leaf of the plant. The electrode was wired through to a transducer to translate the subtle vibrations and the chemical reactions of the leaf into musical sound vibrations. When everything was finally hooked up, the audience settled in to listen to the most amazing symphony of music ever heard. That was just one plant. Can you imagine listening to a whole forest? Nature is a great tranquilizer. Remember, sometimes the most relaxing music can be found in your own backyard with the stereo turned off.

10. Anger Management: Learning to Fine-Tune Expectations

One of the biggest roadblocks on the human path is unresolved anger. If you haven't noticed, there is plenty of anger to go around these days. Every episode of anger, from impatience to rage, is the result of an unmet expectation. From the conquest of the American dream to a troubling economy, to unparalleled civil liberties, we are enculturated with certain expectations. We feel that we are entitled to various benefits in our comfortable lifestyle, and these do not include perpetual rush hour traffic, computer viruses, anthrax hoaxes, and corporate downsizing. Add to these the promise that technology will make our lives easier (not to mention guarantee more leisure time), and unmet expectations are a dime a dozen today.

How many times a day do you get angry? Three? Five? Ten? Twenty-five? Fifty? According to several recent surveys, the average number of times the typical American gets angry in the course of a day is between fifteen and twenty. When you think about how many different ways anger feelings can arise (e.g., impatience, guilt, frustration, envy, indignation, etc.), this number is not all that surprising.

The renowned psychiatrist Elisabeth Kübler-Ross uncovered more than she realized when she outlined the stages of death and dying. In what has now become part of the national consciousness, the stages of the death and dying process are denial (shock), anger, bargaining, withdrawal, and acceptance. Although these stages were first observed with cancer patients, its interesting to note that the same stages are experienced, to a much lesser degree, with the death of unmet expectations. These can range from a postponed flight at the airport to a fender-bender car collision or simply playing phone tag with a colleague.

Does this mean that we should conduct our lives with no expectations? Absolutely not. What it does mean is that we need to be able to fine-tune our expectations when they are not met to our satisfaction, so that we don't fly off the handle, make our blood pressure soar, or get an ulcer. The final stage after acceptance is adaptation, which means to change our perceptions and go with the flow.

ACTION PLAN 10:   There are many aspects to consider when implementing a creative anger-management plan. One of the most important steps is fine-tuning your expectations so that you don't permanently derail off the human journey.

Here are some ideas for creative anger management:

- Refine your expectations. Ask yourself what expectation wasn't met and why you feel threatened by it. Then let it go.

- Count to ten (take a time-out). It's okay to feel frustrated. In fact, it's normal, but your best bet is to cool off before saying or doing something you'll later regret. Counting to ten really helps you to cool off. If you must, count to twenty-five; count as high and as long as it takes to chill out before you come back to begin to resolve the situation.

- Plan in advance for things that you know drive you crazy, like highway construction and prolonged office meetings. Design a strategy so that when the unexpected happens, you are prepared.

- Practice sweet forgiveness. Are you harboring a grudge against someone? Now is the time to let it go and move on.

11. Meditation: Take Five or Even Ten

If you have ever read the directions that come with your cordless phone, you will notice somewhere in the fine print that the phone needs to be recharged regularly, or it won't work properly. Typically, when left out of the cradle for an extended period of time, a red light comes on during its use, indicating a low battery. Human beings don't have red lights on their foreheads that indicate a power failure, although it sure would be helpful if we did. A red light would be an ideal warning to others, saying, keep your distance or, better yet, stay away entirely. Metaphorically speaking, signs of an imminent human power failure or simply low energy at the human level include impatience, rudeness, sarcasm, arrogance, and other less-becoming behaviors, all of which epitomize an overreactive emotional stress response.

Unlike cordless phones, we don't necessarily need a minimum of ten hours of recharging to function properly. Restoring your personal energy can be done in as little as five minutes a day, and that's what meditation is all about: recharging your personal energy after a draining day to return to a sense of inner peace. Again, this is centering.

Meditation became popular in the United States back in the sixties when the Beatles tried Transcendental Meditation (TM). What started as a fad soon became a daily practice for hundreds of thousands of people nationwide. Dr. Herbert Benson, an early TM follower, conducted several scientific research studies at Harvard University to examine the effectiveness of meditation. The studies revealed that regular meditation tends to lower the resting heart rate and the resting blood pressure, boost immune function, improve sleep quality, and improve several other physiological functions associated with relaxation. With this scientific proof backing him up, Benson Americanized TM and called it "The Relaxation Response." The rest, as they say, is history.

In an age of information overload and attention deficit disorder, meditation is a time to unload or purge unnecessary information (e.g., thoughts, feelings, etc.). It is a time to clear the mind of irrelevant chitchat so that more important matters can be addressed. Just like deleting all the e-mails that you no longer care to store in your computer's memory, meditation is the mind's way of doing the same. Meditation is nothing more than clearing the mind of thoughts and feelings that are taking up space and crowding out more important things that really need attention. Some people call meditation "mental disarmament." I like the slogan that says: Meditation, it's not what you think!

ACTION PLAN 11:   The following meditation technique can be done in as little as five minutes. Read through this exercise once to get the idea, and then find a quiet place to practice it or some variation of it.

Breathing Clouds Meditation
The purpose of this meditation is to focus on your breathing and, at the same time, help clear your mind of distracting thoughts and unresolved emotions that no longer serve your highest good. This meditation can be used to initiate the emptying process. As with all meditations that use mental imagery, please feel free to augment these suggestions in your own mind to promote the greatest sense of comfort and peace.

In this meditation, two images are combined with your breathing. The first is an image of a clean, white cloud of air when you inhale; the second is a dark, dirty cloud of air when you exhale. The clean, white cloud of air is symbolic of cleansing the mind. It is pure and fresh and accompanies your intention to cleanse your mind-body and spirit. The dark cloud of air symbolizes any or all thoughts and feelings that you wish to release and let go of, such as fears, frustrations, grudges, physical pains, or any unresolved issues. The inhalation is symbolic of invigoration; the exhalation is symbolic of cleansing and detoxing.

You can do as many breathing clouds cycles as you wish. Ten is a good number to start with. The idea with this meditation is that at some point in this breathing clouds cycle (which will vary from person to person), the air you breathe out will eventually become as pure as the air you breathe in, and as this happens, you become relaxed and peaceful.

1. Begin by closing your eyes and focusing on your breathing. Place all of your attention, focus all of your thoughts on your breathing.

2. Now, as you take your next breath, slowly and comfortably, inhale through your nose and imagine that you are inhaling clean, fresh air, like a white, puffy cloud. Feel the air circulate up through your sinuses, up to the top of your head and down the back of your spine.

3. As you begin to exhale, slowly and comfortably, exhale through your mouth. As you exhale, visualize that the air you breathe out is a dark, dirty cloud of air. As you exhale, bring to mind a thought or a feeling that no longer serves you and let it go as you exhale.

4. Again, inhale clean, fresh air through your nose, let it circulate to the top of your head and down the back of your spine, to reside in your stomach.

5. Exhale very slowly through your mouth, and, as you do, think of a moment of frustration or a feeling of resentment that you have been carrying around for a long time. Now is the time to let it go; as you exhale, visualize the dark, dirty air you breathe out carrying this toxic thought, so that it leaves with the breath.

6. Slowly inhale clean, fresh air through your nose and feel it circulate to the top of your head and down the back of your spine. As it circulates, feel it invigorate your entire body.

7. Exhale slowly through your mouth, and once again bring to mind a thought or a feeling of unresolved stress that begs to be resolved. Letting go is the first step in doing so, and as this cloud of dark, musty air leaves your mouth, give yourself permission to release this stress by letting go as you exhale.

8. Repeat this cycle of breathing clouds—fresh air in and dark, dirty air out—until you come to a greater sense of calm. As you do, notice that the air you exhale becomes as clear as the air you inhale, symbolizing homeostasis of your mind, body, and spirit.

12. Adopt an Attitude of Gratitude:
Counting Your Blessings (and Curses, Too!)

Under moments of stress and duress, the only thing you may want to think about is how bad off you are. While this is certainly a normal response, spending too much time fretting about personal misfortunes can become a mental rut that is very hard to get out of. On the other hand, ignoring your feelings by looking only at the bright side is nothing less than denial, so a compromise is in order. First, take some time to evaluate the situation as objectively as you can. Obviously, each situation will merit its own duration of time for you to do this, but when you have exhausted looking at all the negative aspects of the situation, pause to try to find something good that might come out of it. There is always something good that can come from a bad situation, even if it's what you can learn so that you avoid this hazard again.

Adopting an attitude of gratitude means redirecting your thinking process away from negative patterns, which are so common (and unproductive), to successfully deal with stress. Often, we become myopic when faced with problems, and we fail to see that with lemons comes lemonade and with rain clouds comes rainbows.

By shifting your focus to an attitude of gratitude, you move out of the pattern that is commonly called victim consciousness. And in perhaps not every case, but darn near close to it, people who can get beyond the negative impact of a stressful event soon begin to see that what was once a curse may actually be a blessing in disguise.

ACTION PLAN 12:   When you find yourself in a funk, pull out a pen and a pad of paper and make a list of all the things you are grateful for or take for granted. Start with simple things like your eyesight, the fact that you are breathing, or that the earth spins on its axis, giving us night and day. Then move on to more profound things, such as experiences that have made you who you are. Don't stop till you reach one hundred items. Then, savor everything on the list.

13. Good Nutrition: Avoid Putting Gasoline on the Fire

The best way to keep a car going is to put gasoline in the tank for fuel. The body also needs fuel, but what most people use as a source of energy these days is atrocious. In a country where food choices are amazingly diverse, the standard American diet (SAD) is just that, sad! People survive on foods that hold little, if any, nutritional value: processed foods that are made to last months on a grocery store shelf but barely sustain a low quality of life, let alone a good one. Trans-fatty acids (hydrogenated oils), found in nearly all boxed goods, have been created so that foods that contain it won't go rancid. Bacteria are smarter than humans; they won't go near that stuff. Humans, on the other hand, can't get enough of it. Something is wrong with this picture.

In the course of a stressful day, the body tends to utilize vitamins and minerals to metabolize carbohydrates and fats for energy. The higher the level of stress, the greater the need for these nutrients. It is safe to say that many people are running a deficit of essential nutrients when they are stressed for prolonged periods of time.

As if that's not bad enough, it gets worse. Good nutritional habits are the first casualty of a stress-filled day. People skip meals or snack on foods that offer little, if any, nutritional value (the term is *empty calories*—foods that are high in calories but extremely low in nutrients). As a consequence, the deficit of essential nutrients grows worse. To make matters even more dismal, people often consume foods that either trigger the stress response or add to it, which is akin to throwing gasoline on the fire. Which foods do this? Caffeine is perhaps the biggest culprit. A substance in caffeine (methylated xanthines) acts on the nervous system to promote the release of the stress neurotransmitters epinephrine and norepinephrine. A high consumption of salt is believed to increase blood pressure by causing more water retention. Processed sugar and flour (the legal but addictive white powders) also have an adverse effect on the nervous and immune systems.

Many popular foods are considered a stress on the body, such as processed foods; genetically modified foods; and artificial colors, flavors, sweeteners, and preservatives. According to the author Robert Cohen, who wrote the book *Milk: The Deadly Poison*, milk can have as many as eighty different antibiotics in it, and many fruits and vegetables are coated with just as many pesticides. Sad to say, the synergistic effect of these toxins has never even been looked at by the FDA or the EPA. These toxins are absorbed into the body and are typically stored in the liver, the kidneys, or the adipose tissue. All of this supports the recommendation to eat organic foods, whenever possible.

It's no secret that the American diet is high in calories and low in nutrients. It's also very high in toxins and chemical substances (synthetic estrogens associated with cancer) that are anything but natural. A good rule of thumb is to eat natural whole foods, organic foods whenever possible, and foods that support a healthy immune system, and minimize foods that jack up the stress response. Food, particularly anything with a high sugar content, can also affect one's mood.

ACTION PLAN 13:   Here is a short list of suggestions to enhance your health and boost your immune system through good healthful nutrition:

- *Eat a good amount of fiber.* Fruits and vegetables have plenty of fiber, and this helps to clean the small intestine and the colon to rid the body of toxins. Americans do not get enough fiber, mostly because we don't eat enough vegetables. Vegetables should be at the base of the food guide pyramid. Again, the best choice is "Certified Organic."

- *Consume more essential fatty acids.* Not all fat is bad; in fact, some fats are crucial for life, including the essential fatty acids (omega-3 and omega-6). Most people get too much omega-6 and not enough omega-3. Flaxseed oil and cold-water fish, such as fresh Alaskan salmon, are the best sources of omega-3 fatty acids.

- *Consume a daily supply of antioxidants.* Beta-carotene, vitamin C, vitamin E, and the mineral selenium can be found in a variety of fruits and vegetables. Antioxidants combat free radicals that tend to destroy cells in the body. Free radicals are associated with cancer and coronary heart disease. Remember to choose certified organic foods.

- *Consume a good supply of organic produce.* Organic produce has minimal amounts of pesticides, herbicides, and fungicides, many of which are carcinogenic. Buying and eating organic foods lowers the risk of ingesting these and other dangerous substances, which ultimately tax or suppress the immune system. Organic foods are often nutrient-dense, packed with vitamins and minerals to help restore balance to the body's physiology.

- *Minimize or avoid the consumption of processed foods.* Many foods are processed so that they'll have an extended shelf life. They contain a plethora of synthetic and unnatural substances unfit for human consumption, such as trans-fatty acids.

- *Consume free-range meats whenever possible.* Free-range chicken and beef contain substantially less hormones, pesticides, and antibiotics. Factory-farm chicken and beef are loaded with antibiotics and hormones, which tax or suppress the immune system as it tries to rid the body of these substances. If you really like meat, try free-range buffalo; it's much more healthful.

- *Minimize or avoid the consumption of foods that contain synthetic additives.* These include aspartame, MSG, and nitrates, among others, which are cited as destabilizing brain chemistry—hence, attention span. You can learn more about the effects of synthetic additives in Russell Blaylock's book *Excitotoxins*. Many foods list MSG merely as "spice" on the label, so, again, the best course of action is to eat certified organic products.

- *Include herbal remedies to boost your immune system.* Many herbs, such as astragalus, shiitake mushrooms, and garlic, are used to boost the immune system, with no ill side effects when taken as directed. A good reference on herbs is *The Way of Herbs*, by Michael Tierra.

- *Drink plenty of water all day long.* Rehydration is essential to cleanse toxins from the body. Get in the habit of drinking plenty of water (or caffeine-free tea) to keep cells healthy. Cancer patients on chemotherapy are told to drink plenty of water to flush it out of their systems. Drinking plenty of filtered water is good advice for everyone. Consider beginning each day with a glass of water, too.

- *Minimize or avoid foods that trigger the stress response.* These include caffeine, salt, refined sugars, bleached flour, and processed foods. Your body will surely thank you.

There is an old saying from Hippocrates, the man credited with being the father of modern medicine. In addition to uttering the now-famous words "First, do no harm!" he is remembered for saying, "Let food be your medicine and let medicine be your food." This is always good advice.

14. Empowerment: Remember, You've Got the Goods

At times, stress can seem not only overwhelming but also disempowering, if for no other reason than by making you feel as if you have no control over a particular circumstance. One of the basic human fears is the fear of losing control in any given situation. The consequences can be paralyzing. One of the ironies of human nature is our desire to manipulate things we have no control over and to neglect or abandon the things we have complete control over. So, what do we have control over? First and foremost, we have control over our own thoughts. But we are also empowered to use our inner resources, or the muscles of the soul, described in chapter 4. When you acknowledge the amazing potential of these resources, your wealth is immeasurable. To reiterate an important point: these are the attributes that we recognize, consciously or unconsciously, in the people we call our heroes, role models, or mentors.

Empowerment and mentors, along with support groups and uniqueness, constitute the four pillars of high self-esteem, and high self-esteem is paramount in dealing effectively with stress. Reflect for a moment on someone whom you would identify as your mentor or role model. Once you have a specific person in mind, ask yourself what you admire in this person. Finally, ask yourself what steps can you take to enhance the same qualities in yourself. That's empowerment. Empowerment is also knowing the difference between assertiveness and aggression.

ACTION PLAN 14:   Before you can claim your power, you have to reclaim it from anyone and anything you might have given it away to. Have you given your personal power away to others (movie stars, spiritual gurus, sports teams, physicians, spouse), thus denying yourself a full sense of empowerment? Giving your power away is akin to leaking energy from your body. Empowerment comes from believing in your personal power, reclaiming your personal energy. This is reinforced by positive affirmation statements: positive feedback that you give yourself, particularly when the chips are down. Take a moment to write down three positive affirmation statements that help to instill a sense of calm. Begin each phrase with the words *I am* (e.g., "I am calm and relaxed").

1. I am _____

2. I am _____

3. I am _____

Make a habit of giving yourself empowering feedback so that when the shadow of fear lurks nearby, you can use these affirmations as a light in the darkness.

15. Friends in Need: Having a Good Support System

One thing that became quite evident from the attack on the World Trade Center and the Pentagon was how people reached out to help those in need. Within minutes, if not seconds, people took steps to assist others, from donating blood for the residents of New York City and Washington, D.C., to organizing community action groups for disaster relief. People, some of them for the first time, were talking to their neighbors, learning their names.

Psychologists have known for decades about the importance of a good support system to maintain one's health. Reaching out to friends and family in times of need is perhaps one of the oldest coping techniques for stress. In the now-famous words of John Donne, "No man is an island." What used to be called "six degrees of separation" has been reduced down to two degrees, and when it comes to knowing somebody who's under stress, it may be less than that. Emphatically speaking, human beings are very social animals, yet in the hustle and bustle of a fast-paced life, contact— real quality time between friends and family—is decreasing. More time spent on the Internet or watching television means that less quality time is devoted to family and friends. The result can be a feeling of isolation, which is commonly known to create a fertile ground for bouts of depression.

What is quality time among friends? Quality time includes activities where an experience is shared to strengthen the bonds of friendship. Playing musical instruments or games of tennis or golf, throwing potluck dinners, going on bike rides or hikes, and attending music concerts are just a few ideas. There are hundreds of others. To paraphrase the words of Khalil Gibran, "Find hours to live, not time to kill."

ACTION PLAN 15:   Take a moment to list five of your friends whom you could call at a moment's notice to spend time with. Or try this: make a list of the things you always wanted to do, and then call your friends and see who has an interest in joining you. If your list of things to do or creative ideas is short, and your list of friends is shorter, find ways to meet people with similar interests. If you're not sure where to start, check the local paper for upcoming events. Some stores (such as those selling outdoor gear) host events and socials, too, which can become a great place to meet others who have similar interests. Bookstores have author signings and churches have potlucks. Last, but not least, volunteering your time at a nonprofit organization is a great way to meet others who have open hearts. Make time to reconnect.

16. Back to Nature: Getting and Staying Grounded

Our bodies operate on an internal clock. The scientific name is "biorhythms" or circadian variations, and this clock seems to run on a twenty-four- to twenty-five-hour interval. Our physiological dynamics appear to be based on the earth's spin on its axis, in relationship to the sun, and this affects everything from our sleep cycles to cell metabolism, and perhaps a lot more that we are not even aware of. One thing is certain: sitting in front of a computer screen for eight to ten hours a day and snacking on processed food under fluorescent lights is not natural. In fact, this doesn't even come close to nature!

It is no exaggeration to say that we, in the Western world, are quite removed from nature. It used to be that people were well aware of the phases of the moon, the seasons of the earth, and little nuances observed in nature, from the brown bands on fuzzy caterpillars to subtle differences in the tides. If you were to ask the average person on the street what phase the moon is in tonight, aside from receiving a funny look, you would be hard-pressed to get a correct answer. One of my friends, who happens to live in New York City, says the closest she gets to nature is *Animal Planet*. That says it all. Unfortunately, she's not alone. Millions of people know all too well what she means. Today it is commonplace to get up, drive to and from work, and never even have a natural ray of sunshine hit your skin. Instead, we are surrounded with stale office air and bombarded by electromagnetic pollution.

The flow of life is closely associated with the cycles of nature—the ebb and the flow of rhythms. The changing of the leaves, the scent of flowers in the air, butterflies and geese in migration, and frost on the windows all provide signals for us to be a part of, not separate from, the natural world. If nothing more, getting in touch with nature keeps us grounded. First and foremost, nature is a sanctuary, and it beckons us to come outside on a regular basis.

With all puns intended, nature is very grounding. Not only does a walk in the woods or on a beach cleanse the mind and the soul of life's daily hassles, the sights, the sounds, and the scents of nature strike a primordial chime of balance (the balance of nature) in the unconscious mind. Moreover, when we align ourselves with the sacredness of nature, we honor the divine connection of which we are always a part.

ACTION PLAN 16:   What can you do to get back to nature? Find the nearest park and go for a walk. If possible, drive to the ocean or a lake and walk or sit on the beach. Pull out a blanket some evening and lie down to watch the stars for a few hours (especially during a meteor shower). Plant a garden. Get out the binoculars and go bird watching. Visit the nearest botanical gardens or local greenhouse. The options are endless. Every person I have ever talked to says that getting back to nature is nothing less than invigorating, and although a million distractions may tempt you to put it off, there are no valid reasons not to return to the source. So, what phase is the moon in tonight? Don't cheat and look at a calendar. Walk outside tonight and take a look!

Keeping a strong connection to nature can also mean bringing a part of nature indoors, such as houseplants and small water fountains. Even if you already have these in your house, reconfigure them in a sacred space that truly honors this basic connection.

17. Diversify Your Interests: Place Your Eggs in More Than One Basket

Bill took up pottery as something to do on weekends. He admits that he didn't know the first thing about it when he took his first pottery class ten years ago. It was something he had had an interest in as a kid. A foot injury curtailed his leisure pursuit of golf, and making pottery just seemed to fill the void. He must have had a knack for it, because his wife's friends began to express an interest in buying some of his pieces. Bill was amused. Within two months, he could barely keep any of his pieces in stock. At first, Bill often described himself as living in two worlds, but now he compares the passion between work and play to being bilingual.

As a hobby, Bill found that making pottery served as a great distraction from the strife at his workplace. Whenever he sat down at the potter's wheel, he was in another world. But what he also noticed was that the creative aspect of making pottery transferred from home to his work-related projects. His colleagues at work noticed it, too. He quickly learned the wisdom of not placing all of his eggs in one basket or, in his case, one ceramic bowl. When his company went through a restructuring process, rather than waiting to see if the ax would fall on his head, Bill took the early retirement program that was offered. His hobby of making pottery became his golden parachute, many times over.

Hobbies serve as a great diversion from day-to-day work responsibilities that can weigh us down. Outside interests, whatever they might be, can provide much-needed equilibrium in an otherwise unbalanced life. Not only do hobbies involve an attempt to make order out of chaos, as well as foster creativity; these skills also transfer over to work-related responsibilities. If nothing else, the activities tend to open the mind to new ways of thinking and problem solving, and that's always helpful.

ACTION PLAN 17: What are your current hobbies or nonwork-related interests? If you come up blank, with no answer, then start with this question: What are your current interests or fascinations? What are five things that you've always wanted to do but put off for lack of time and/or money? By the way, hobbies don't have to be time-consuming or expensive, so those excuses are not viable.

If you are unsure where to start, take a continuing education course at your local community college, YMCA, or church.

18. Amazing Grace: The Healing Power of Prayer

One of the greatest paradoxes of life is this: throughout the course of human history each life appears infinitely insignificant, yet each life is absolutely essential to the grand scheme of the cosmos. At some point in life we realize that we are a small part of something much bigger than we can ever imagine. It's a given that we will never fully understand the greater mysteries of life. The wisest sages and prophets have as much as told us so. But they have also given these words of insight: prayer gives us perspective on this seemingly incomprehensible picture.

The illusion of life is that we are separate beings. The reality of life is that we are all connected. During moments of stress, the perception of separation wins out. Faith is the metaphorical ray of sunlight that breaks through the clouds of illusion to reveal our divine connection, a connection that always has been and always will be there. Prayer is the realization of this connection. Prayer doesn't unfailingly provide the answers we seek, but it does provide a level of comfort that can be found nowhere else.

So, in times of stress, we pray. We pray to God—whatever we perceive God to be. We pray for help and assistance to make it through the moments of stress and tribulation. If we are not too consumed with the gravity of the situation, we might also pray for insight and understanding to make sense of it all. If we are feeling truly altruistic, we may pray for others as well. Some people say that there are two types of prayer: thoughts and desires asking for divine intervention, and praise and gratitude for the wondrous blessings bestowed upon us. Other people say that all thought is prayer.

Joseph Campbell noted that one hallmark of every great mythical story is the presence of what he called spiritual aids, a special alchemy between one's inner resources and divine assistance, which provides needed help in times of crisis. Prayer is the call for assistance.

During stress, more than at any other time, our faith has its greatest test. No sooner did the four hijacked planes crash on the morning of September 11, 2001, than people around the world, of all faiths, began to form prayer vigils (in and out of churches, temples, and mosques), in an effort to console the hearts and the minds of those left behind to pick up the pieces of the tragedy.

At the cusp of the twentieth and the twenty-first centuries, the topic of intercessory prayer has gained much attention outside the parameters of conventional theology. Only a few years ago it would have seemed like heresy in the halls of academia, yet prayer is now accepted as a viable topic of investigation. As such, scientific studies have examined the healing power and the potential of prayer (do a quick search on the Internet and you'll be amazed!). Perhaps it's no surprise that conclusions drawn from these studies suggest that intentions that honor the divine connection of the universe do indeed appear to have a significant impact on the lives of people involved in the healing process. Although we may never really understand the dynamics involved (remember to embrace the mystery), the outcomes appear certain: prayer works, even when prayers seem to go unanswered.

ACTION PLAN 18:   Is there a right way to pray? Given the complexity of world religions, the answer might seem to be yes, but, as it turns out, religion and religious practice really have nothing to do with either the mystery or the power of prayer. There are many similarities between the techniques of mental imagery and visualization and prayer. In fact, they follow the same template. The following five suggestions are inspired by the writing of Sophy Burnham, the author of *A Book of Angels* and *The Path of Prayer*, who synthesized them from the ageless wisdom found in all the world's religions.

1. *Send a clear transmission of thought.* First, think of your mind as if it were a radio transmitter that can send and receive messages. Then think about how your ears tend to prefer a clear signal, rather than loud static. When our minds are racing with dozens of thoughts at the same time, the result is mental static. Praying in the midst of this mental chatter is like talking over static—the message is unclear. More often than not, the mind tunes out. When sending a prayer to the heavens, the last thing you want is static or even a mixed message. To send a clear

transmission, quiet the mind by taking time to clear away feelings of anger, fear, frustration, or anxiety, which tend to distort the intended message.

2. *Express prayers in a positive context.* Various studies have shown that the unconscious mind understands positive thoughts extremely well but doesn't process negative thoughts well at all. For example, if you were to say, "I hope I'm not late," the unconscious mind translates this to "I hope I'm late," and this in turn can become a self-fulfilling prophecy. The universal mind, of which the human mind is a part, also understands positive thoughts so much better than it does negative ones. So, when you pray, do it in a positive context, so that nothing gets lost in the translation.

3. *Express prayers in the present tense.* The cosmic clock is calibrated quite differently from basic earth time. Even Einstein proposed that time is a very relative matter. Mystics and sages have shared the thought that there is no past or future when it comes to the mind of God; all things are in the present tense. So, with this in mind, phrase your thoughts in the present moment. Regardless of when, ask as if you need to be answered now.

4. *Close with a thought of gratitude.* In many cultures, it is customary to make an offering to the divine spirit, after asking for assistance. The gift is a token of appreciation. Gratitude can be expressed in many ways. Through prayer, a simple intention or a sincere word of thanks is all that is required. With this thought of gratitude comes the requirement that you be detached from the results. In other words, make your intention known, offer thanks, and then let go of the outcome, knowing that a bigger game plan is in the works.

5. *Be open for any type of response or sign.* All prayers are answered, but not all answers are received. Sometimes there's too much static in the receiver (mental chatter). Sometimes the answer may be different from what we are looking for or even expect. Being open to a response or a sign means being receptive to what is in our best interest, even if we don't realize it at the

time. And it also means dropping all expectations of what we think is the right answer, trusting that what does result is indeed in our best interest.

19. Reserving Judgment: The Power of Acceptance

The human mind is amazing. It can create, analyze, incubate, rationalize, calculate, organize, and judge ideas and perceptions with a speed so rapid that no computer can begin to match it. Each of these capabilities is remarkable unto itself, yet the integration of these mental processes is truly extraordinary. No less extraordinary are the dynamics through which these thinking processes work together. One additional element in this collection of cognitive gifts is timing: knowing the best time to organize ideas versus the best time to judge aspects of a given situation. Any good comedian will tell you that when it comes to delivering a joke, timing is everything. The same can be said about the thinking processes—specifically, about using good judgment. At best, engaging in a mental process at the wrong time can be embarrassing; at worst, it can be deadly.

One of the more dangerous thinking processes is the power of judgment. Perhaps more than any other cognitive skill, it causes the most problems, if for no other reason than that it tends to dominate our thinking patterns. In times of physical danger, the power of judgment is essential for survival. In the best of times, judgment is the last in a series of steps we should use in our thinking process. A lesson can be learned from the creative process regarding the order of judgment. Remember that should a judge step in too soon, before an idea has had time to germinate, then this ends the promise of our potential creativity. Unlike judges in our national judicial system, the ego acting in the role of a judge says, "Guilty until proven innocent." It is this mental tape that often gets us into trouble.

Our judgments are made from a combination of past experiences, current facts, and some element of intuitive perceptions. In the right order, with the right mix, judgment is a wonderful tool. In the wrong order of mental processing, judgment sabotages our best efforts. Poor judgment is directly tied to intolerance, prejudice, and a score of other less-than-desirable human traits. Simply stated, our judgment can be our best friend or our worst enemy. It can either be the navigator or the pirate controlling the fate of our own human journey. At each bend in the road in our life's sojourn, consciously or unconsciously, we decide which role it plays. Reserving judgment is a skill that enables us to become more conscious and responsible for our thought processes.

So, remember, not only is it okay to use judgment in the thinking process, it's strongly encouraged. But as you become more conscious of your own thoughts, ask yourself whether you have questioned judgments in your thought processes. This is what it means to reserve judgment.

One morning while driving down a country road in Hawaii, I passed a guy who was hitchhiking. He had shoulder-length hair and a full beard, and my first thought was very judgmental. I passed him by. As I continued to drive, however, I found myself asking what it was about him that I didn't like. It didn't take me long to realize that I didn't have a good answer. To be honest, on first appearance, he looked quite biblical. He was even wearing sandals. He also had a huge backpack, and from the looks of things, it was quite heavy. Despite knowing the risk involved, I slowed down, turned the car around, and drove back. He was still there, waiting, so I offered him a ride.

Dan was traveling around the islands and had begun to make his way home to Ohio for Christmas. The more we talked, the more interesting he became. We ended up having lunch and spent the better part of the day together before he made his way to the airport. Before we parted company, we exchanged addresses. Back on the mainland, we corresponded several times. Five years later we have become the best of friends, and I am now the proud godfather of his son, Noah. I realize how enriched my life has become by his friendship, and I sometimes wonder what else I might have missed out on by being too quick to judge others.

ACTION PLAN 19:   Reserving judgment has many side benefits, but we will never know what they are until we become less judgmental and more receptive to the greater good that life has to offer. Although we all have moments of being judgmental, begin to observe your thoughts. When you find yourself passing judgment,

open your mind by changing your mental perspective and consider-
ing other viewpoints. The next time you find yourself passing
judgment, ask yourself what you might be missing out on.

20. Seizing the Day: The Future Is Now

One day while attending an outdoor art festival, I happened to hear
a song from one of my favorite CDs, *Northern Seascape*. I looked
up and there was the artist at the keyboards, giving a small public
concert to people, like me, who were strolling by. When he had
finished playing, the pianist Jim Wilson took a break to sign
autographs and chitchat with people at his booth. I walked over to
say hi, and he invited me to sit down and talk with him for a while.
In the course of our visit, Jim shared the story of his first recording,
and it became quite apparent to me that this man had learned the
meaning of the expression "Seize the day!" Here is Jim's story.

"Like many people, I wanted to become a famous musician
many years ago, but it is tough breaking into the business. I always
wanted to cut an album, but I found myself putting it off, waiting
for the right moment, except that the right moment never seemed
to be within sight. Although I really wanted to play piano, I ended
up becoming a piano tuner in Los Angeles. I guess I was rather
good, because I ended up tuning the pianos of performers like
Billy Joel; Crosby, Stills, and Nash; Carole King; Paul McCartney;
Burt Bacharach; Dan Fogelberg; and Elton John! I actually made
a pretty good career out of piano tuning. But then one day my best
friend died of a heart attack. He was only thirty-seven years old.
He had a lot of unfinished dreams. His death was like a knock on the
head for me to start finishing some of my own dreams—specifically,
to record my first album. I quickly got all the pieces in place, and
that's how *Northern Seascape* was born. You could say it was a
twenty-year project in the making, but in many ways, its origins
began after the death of my buddy." Prompted by that event, Jim
seized the day and has never let go since.

What is it that motivates some people to get up and go, while
others simply sit around, waiting for a ride? It's not fear or apathy.
This age-old question has as many answers as it does people who
get off their duffs and start moving. But what they all seem to have

in common is a means to capture the winds of inspiration, to fill their sails, and head out on an adventure, oftentimes into uncharted waters. And while many people are attached to the security of staying home, bathed in the comfort of familiarity, they will also tell you that this routine eventually leads to mediocrity and boredom.

Today, participating in life has become more passive than active. In an age of reality television and virtual technology, many people would rather sit and watch someone else have an adventure than take the time to have their own. The ultimate virtual, vicarious experience inevitably becomes a shallow adventure at best. At worst, it becomes one more nail in the coffin of our human potential.

Seizing the day begins with hoisting the sails of ambition to catch the winds of inspiration, but it also includes accessing your imagination and creativity to gather resources with which to make dreams come true. The goal can be small, such as running a marathon, or huge, like telling an estranged parent that you love him or her. Let there be no doubt, risks are involved with seizing the day—most notably, the risk of failure. But ask anyone who returns home from a personal adventure, and that person will say that the real failure is not in the doing. The real failure is in not even trying to seize the day. Seizing the day isn't so much an action or an action plan as it is an attitude. It's the voice of opportunity riding on the winds of change that begs to be heard. Seizing the day is the hero's call to action.

ACTION PLAN 20:   I ask this question with the intention of sending you on a quest: what are three personal lifetime goals that you wish to accomplish in the near future? Write them down here:

1. _____

2. _____

3. _____

This list is really just an invitation. Now comes the real quest: pick one of these goals and map out a strategy to make it happen. Fill in the specifics; identify what resources you need to accomplish it. Give it an estimated completion date. Seize the day today and start to make it happen, step by step.

21. Forgiveness: The Last Frontier

Several years ago someone shared with me a story of forgiveness that has left an indelible mark on my soul, so much so, that I wanted to share it with you. As it turns out, her father had read a passage in my book *Stand Like Mountain, Flow Like Water*, which she had given him as a birthday present. The passage was on the topic of forgiveness, in a story where a father came to terms with his estranged son. The story must have struck a chord because this woman's father, who also had an estranged child, decided that it was time to let bygones be bygones. The woman who told me this story explained that she had a sister living in New York City, whom her father had been estranged from for over a decade. Something had come between them, and he just couldn't let it go. All the estranged daughter's attempts to reconcile failed to repair the fragile relationship. In that time, she had gotten married, had a son, and gone on with her life. Not only had the man never seen his grandson, he refused to acknowledge that he even had one. But now something stirred in his soul, and within several days of finishing the book, he made what must have been a very difficult phone call to New York. Within a month's time, after several healing conversations over the phone, there was a reunion, and soon everything was back on track.

Carrying the weight of a grudge becomes immobilizing over time. It is human nature to feel hurt when we have been violated by another person. It is also human nature to seek revenge, even if revenge consists of withholding any attempts at reconciliation. A well-known expression says, "To err is human, to forgive divine." What often gets forgotten in this adage is that we hold a spark of divinity that enables us to do God's work ourselves. Nothing is more paramount to removing roadblocks of unresolved anger than the act of forgiveness. Carl Jung once said that we each have a responsibility to bring light into our being. When we engage in the process of forgiveness, not only do we bring light to our heart, but the whole world benefits as well.

What makes forgiveness hard to initiate is the feeling that we are letting someone off the hook for wrongs this person has committed. That's not what forgiveness is all about. Forgiveness is not about changing someone's behavior. Forgiveness is about letting go of anger and resentment and moving on with your life. Acts of forgiveness don't result in apologies (although this may happen). Many people confuse forgiveness with reconciliation; however, these are two very different concepts. Forgiveness is something you do for yourself so that you can move on. If the other person benefits, that's great, but that's not what forgiveness is all about. Another aspect of forgiveness includes learning to forgive ourselves for holding a grudge or having less-than-becoming thoughts and behaviors, which pull us down and deflate our human potential. Self-righteousness is the biggest roadblock to forgiveness. It can be rather upsetting to realize that we are just as capable of doing an injustice as are people whom we find fault with. Forgiveness is good not just for the soul but for the body as well. Research by the Stanford University psychologist Carl Thoreson reveals that acts of forgiveness reduce stress-related illnesses such as headaches and ulcers and perhaps many more.

ACTION PLAN 21:   What are some ways to initiate the first steps of forgiveness? First, try to get a perspective, looking at the situation from a neutral point of view. Next, begin to process an acceptance of how things are, which in turn will lead you to the realization that moving ahead with your life is the most productive thing you can do. Finally, do some soul-searching to see what it is in you that has allowed you to hold onto these negative feelings for so long, and let that go, too. Sometimes outside resources help you to make sense of the chaos that anger stirs in the soul. A great book on the topic is *Forgive for Good*, by Fred Luskin, which is based on the renowned Stanford program.

A Change for the Better

Ironically, despite the rapid social and technological changes that are occurring today, human behavior is slow to change, particularly when it comes to our own health status. If you need proof of how challenging it is to steer our lives in a positive direction, just look at the poor record of weight-loss programs, with their 95 percent failure rate. So, what is the secret of being able to successfully change? First, all issues of anger and fear must be addressed, lest they hold you back from making further progress. Second, don't try to make a lot of changes at once. If you do, you'll drive yourself crazy, which will only lead to more stress. Start by selecting one suggestion in this chapter that you wish to incorporate into your life, and integrate this into your daily routine for several weeks until you have mastered it. Then, if you wish, try something else. As we have learned from observing the successes in addiction treatment, support from friends and family is essential for positive changes to become permanent, so have the courage to ask for help. Finally, during times when your motivation is waning, call a like-minded friend to join you. Camaraderie is also essential, to nurture the health of the human spirit.

Lifestyle changes aren't as physically dramatic as an extreme makeover, but they tend to last much longer because of the virtues and the values adopted with the changes. As the hero matures from the experiences and the wisdom gained from the journey, he or she is not only recognized but admired when walking up the path, to rest confidently on home's doorstep. Camaraderie also makes the welcome-home celebration all the sweeter, when you have friends with whom to share your experience.

PART IV

Back Home Again

Every journey away from home ultimately ends back at the front doorstep, whether you attain the comfort of home or a sense of inner peace. The common denominator is that the unknown has been conquered, and the hero is recognized for his valor. Campbell called the hero who returns home "a master of two worlds": the world he initially left and the world he conquered so that he could return home. Returning home is itself a metaphor for a sense of resolution, the realization of an aspiration, which promotes a sense of inner peace. May these final stories serve as a reminder that you, too, will make it home again as the master of two worlds.

7

The Winds of Grace

There are two ways to live your life.

One as if nothing is a miracle.

The other as if everything is a miracle.

—ALBERT EINSTEIN

As a way to end each year with a reward, I head off to Hawaii to rest and rejuvenate my soul. Hawaii has become an archetypal sanctuary for me, particularly after I first read Anne Morrow Lindbergh's book *Gift from the Sea* in 1982. She and Charles took refuge there after the kidnapping and the ultimate death of their first child, in what became known as the crime of the twentieth century. Her book began as a collection of personal thoughts and reflections on her life in the form of a journal. Since it was first published in 1955, *Gift from the Sea* has become a classic primer of self-reflection and personal triumph for women (and men) of all ages.

At workshops and conferences during the span of my twenty-five-year career, I have usually encountered many more women than men who have shown a yearning for wholeness. Men have been enculturated to show strength and courage, while at the same time to hide any signs of vulnerability. It would be foolish to think that men are less spiritual than women or even have less of a yearning for wholeness. Most men are simply trapped in the confines of their own social structure. I believe that no gender has an advantage in feeling life's pain or intuiting special insights on the path to wholeness. Spiritual hunger knows no difference between men or women. Just as the Taoist circle contains male and female aspects, we are all in this life journey together and we can certainly learn from each other.

So, like Anne Morrow Lindbergh, I, too, go to the north coast of Hawaii and sit upon the beach for days, listening to the sound of waves hitting the sand—something I don't hear in Colorado, no matter how hard I try. For over five years now, Hawaii has become a retreat, a home away from home, a place for me to sort through various aspects of my life, find inspiration, resolve issues, begin new projects, and enjoy the pristine beauty of nature at her finest. I particularly like Hawaii at this time of year, because there are very few tourists, and it seems to me that unlike the mainlanders, the island residents haven't become overly commercial in their celebration of the holiday season. My annual trip to Hawaii is more accurately described as a pilgrimage, a journey where I pause to gracefully remember all the many blessings that have come into my life. It is also a time of self-reflection, when I ask myself how I can continue to make this a better world in which to live.

Of Attempted Suicide and Service

The flight from Denver to Hawaii is a long one, and the airlines have figured out that if they can keep passengers sedated with a movie and food, sitting still for eight hours doesn't seem nearly as torturous. On this particular flight, the movie was *It's a Wonderful Life*, starring Jimmy Stewart and Donna Reed. I had seen it once before as a child, but this edition had been transformed into color. Despite the voice in my head that begged me not to be a traitor to the original black-and-white version, I found myself immediately drawn in, as if watching the movie for the first time. For the few people who may never have seen this classic (and even for those who have), a quick review is in order. Jimmy Stewart's character, George Bailey, sacrifices a life of dreams and ambitions when his father dies, to serve the town of Bedford Falls as the head of the Savings & Loan. Just when things seem to turn for the better, instead they get worse—at every turn. Eventually, George decides to end it all one Christmas Eve and commit suicide by jumping off a bridge into ice-cold water.

    With the help of an angel (and accompanied by the ever-present ringing of bells), George is shown what the town would have been like in the grips of a greedy banker, had George never lived and, specifically, all the people's lives that he so greatly influenced with acts of kindness. Perhaps what has endeared the movie to so many Americans for six decades are these inherent questions: Whose lives have we positively affected? and How have we made this world a better place to live? As was made clear in the movie, the beauty of life is that more often than not, we may never really know whose lives we positively affect as we navigate the course of our own human journey. But rest assured that the ripple each of our lives makes on the huge lake of humanity goes well beyond our own vision, to affect countless people in ways we cannot even imagine.

Perhaps it was not a coincidence that the day after I arrived on the "Garden Island" and headed to a local bookstore to do a book signing, I met Derek. He was a young man, about twenty-five years old, and the first thing I noticed about him was his warm smile, dark wavy hair, and sapphire eyes. He was one of the first people to show up that night, but before I could start a conversation with him, the room quickly filled with people. As I began my presentation, I looked over at Derek. Although his smile was still present, this time I observed something else. Glancing at his arms, I noticed long scars on the inside of his wrists, the undeniable marks of a suicide attempt. I continued my talk, sharing stories about people who emerged from stressful events with grace and dignity. When I was done, a line quickly formed at the table where I was to sign books. Derek waited patiently until all the other people had left and then pulled up a chair to talk.

"I just wanted to say how much I enjoyed your presentation tonight. I have been working on some major issues in the past year, and I feel like I am really making some headway. I have been fighting depression for several years now," he explained, pointing to his wrists. "I ended up going to see a new doctor this year, who discovered I have a chemical imbalance, and I am doing so much better. But I sense that in my case, it's more than just a chemical imbalance. As I lay dying on the floor in a pool of blood that day, and I might have been dead, for all I know, I heard a voice—a very distinct voice. It said to me that love is the divine force that holds the universe together. This is why we are all here. Fear, in all its many forms, is the absence of love. In giving love, we receive it tenfold. Love is far more subtle than it is dynamic. I now know this to be true." He paused for a moment and then continued.

"Something you said reminded me of that mystical experience. I wasn't sure why I came here tonight. I guess we all need to be reminded every chance we get. Thanks for your message about the healing power of love."

The look in Derek's crystal-blue eyes had a unique blend of confidence and enthusiasm, as well as a wisdom far beyond his years. I could tell that he had made the voyage home.

"There is an expression here in Hawaii I thought you might like, as it resonates with everything you speak about. It goes like this: 'No rain, no rainbows.'" Then, with a strong handshake and a warm smile, he turned toward the door and disappeared.

Derek's story reminded me of a similar exchange. Several years ago I took a trip to St. Moritz, Switzerland, to do some photography. In what can only be described as unsurpassed mountain splendor, a series of lakes rests strategically in a valley between two small mountain ranges. One afternoon, I went exploring with my camera and was delighted to see people flying kites in a field near one of the lakes. The image of colorful kites against a backdrop of rugged mountains and blue sky has been imprinted on my mind ever since. I took several shots with my telephoto lens, but as I approached, I realized that the three people flying kites were seated in wheelchairs. After taking a few more photos, I struck up a conversation with the nearest kite flyer, who was named Peter. He told me that he had taken up kite flying quite unexpectedly.

"See that lake over there? I was going to end my life one cloudy afternoon by wheeling up to the edge of the dock and dropping myself over when no one was looking. The lake is actually quite deep. I had it calculated that by the time someone might help me, it would be too late to save me. I didn't plan on some teenage kid with a kite asking me to help him fly the damn thing. You see, it really takes two people to get this thing up in the air, and there was no one else around that day. He was determined to fly that kite, and he wouldn't take no for an answer. Perhaps at some level he knew what my plan was. So I postponed my rendezvous with death, and it's been on hold ever since. That day, what I call Independence Day, I came to realize how much more important giving is than receiving. That's really what life is all about. I also realized how much fun it is to fly a kite. The element of fun had been missing in my life, and he brought it back with something as simple as flying a kite. The odd thing is, I've come back here every day since and have never seen that kid. What do you make of that? I ended up buying a kite, and I definitely need help to get it off the ground. So now, when I see someone who looks lonely and dejected, I ask him or her for assistance. The person never says no." He smiled. As I shook his hand, he said, "Kite therapy! I can't walk, but I can fly."

Peter's smile was contagious, and I, too, walked away with a huge smile on my face, thinking, once again, that you just never know whose lives you touch enough to make a difference. Like Derek, Peter had also made it home. Indeed, it's a wonderful life! Somewhere, I know there was an angel flying a kite because the winds of grace were blowing strong that day.

The Never-Ending Story
(Laughing Again and Again)

If I've learned one thing from the experience of storytelling, it's that just when you think you have finished a story, there is always something more to share. As the proverbial expression says: Life goes on, and so do the stories that try to contain each human life within the linear confine of words. In my book *Stressed Is Desserts Spelled Backward*, I told several stories of remarkable people who had come into my life, people who exemplified grace and dignity through the worst of human experiences. One such chapter, "Making Andrew Laugh," was the story of Andrew Adams, a quadriplegic who used humor as his muscle of the soul to aid in his healing process.

As often happens with acquaintances over the years, I had lost touch with Andrew, a student at American University, but fate brought us back together again in the summer of 2000. It was ten years after we first met. Andrew was now married to a beautiful woman named Lauren, and they were expecting their first child, Alexis, within a week's time. As he does each time we part company, Andrew reminded me of my lifelong promise to him that I would make people laugh. In the spirit of what goes around comes around, this particular reminder became an investment of sorts, which paid untold dividends for Andrew in the months ahead. Before I left the bookstore that night, I gave Andrew my e-mail address, knowing that we would indeed be in touch soon. One morning I turned on my computer to retrieve my e-mail and got this message from his wife:

> Dear Friends, like the song says, it's been a long, cold, lonely winter. The reason you haven't heard from me in a while is because I've had nothing good to say. Andrew's been in and out of hospitals with infections and abscesses that antibiotics can't seem to beat. He was in for a week in January, three weeks in February, and has been in again since having emergency surgery last Tuesday. He's now in a rehab hospital where he'll be for at least five more weeks, best-case scenario, and on IV antibiotics for two and a half months. Andrew figures he's been in bed for six of the nine months we've lived in New England, and he's sick and tired of being sick and tired. We both are.

—Lauren

Remembering my promise to Andrew, I quickly drafted a letter and decided to try something. Knowing how the Internet can serve to rally a crowd, I sent it out as a personal letter to over fifty people, in the hopes that friends, acquaintances, and colleagues might pull together to lend a helping hand. Sometimes, we must act as "spiritual aids" for others on their quests. Here is what I wrote:

May 10, 2001
Dear Friends and Family: a small favor please?

> I just got word that Andrew is back in the hospital. As you might remember, Andrew was featured in my book *Stressed Is Desserts Spelled Backward*, in the chapter "Making Andrew Laugh." Andrew became a quadriplegic at age thirteen, and it was humor that helped him get through this terrible ordeal. Once again, he needs our help!
>
> Last fall, Andrew was hospitalized with a bed sore infection. Major surgery was required. Apparently, there is now an infection, and Andrew is back in the hospital for an undetermined and indefinite length of time, possibly more surgery, and God knows what else. As you can imagine, this has been a huge hardship on him, his wife, Lauren, and, of course, their baby daughter.

When I was on a national TV talk show last week, I mentioned that Andrew was back in the hospital. His wife called me to tell me that he actually saw the show live and was very touched that he was remembered. Knowing the power of e-mail, and the power of love, I'd like to ask you (and anyone you know who may wish to do the same) once again for your help in dropping Andrew a card or a joke. I truly believe that love is the greatest healing energy of all, and it comes in a great many ways: humor, patience, optimism, and compassion. So if you feel so moved, here is his address. I know he would appreciate it.

Thanks so much! In love and peace,
Brian Luke Seaward

Over the next several months, I too, wrote Andrew several times and sent him a stack of jokes (contents from my tickler note-book) that have been e-mailed to me over the years. We also talked on the phone several times. On one occasion, he was elated to tell me that he had received well over two hundred cards, letters, and jokes. He was astonished because he had no idea that he had so many fans out there. (Can you imagine if you were in his shoes?) One day, I got an e-mail from Lauren, with the great news that Andrew was home from the hospital. Within the next few days, this e-mail showed up in my mailbox.

Hi, Luke, Yes, I'm home. It's been a long time but I'm back. I still have some healing to do, and I am only allowed to get up in my chair for an hour at a time, but it's good to be back home. All the cards and good wishes have been wonderful; they have really helped me to get through this with a smile on my face. Every time I received a letter, card, joke, or message of hope and goodwill (especially the mural!), I could feel my spirit rise. I want to thank you so much; even though this has been a VERY LONG haul, it has been easier since I have taken your class and with the gen-erous acts of kindness from everyone you have told about my hospitalization. Please forward this message to all of those you asked to help me through this. I have always loved the phrase "no matter where you go, there you are," only this time I was there with so many people letting me know "we're here with you, and we're going to help you get through this." I look forward to hearing from you.

All the best,

Andrew

P.S. I was coming back home from a new doctor's appointment, where I got another opinion, when Lauren and I decided to stop and have lunch. We stopped at a Chinese restaurant and had some good food, and our fortune cookies came up next. Well, guess what my fortune said: "A merry heart does good like a medicine." How about that!

Holding his letter in my hand, I walked up the path to my front door. As I reached for the doorknob, the winds of grace blew gently across my face and reminded me once again that it's a wonderful life.

The Germination of Seeds

As any parent knows, you can impart some morsel of wisdom to your child thousands of times, until the cows come home, and no matter how many times you say it, you really wonder if it will ever sink in. You just hope it does, and you hope you live long enough to see the fruits of your labor pay off.

Teaching is much the same way. As a teacher, you just hope that the seeds of knowledge you cast out among the fields of aspiring young minds will take root someday. Unlike a parent, however, a teacher never really knows if or when these seeds will take root. As the expression goes, you cannot push water uphill. Indeed, water always finds its own level. That's where faith steps in; you just trust that all will work out as it should. Unless a student makes the effort to get in touch, you just never really know. A few students do in fact locate their former teachers. When this happens, you feel like you have died and gone to heaven. That's how I felt the day I came home to find this letter in my mailbox.

January 14, 2000
Dear Luke,

Ahoy from the peaceful shores of Seattle! This is a long overdue letter from one of your American University students, class of '93, your last semester, I believe. I should have written much sooner; there's been something I've been meaning to tell you. Remember when you told us that the things you were teaching might take on greater significance as we aged and matured (or failed to mature)? That was a major understatement! In fact, you may have saved my life. This is my story:

I'm an alcoholic. I've been one since I was in my teens, and I was headed for more advanced stages when we crossed paths. I had a DWI and was charged with another misdemeanor before I reached twenty. And that's when they caught me. But my legal difficulties were the least of my problems. I was becoming a vicious, animalistic monster, the very antithesis of who I really was. I was alienating everyone I loved and I had lost all self-respect. But try to tell me that back then and you would've been treated to the work of a master manipulator with true genius toward rationalization and self-deceit.

And then, I had the beginnings of what I now see to be a spiritual awakening. It was suggested that I go to Alcoholics Anonymous. I went and my first instinct was to run out the door. They used words like *God* and *spirituality*. What the hell did God and spirituality have to do with my problems? I am sure you know the answer to this question better than I. But, of course, my ego told me that these people were freaks, thinking that spirituality was the answer for them.

When was the last time I heard of talk like this? It was from you. And you certainly weren't a freak. You possessed a sincere inner calm. You helped people, and I believed you were behind the concepts you taught. I remembered how impressive some of your presentations were, how you could get a group of students to open their minds and try meditation. I remember when you had a Native American shaman visit the class and how impressed I was with what he shared. I remembered when you told us that drugs and alcohol did not enhance spiritual development; they put up walls. I did feel a spiritual link back then, for all my faults, and I saw some of the things you covered in the Twelve Steps. So maybe there was something to this spiritual angle they talked about in AA, I thought. And I stayed.

I celebrated four years of sobriety on December 10, 1999, and am still sober as I write this letter. I have gained a deep and very personal appreciation for the concepts you introduced me to and promised would become important further down the road. Thank you.

Sincerely,
Steven M.

On the day I received this letter, I could have sworn I heard tiny bells ringing everywhere, a reminder that indeed, it's a wonderful life! I also thought I could hear the faint voice of Joseph Campbell whispering in the winds, telling me that the return home is glorious indeed.

Reason for Hope: Breaking Bread with Jane Goodall

In 1960, a young woman hiked into the jungle of Gombe, Tanzania to begin a study of chimpanzees that would last several decades and that continues to this day. Her name is Jane Goodall. She is recognized for her discovery that human beings are not the only species to make and use tools and also for her tireless efforts as an environmental activist to save wildlife habitats around the globe. In a wonderful display of serendipity, our paths converged, and I found myself having breakfast with Jane in the spring of 2004. She had invited me to join her in a new environmental fund-raising project. During our time together, we revealed our concerns and our passion for the environment. It is no understatement to say that as a species, humanity is on a Hero's Journey, and humankind has never confronted a bigger challenge than the obstacles we face now.

Despite the clouds of uncertainty overshadowing our planet, Jane shared with me her desire to make this a better world to live in and the reasons she has hope for a better tomorrow. The first two reasons were embodied in gifts she received from other people: symbols of achievement that transcend the limitations of ego. One was a California condor feather given to her by the individuals who were responsible for bringing this magnificent bird back from the brink of extinction; this is a symbol of what is possible. The second gift was given to her by Nelson Mandela: a piece of rock from the prison quarry where he had been confined for more than twenty-six years under the rule of apartheid. She carries it with her as a sign of both forgiveness and powerful, peaceful transformation. The third reason for hope was a spiritual gift: a mystical experience she had in Nebraska, watching the migration of the sand hill cranes. It occurred on the same day in 2003 that the war broke out in Iraq: a sign that in a world of chaos, there is still beauty, and this beauty is worth saving.

"Despite signs of imbalance, I believe in the power of the human spirit, but we must act now," she said.

To sit in the presence of Jane Goodall is to experience grace firsthand. Moreover, to see her work take root around the world, through programs like "Roots and Shoots," is proof not only that one person can indeed make a difference, but that we are all called upon to be the winds of change that produce the winds of grace.

The Winds of Grace

One day I got a call from my good friend and colleague Elizabeth "Rabia" Roberts. She invited me to lunch. She was excited about her new book project and wanted to share some ideas. I arrived at the Sunflower Café to find both her and her husband, Elias, and they couldn't wait to talk about this exciting endeavor. Their new book idea was the third in a sequence of collected poems and prayers, following the success of *Earth Prayers* and *Life Prayers*. This manuscript, *Prayers for a Thousand Years*, was unique, in that a host of people had been asked to contribute new poems, prayers, thoughts, and reflections on the future of humanity. Elias explained the premise of the book this way: "We are concerned with all this talk about despair as we turn the corner into the new millennium. There is a cloud of gloom and doom over the planet. There seems to be little hope for future generations and much anguish and frustration among members of the younger generation. We want to try to bring forth a sense of hope and faith where there is despair, and turn this perception around for the better."

Elizabeth added, "To be honest, we are concerned with the attitude of humanity. There is no doubt that we are at the crossroads, with many decisions to be made. This book project is our attempt to lift the spirits of men and women everywhere. We have asked people like Nelson Mandela, Rosa Parks, James Taylor, Jane Goodall, Jimmy Carter, Desmond Tutu, and scores of others to write a passage of inspiration."

Taking his cue, Elias stepped in. "So, with that in mind, we would like to ask you to make a contribution as well. Would you be willing?" And with that, he passed me a folder with a copy of the book proposal and the guidelines to follow. I placed the folder in front of me and shook their hands in admiration.

"Sure," I said. "I would be honored."

I thought long and hard about what kind of message I could impart to the kids of tomorrow, what lasting words I could share in a simple message. Then it dawned on me that the only answer was to share the message that had been given to me by the special people who had blessed my life with the colors of love's rainbow.

Within the next few days, I found myself seated on a jet flying over the great plains of the Midwest. I sat with pen in hand, as thoughts of inspiration circled inside my head. This prayer practically wrote itself. Actually, I based my prayer on a line that had been surfacing in my mind for several months. The line "the winds of change are the winds of grace" became the anchor for the poem. Unlike the many people whom Elizabeth and Elias had spoken of, I saw and continue to see great hope for the family of humanity on the planet earth. As it turned out, there were so many submissions of poems and prayers, they couldn't all be used. In fact, Elizabeth and Elias received so many contributed prayers, there were enough for three volumes. As a result, my prayer was never included, but I sensed that one day, it might find a home somewhere.

I have met many wonderful and brave people who have endured the most hellacious events that life can offer. They have conveyed to me that some good can always come from a bad situation, if we choose to learn from it—hence, the phrase "the winds of change are the winds of grace." Once I shared the following poem at a national conference and was inundated with requests, perhaps to serve as an inspiration to chart a new course for home. I have learned that since that time, this poem has been recited at many gatherings and memorial services. It feels appropriate to share it once again at the end of this book. Peace!

The Winds of Grace

Disturbing are the winds of change,
As they produce growing pains.
Oh God, I seek a safe port
To harbor my fears and worries.
Grant me the courage,
To endure the winds of change.

Comforting are the winds of grace,
As they instill a sense of faith.
Oh God, fill my sails with love
On this journey of self-exploration.
Grant me the insight,
To enjoy the winds of grace.

Blessed are the winds of grace,
As they invigorate my human spirit.
Oh God, I seek to know my purpose
In the community we know as "one people."
Grant me the strength to do my work.
The winds of change *are* the winds of grace.

Epilogue

Sacred Spaces
and Divine Inspiration

I t is autumn. I am walking in front of the majestic snow-covered Tetons. Mount Moran stands tall at sunset, with its clear reflection in the calm waters of Jackson Lake. To my left and right stand aspen trees dressed in their fall regalia: golden leaves that shimmer with the slightest breeze. Streaks of sunlight reach beyond the clouds and find their way to the waters below, setting the lake on fire. To the east, the moon, nearly full, is seconds away from beginning its journey across earth's sky. My eyes are saturated with this undisturbed beauty, and my heart is filled with unimaginable joy. If heaven exists on earth, and I know it does, then I am surely here in a sacred space.

Scientists can postulate theories for the splendor of the Grand Tetons, such as the movement of the earth's surface on a fault line, but geological facts don't adequately account for a definite element of divine spirituality, one that cannot be ignored by the human heart. I certainly cannot deny it. Nor can the other tourists who, like me, have gathered in this spot at this moment, to soak in every detail through the five senses, in unison with each breath and heartbeat. Above all else, human spirituality is experiential, and the holiness of this moment allows me to retain its memory in each and every cell of my body. The winds of grace have blown gently on the embers of my soul, and I ignite on fire.

Cathedral spires of rock, carved by wind, rain, and ice, reach toward the celestial heavens and stand ever so humble against the backdrop of an amber and crimson sky. The Tetons are a creation of biblical proportions, yet each detail, from the simplest blade of grass at their base, to the crevasses that hold the glaciers, and beyond to the most complex astrological galaxy far above, pays homage to God's creative energies. I have come many times to the Tetons for a spiritual retreat, to find peace of mind and comfort of soul. In this visit, as in every other, it happens instantaneously when the Tetons first come into view. These mountains speak to me; sometimes they whisper, sometimes they shout, but they always call to me. Today I listen, and I am speechless. I nod in silence. As with each previous visit, my cares and worries quickly melt, then evaporate. Now I can only give thanks—thanks to the recurring recognition that I am part of the whole, an infinitesimal, yet essential, part of the universe.

Nature has been my therapist for over forty years. From my days as a small boy, I would flee to the primeval forest and rock cliffs behind my house, escaping the frenetic household, captive under the dark aura of alcoholism. The pine trees were my friends and confidants, the lake was my teacher, the clouds high above my silent partner and, oftentimes, my guardians. They remain so today. God, in all its many faces, surrounds me and comforts me. More than once, I have heard these words whispered on the wind, "God is not a noun, but a verb." I know the verb is love, and now years of experience have shown me that love is more subtle than dynamic, manifesting through acts of optimism, humor, patience, courage, faith, humbleness, forgiveness, curiosity, persistence, and compassion. Years later, I heard these same words again by the philosopher/inventor Buckminster Fuller, "God is not a noun, but a verb." One can only guess whether Bucky Fuller took walks in the woods as a young boy, but I know that he must have listened to the same divine whispers that fell on my ears so many years ago.

I am in a taxi cab, riding from the airport to a hotel on what is known internationally as the Strip, where millions of neon lights put the central nervous system on full alert. To say that this even-mile stretch of concrete and electricity is sensory overload is no slight exaggeration. This is my first time to Las Vegas, for decades known affectionately as "Sin City." I am here to speak at an addictions treatment counselor conference in a city renown for its addictions. The cab driver laughs at the incongruity. So do I. The next morning I walk the empty streets, which oozed with people just hours before. This city never sleeps, but I have caught it in quiet repose, and I take full advantage of it. I quickly notice that Vegas is surrounded by mountains, and I smile. A subtle magic in the mountains stirs the imagination. Only a few steps on the Strip and it becomes obvious. With canals, a pyramid, and skyscraper replicas, Las Vegas is no stranger to imagination.

To see a city of blinking lights and water fountains blossom in an unforgiving desert is to marvel at human ingenuity. What might look like a large blight, an atrocity of greed to some people, is nothing less than a miracle of consciousness to others. I pause to think how powerfully resourceful the human species is. I think that if this can be accomplished, so, too, can a cure for cancer be discovered and an end to all wars be found. I know that divine miracles abound in human creativity. As such, I know that human potential is limitless. Early settlers on their way to California, dehydrated in the Mojave desert heat, referred to the area now known as Las Vegas as hell. Some people today say the same thing, albeit for different reasons. Perhaps heaven and hell are nothing more than perceptions of the mind, human creations. I reserve judgment on this once-desert vista, now a booming metropolis. If nothing more, this artificial oasis has become a testament to human endeavors. I know that God doesn't reside solely in pockets of uninhabited landscapes. The spirit of God is found everywhere, even on the Las Vegas Strip.

It is winter in the South Pacific. I am walking along one of the northern beaches on the isle of Kauai. I have the beach to myself, but I am not alone. Spirit fills land, sea, and sky. The water here is no ordinary shade of blue: azure here, sapphire there, indigo farther from the shore, and perhaps several more colors that I cannot adequately describe in words. The mountain of Kauai, a dormant volcano, stands like a crystal-clear green emerald in a setting of golden sand. Unlike the Teton range, which so often is covered in snow, each mountain ridge along the Na Pali coast is lush green every day of the year. Barely an inch of naked rock can be seen anywhere. Unlike the desert of Nevada, Kauai is known to be the wettest place on the planet. I marvel at the opposites and once again applaud the simplicity of the Tao.

I stand between land and water. Between earth and sky. Between here and the hereafter. If there is heaven on earth, and I know there is, I am surely here once again.

This is my first time to the Garden Island, as Kauai, the oldest of the Hawaiian Islands, is affectionately known. It's a place of magic and divine essence. Every expectation of paradise has been met and then some. I came to heal from a relationship that ended abruptly, the pain intense. Nature has a certain way of healing that Western medicine has yet to discover. I walk the beaches, I hike the trails, I bathe in the Pacific and become whole again. The land of the Kahunas has imparted a sacred space to open my closed heart once more. During my stay in Kauai, I have a vision. In the veil of a crimson sky, I close my eyes in meditation. Within moments, I am transported through space and time to become surrounded by a brilliant golden-white light, a loving light that I cannot articulate in words, yet I know is very real. My hands, feet, and body dissolve into the light. Now, I am the light. I am love. It is euphoric. In knowing this, I kiss the face of God. Moments later, I return to the confines of my body and the room where I sit, forever changed. Now twilight surrounds the island. The Milky Way appears to the soundtrack of rushing waves at high tide.

The psychologist Carl Jung once argued with his mentor Freud by saying that we are not animals, with each action attributed to an instinct. Rather, he insisted, we are spiritual beings, unfolding our divine nature as we explore the deepest reaches of the unconscious mind. Prior to his death in 1961, Jung was asked whether he believed in God. Without hesitating, he answered, "No." Then he paused for what seemed like an eternity. He slowly took the pipe out of his mouth and said, "I know."

If I were asked the same question, I would give the same response. I don't believe in God. I know.

References
and Resources

Armstrong, L. (with Sally Jenkins). *It's Not about the Bike*. New York: Putnam, 2002.

Burnham, S. *The Path of Prayer*, New York: Viking Compass, 2002.

Buscaglia, L. *Living, Loving and Learning*. New York: Fawcett Books, 1982.

Campbell, D. *The Mozart Effect*. New York: Avon Books, 1997.

Campbell, J. *Hero with a Thousand Faces*. Princeton, N.J.: Princeton/Bollinen, 1949.

———. (with Bill Moyers). *The Power of Myth*. New York: Doubleday, 1988.

Capra, F. *The Tao of Physics*. Boston: Shambhala Books, 1975.

Carlson, R., and B. Shields. *Handbook for the Soul*. Boston: Little, Brown & Company, 1995.

Castenada, C. *The Teachings of Don Juan*. New York: Pocket Books, 1968.

Cheng, N. *Life and Death in Shanghai*. New York: Penguin Books, 1986.

Chopra, D. *Quantum Healing*. New York: Bantam New Age Books, 1989.

Cimino, R., and D. Lattin. "Choosing My Religion." *American Demographics* (April 1999): 60–65.

Cohen, R. Milk: *The Deadly Poison*. Englewood, N.J.: Argus, 1998.

Cousineau, P. *The Hero's Journey*. Dorset, England: Element Books, 1999.

Cousins, N. *Anatomy of an Illness*. New York: Norton, 1976.

DeGraaf, J., et al. *Affluenza: The All-Consuming Epidemic*. San Francisco: Berret-Koehler, 2002.

Dreher, D. *The Tao of Inner Peace*. New York: Harper Perennial, 1990.

Frankl, V. *Man's Search for Meaning* (3rd edition). New York: Pocket Books, 1984.

Gelb, M. *Thinking Like Da Vinci*. New York: Dell Books, 1998.

Gerber, R. *Vibrational Medicine* (3rd edition). Rochester, Vt.: Inner Traditions, 2001.

Gibran, K. *The Prophet*. New York: Alfred A. Knopf, 1923.

Goleman, A. *Emotional Intelligence*. New York: Bantam Books, 1995.

Goodall, J. *Reason for Hope*. New York: Warner Books, 1999.

Graham, R. L. *The Dove*. New York: Harper & Row, 1972.

Hawkins, D. *Power vs. Force*. Sedona, Ariz.: Veritas, 1995.

Hoff, B. *The Tao of Pooh*. New York: Penguin Books, 1982.

Huxley, A. *Brave New World*. New York: Perennial, 1939.

———. *The Perennial Philosophy*. New York: Perennial Library, 1945.

Janis, S. *Spirituality for Dummies*. Foster City, Calif.: IDG Books, 2000.

Jung, C. *Memories, Dreams, Reflections*. New York: Vintage Books, 1961.
———. *Man and His Symbols*. New York: Anchor/Doubleday, 1964.
Krackauer, J. *Into Thin Air*. New York: Anchor Books, 1997.
Lindberg, A. M. *Gift from the Sea*. New York: Vintage Books, 1955.
Luskin, F. *Forgive for Good*. San Francisco: HarperSanFrancisco, 2002.
Lyman, H. *The Mad Cowboy*. Scribner: New York, 2001.
Maslow, A. *Toward a Psychology of Being*. New York: Van Nostrand Reinhold, 1968.
McEwen, B. *The End of Stress As We Know It*. Washington, D.C.: Joseph Henry Press, 2002.
Ming-Dao, D. *356 Tao*. San Francisco: HarperSanFrancisco, 1992.
———. *Chronicles of Tao*. San Francisco: HarperSanFrancisco, 1993.
Mitchell, S. *Tao Te Ching*. New York: HarperCollins, 1988.
Narby, J. *The Cosmic Serpent. DNA and the Origins of Consciousness*. New York: Tarcher/Putnam, 1999.
Newburg, A., et al. *Why God Won't Go Away*. New York: Ballantine Books, 2001.
O' Reagan, B., and C. Hirshberg, *Spontaneous Remission—An Annotated Bibliography*. Sausalito, Calif.: Institute of Noetic Sciences, 1993.
Peck, M. S. *The Road Less Traveled*. New York: Touchstone Books, 1978.
———. *The Different Drum*. New York: Simon & Schuster, 1987.
Pelletier, K. *The Best Alternative Medicine*. New York: Simon & Schuster, 2000.
Pert, C. *Molecules of Emotion*. New York: Scribner, 1997.
Robbins, T. *Still Life with Woodpecker* (revised edition). New York: Bantam Doubleday, 1994.
Samuelson, M. *Voices from the Edge*. Marietta, Ga.: Longstreet Press, 2002.
Seaward, B. L. *Stand Like Mountain, Flow Like Water*. Deerfield Beach, Fla.: Health Communications, 1997.
———. *Stressed Is Desserts Spelled Backward*. Berkeley, Calif.: Conari Press, 1999.
———. *Health of the Human Spirit*. Allyn & Bacon: Boston, 2001.
Siegel, B. *Love, Medicine and Miracles*. New York: Perennial Books, 1981.
Tierra, M. *The Way of Herbs*. New York: Pocket Books, 1998.
Tolkien, J. R. R. *Lord of the Rings*. Boston: Houghton Mifflin, 1954.
Travino, H. *The Tao of Healing: Meditations for Body and Spirit*. Novato, Calif.: New World Library, 1993.
Tzu, L. *Tao Teh Ching* (translated by John C. H. Wu). Boston: Shamhala Pocket Classics, 1961.
Von Oech, R. *A Whack on the Side of the Head* (revised edition). New York: Warner Books, 1998.
———. *A Kick in the Seat of the Pants*. New York: Perennial Library, 1986.
Weil, A. *Spontaneous Healing*. New York: Fawcett Columbine, 1995.
Yogananda, P. *The Divine Romance*. Los Angeles: Self-Realization Fellowship, 1986.

INDEX

ABOUT THE AUTHOR

Brian Luke Seaward, Ph.D., is considered a pioneer in the field of health psychology and is internationally recognized for his contributions in the areas of holistic stress management, human spirituality, and mind-body-spirit healing. The wisdom of Dr. Seaward is often quoted in PBS specials, college graduation speeches, medical seminars, boardroom meetings, church sermons and keynote addresses all over the world. Dr. Seaward is highly respected throughout the international community as an accomplished teacher, a consultant, a motivational speaker, an author, and a mentor. It's been said several times that Brian Luke Seaward looks like James Taylor, dresses like Indiana Jones, and writes like Mark Twain. He is the author of several books, including *Stressed Is Desserts Spelled Backward*, *The Art of Calm*, *Health of the Human Spirit*, and the popular *Stand Like Mountain, Flow Like Water*. Many of the meditation and visualization exercises found in this book are narrated by the author and are available on CD for purchase through his Web site. Dr. Seaward can be reached at www.brianlukeseaward.net.

ABOUT THE
ONE QUIET NIGHT CD
AND EVERSOUND MUSIC

It's been said that when you listen to great music, you eavesdrop on the thoughts of God. I love music, and perhaps that is why I am often asked by people who know me whether I could recommend a selection of great music that promotes relaxation. I have made several compilation CDs of my favorite instrumental songs and often let the music waft through my house. In the fall of 2003, I was approached by my friend and colleague Javier Sanz, the creative director of EverSound Music, to compile my favorite pieces from the EverSound Music collection to make a CD that will be released in conjunction with this book. From soft guitar melodies and romantic cello interludes to piano and flute pieces composed and performed by the likes of Lino, John Mills, Manuel Iman, and John Adorney, it wasn't easy to edit this collection down to sixteen songs. The result, *One Quiet Night*, quickly became a labor of love, and I am delighted to be able to recommend this CD as my favorite collection of instrumental songs to promote relaxation. I think you will agree. You can visit EverSound Music at www.eversound.com.